Consuming Scenography

Performance + Design is a series of monographs and essay collections that explore understandings of performance design and scenography, examining the potential of the visual, spatial, material and environmental to shape performative encounters and to offer sites for imaginative exchange. This series focuses on design both for and as performance in a variety of contexts, including theatre, art installations, museum displays, mega-events, site-specific and community-based performance, street theatre, design of public space, festivals, protests and state-sanctioned spectacle.

Performance + Design takes as its starting point the growth of scenography and the expansion from theatre or stage design to a wider notion of scenography as a spatial practice. As such, it recognises the recent accompanying interest from a number of converging scholarly disciplines (theatre, performance, art, architecture, design) and examines twenty-first-century practices of performance design in the context of debates about postdramatic theatre, aesthetic representation, visual and material culture, spectatorship, participation and co-authorship.

Series Editors
Stephen Di Benedetto, Joslin McKinney and Scott Palmer

Contemporary Scenography: Practices and Aesthetics in German Theatre, Arts and Design
Edited by Birgit Wiens
978-1-3500-6447-8

The History and Theory of Environmental Scenography: Second Edition
Arnold Aronson
978-1-4742-8396-0

Immersion and Participation in Punchdrunk's Theatrical Worlds
Carina E. I. Westling
978-1-3501-0195-1

The Model as Performance: Staging Space in Theatre and Architecture
Thea Brejzek and Lawrence Wallen
978-1-350-09590-8

Scenography Expanded: An Introduction to Contemporary Performance Design
Edited by Joslin McKinney and Scott Palmer
978-1-4742-4439-8

Sound Effect: The Theatre We Hear
Ross Brown
978-1-3500-4590-3

Forthcoming Titles

Digital Scenography: 30 Years of Experimentation and Innovation in Performance and Interactive Media
Neill O'Dwyer
978-1-3501-0731-1

Sites of Transformation: Applied and Socially Engaged Scenography in Rural Landscapes
Louise Ann Wilson
978-1-3501-0444-0

Consuming Scenography

The Shopping Mall as a Theatrical Experience

NEBOJŠA TABAČKI

methuen | drama
LONDON • NEW YORK • OXFORD • NEW DELHI • SYDNEY

METHUEN DRAMA
Bloomsbury Publishing Plc
50 Bedford Square, London, WC1B 3DP, UK
1385 Broadway, New York, NY 10018, USA
29 Earlsfort Terrace, Dublin 2, Ireland

BLOOMSBURY, METHUEN DRAMA and the Methuen Drama logo are
trademarks of Bloomsbury Publishing Plc

First published in Great Britain 2020
This paperback edition published in 2022

Copyright © Nebojša Tabački, 2020

Nebojša Tabački has asserted his right under the Copyright, Designs and
Patents Act, 1988, to be identified as the author of this work.

For legal purposes the Acknowledgements on p. xi constitute an
extension of this copyright page.

Series design by Burge Agency
Cover image: Ibn Battuta Mall in Dubai,
UAE (© Sami Moda / Alamy Stock Photo)

All rights reserved. No part of this publication may be reproduced or
transmitted in any form or by any means, electronic or mechanical,
including photocopying, recording, or any information storage or retrieval
system, without prior permission in writing from the publishers.

Bloomsbury Publishing Plc does not have any control over, or responsibility for,
any third-party websites referred to or in this book. All internet addresses given in this
book were correct at the time of going to press. The author and publisher regret
any inconvenience caused if addresses have changed or sites have ceased to exist,
but can accept no responsibility for any such changes.

A catalogue record for this book is available from the British Library.

Library of Congress Cataloging-in-Publication Data

Names: Tabački, Nebojša, author.
Title: Consuming scenography : the shopping mall as a theatrical experience
 / Nebojša Tabacki.
Description: London ; New York : Methuen Drama, 2020. | Series: Performance + design | Includes
bibliographical references and index. | Summary: "Consuming Scenography offers an insight into
contemporary scenographic practice beyond the theatre. It explores the ways in which scenography
is used to create a global cultural impact and accelerate profits in the site-specific context of themed
shopping malls. It analyses the effect of the architectural, aesthetic, spatial, material and sensory
aspects of design through their performative encounters with consumers in order to offer a better
understanding of performance design. In the first part the author explores the spatial seduction of an
enclosed market space and traces the origins of scenographic temporality in permanent architectonic
spaces for trade and commerce, from early Roman arched markets and Oriental bazaars, to 19th century
arcades and department stores, though to modern-day shopping malls. The second section addresses
the site-specific theatricality of the shopping mall, considering the exploitation of performative aspects
of scenography in the creation of corporate identity. It engages with how casual shoppers are modified
and transformed into spectators, sales personnel into performers, and shop-filled alleys into stages in
themed malls. In the final section, the author investigates the consumption of scenographic experience
and scenography's sensory influence on consumers through their immersion in themed shopping malls.
Considering a variety of case studies of themed shopping malls, including the Ibn Battuta Mall in Dubai,
Terminal 21 in Bangkok, the Villaggio in Doha and Montecasino in Johannesburg, as well as further
examples from Europe, USA and Asia - this book provides a wide-ranging critical examination of the
ways in which scenographic thinking and practices are exploited in wider cultural contexts for impact,
branding, and higher profits"– Provided by publisher.
Identifiers: LCCN 2020007611 (print) | LCCN 2020007612 (ebook) | ISBN 9781350110892 (hardback) |
ISBN 9781350110915 (ebook) | ISBN 9781350110908 (epub)
Subjects: LCSH: Shopping malls. | Marketing. | Theaters–Stage-setting and scenery. | Retail trade.
Classification: LCC HF5430 .T33 2020 (print) | LCC HF5430 (ebook) | DDC 381/.11–dc23
LC record available at https://lccn.loc.gov/2020007611
LC ebook record available at https://lccn.loc.gov/2020007612

ISBN:	HB:	978-1-3501-1089-2
	PB:	978-1-3502-4666-9
	ePDF:	978-1-3501-1091-5
	eBook:	978-1-3501-1090-8

Series: Performance and Design

Typeset by Integra Software Services Pvt. Ltd.

To find out more about our authors and books visit www.bloomsbury.com
and sign up for our newsletters.

Whoever said money can't buy happiness simply didn't know where to go shopping.
　　　　　　　　　　　　　　　Bo Derek

Contents

List of Figures ix
Acknowledgements xi

Introducing *Consuming Scenography* 1

1 Staging Consumer Seduction: A Brief History 9

1.1 The market enclosure as a scenographic principle 9
1.2 Industrialising pleasure: Shopping arcades and department stores 14
1.3 Post-war functionalism: Shopping malls 23

2 Framing Consumption in Late Capitalism 27

2.1 Entertainment, please! 27
2.2 Theming the identity of consumption 32
2.3 Drama on sale 40

3 Themed Malls as a Global Trend 51

3.1 Make me look older: Montecasino 51
3.2 Shopping for education: The Ibn Battuta Mall 57
3.3 A boat trip to fantasy land: The Villaggio Mall 62
3.4 Have a safe flight: Terminal 21 69

4 Producing Experience 75

4.1 The magic of Disneyization 75
4.2 Technological wizardry 84
4.3 Aquatic fairy tales 92

5 Consuming Experience 99

5.1 Flâneurs or active consumers? 99
5.2 Surface semiotics 108
5.3 The body in the forged reality 114

6 The Deceitful Charm of Scenography 119

    6.1 The echoes of history 119
    6.2 The aesthetic universe 126
    6.3 Social interaction with a price tag 130
    6.4 Public space as a political stage 133

7 Spatial Flexibility: A Yearning 139

    7.1 The fluidity of market changes 139
    7.2 Flexibility matters 147
    7.3 Double-crossed by urban dreams 151
    7.4 Responsibility in the final act 155

Notes 164
References 178
Index 190

List of Figures

1 Montecasino, Johannesburg, South Africa. © Image Philip Mostert. 50

2 Montecasino, Johannesburg, South Africa. © Image Philip Mostert. 53

3 Montecasino, Johannesburg, South Africa. © Image Philip Mostert. 55

4 Ibn Battuta Mall, Tunisia court, Dubai, UAE. © Manowar 1973, Dreamstime.com. 58

5 Ibn Battuta Mall, Egypt court, Dubai, UAE. © Manowar 1973, Dreamstime.com. 58

6 Ibn Battuta Mall, Persia court, Dubai, UAE. © Manowar 1973, Dreamstime.com. 60

7 Ibn Battuta Mall, China court, Dubai, UAE. © Manowar 1973, Dreamstime.com. 60

8 Villaggio Mall, Doha, Qatar. © Wing Travelling, Dreamstime.com. 63

9 Villaggio Mall, Doha, Qatar. © Wing Travelling, Dreamstime.com. 63

10 Villaggio Mall, Doha, Qatar. © Hakan Can Yalcin, Dreamstime.com. 66

LIST OF FIGURES

11 Villaggio Mall, Doha, Qatar. © Hakan Can Yalcin, Dreamstime.com. 66

12 Terminal 21, Bangkok, Thailand. © Biserko, Dreamstime.com. 68

13 Terminal 21, Bangkok, Thailand. © Chingyunsong, Dreamstime.com. 68

14 Terminal 21, Bangkok, Thailand. © Mooindy, Dreamstime.com. 72

15 Terminal 21, Bangkok, Thailand. © Geargodz, Dreamstime.com. 72

Acknowledgements

This monograph came about thanks largely to Stephen Di Benedetto, who kindly encouraged me to publish my research on the theatricality of the shopping mall after I presented the topic at the annual conference of the International Federation for Theatre Research in Stockholm in 2016. The confidence to pursue this adventure also came from Thea Brejzek, Joslin McKinney and Scott Palmer. My sincere gratitude goes out to all of them.

I would also like to thank Biljana Sovilj for her generous contributions to my analysis of the historical references and architectural styles applied in themed malls, which I used here as case studies.

My sincere gratitude goes to Philip Mostert for permission to use his photographs of Montecasino in Johannesburg. I would also like to thank Toma Tasovac, Vanja Savić, Dimitris Donias, Sofia Pantouvaki, Rachel Hann, Tarek Mamdouh, Taiko Saito and Yuka Yanagihara for all of their support. Finally, I wish to express my appreciation for Katia Sand at Kalliscript for all her editing advice.

Introducing *Consuming Scenography*

Contemporary scenographic discourse acknowledges scenography as a cultural practice that goes beyond the theatre, exploring a wide range of artistic interventions in urban spaces. Accordingly, this monograph looks at one particular manifestation of scenography in themed shopping malls. In regard to evolving terminology for the increasingly complex architectural typology of shopping environments, themed shopping malls are not to be confused with themed retail centres, which offer one specific type of goods and services (Coleman 2006: 228). Here, theming refers to a unique approach to branding: the implementation of scenographic techniques to convey a unifying visual identity for a place conceived to realise capital. Using a commercial setting as a backdrop, my aim is to critically assess the consumerist aspects of an artistic discipline embedded in the neoliberal exploitation of creative industries and from there to open a discussion on the sociopolitical responsibility accompanying the design of public spaces (De Cauter 2014: 30). Stepping into the realm of 'disneyization', consumption and globalisation, outlined by Alan Bryman (2004: 157), my goal is to examine theming as an aspect of expanded scenography alongside the role played by the latter in themed consumption around the world. Because of an increasing tendency to interact with things instead of people, the consumption of scenography in commercial spaces has been established as a relevant subject of scholarly interest (Ritzer 2005: 37, 102). Rather than the features of globalisation that are commonly debated, such as the broad dissemination of products and brands, this study looks instead to Bryman's notion of 'anticipatory localization':[1] the attempt to individualise global strategies through the scenography of themed environments and adapt them, at least to some extent, to a specific regional context. The concept of 'consumption', generally applied to describe the use, utilisation and deployment of goods and services,[2] Lieven De Cauter observes, relates to scenography in the advanced phase of capitalism in terms of selling scenographic atmospheres and experiences (2014: 30). According to Mark Gottdiener, the consumption of a themed environment is defined as an individual symbolic interpretation of a constructed space to which meanings are added that influence consumer behaviour (1997: 5). After all, as Bryman explains, Disneyization is not about the production of goods and services; it is 'a mode of delivery in the sense of the *staging* of goods and services for consumption' (2004: 159). In an affluent consumer society, human needs have been sidelined to make room for individual and cultural desires.[3] Echoing this transition, malls have reached out to satisfy consumers' search for new experiences and variety-oriented shopping. The exploitation of their desires is carried out through visitors' immersion in scenographic surroundings, pushed to the extreme in themed shopping malls. Nowadays, such malls are a global phenomenon and are realised through design approaches that create a unique shopping experience by encouraging the consumption of visual, tangible and atmospheric spatial elements. In order to better understand consumer behaviour in these environments, we need to examine the scenographic characteristics of the shopping malls' interiors. Consequently, this monograph focuses on the performative aspects of themed design and how they relate to the consumption experienced in the malls. A fuller grasp of the consumption of scenography and theatricality in commercial spaces offers, in turn, deeper insights into the implications of the consumption of popular culture as a social practice.

The advent of themed malls corresponds with the Postmodern embrace of theatricality and the emergence of the term 'scenography' in theoretical architectural discourse in the 1980s (Brejzek 2015: 25). In the Postmodern tradition of stylistic eclecticism and playfulness, shop-lined alleys in themed malls are transformed into a stage. As a special kind of urban entertainment centre,[4] they rely heavily on scenography and techniques rooted in the long history of the theatre. According to Richard Schechner, malls evoke a comparison with Frederick Kiesler's endless spiral (1994: xxxi). The simple act of walking through this 'spiral' absorbs consumers in a world very different from reality while also effecting a fluid exchange of roles – from spectators to performers and back again (Bryman 2004: 103ff). By adapting the site-specific theatrical form,[5] which blurs the distinction between stage and auditorium, themed malls have brought traditional scenographic techniques and theatrical effects into close proximity with the viewer. Simplification or exaggeration in design, skilful scaling, forced perspective, imaginative architectural styles and materiality, all originally admired from a distance, have bridged the historical gap between the audience and the performance. This has, inevitably, exposed all our senses to scenography, leading to an adjustment of the building techniques used for the stage. Traditional materials, used for centuries to represent architecture in the theatre, have been exchanged for iron, concrete, brick and plaster. The temporality and adaptability of scenography have thus been replaced with the permanent and invariable character of architecture.

On another level, the urge to pursue what is real and tangible, visible in Walt Disney's concept for Disneyland, from which themed malls still draw inspiration, aims to make illusion believable. The attempt to translate the design of animated films, single images repeated twenty-four times per second, each one slightly different from the last, into the building principles of architecture has caused a shift from form to iconography. The result is a self-contradictory blend of scenography and architecture – two related but fundamentally different methods of perceiving and designing space.[6] The encounter between these two disciplines raises several issues, including the influence of scenography as architecture (or architecture as scenography) on our own perception and on our behaviour as consumers in themed environments. To address these questions, I have chosen to look specifically at themed shopping malls, as they offer the ideal playground to study the complex relationship between architecture and scenography and extend a theoretical discourse begun in discussions of Las Vegas.[7] In the process of critically exploring the promise of freedom through consumption, I hope that this book will shed some light on how scenography changes our behaviour by manipulating our spatial awareness beyond the theatre. Confronting debate over the legitimacy of a theatrical approach to analysing shopping malls, I argue that neglecting the theatricality embedded in the history of enclosed markets means we ignore key aspects of the shopping mall's identity and locality. This wilful loss undermines the validity of our perception in the experience of the mall's tangible and ephemeral features, as well as the power of theatrical immersion.

This book is divided into seven chapters. The first chapter, 'Staging Consumer Seduction: A Brief History', traces the origins of scenographic temporality in enclosed architectonic spaces for trade and commerce. Looking at the concept of 'scenographic seduction' described by Rachel Hann, this chapter trains a historical lens on the 'application of scenographics to manipulate the potential of an affective atmosphere to inform decision-making' (2019: 108). It depicts the different stages of scenographic practice, from ancient Greek and Roman roofed markets and Oriental bazaars to nineteenth-century arcades and department stores to modern-day shopping malls. Even though the history of the marketplace continues to be discussed in depth by historians and scholars from various disciplines, I nevertheless felt it necessary to highlight some specific typologies that have cultivated the evolution of scenographic seduction over a long period of time. My purpose is to put current practice in the field into perspective and 'better sense our historical-cultural moment', from which a critical assessment can then be made (Rufford 2018: 13). Special focus is placed on the influence of the Industrial Revolution and the subsequent shift in perception and attention that took place in the nineteenth century, which heavily influenced the seductive techniques of commodity presentation and theming we see today. In the course of this brief historical overview, we can follow the development of the enclosed market conceived as an autonomous scenographic space, independent from its surroundings. This section not only prepares the ground for further discussion but also discloses the logic of seduction propelled through capital and facilitated using a variety of theatrical approaches that have created in-between places of 'filtered' reality.

The second chapter, 'Framing Consumption in Late Capitalism', reviews the evolution of context-specific scenography in the creation of corporate identity, as well as the use of scenographic narratives to serve capitalism as part of the experience economy. It follows the agency of theatricality and performativity in scenographic interventions in malls during the twentieth century, examining the gradually advancing simulacra introduced by enhancing staged realities and becoming detached from the world. Taking into consideration the challenges surrounding audiences' reception of theatricality, this chapter tries to reach beyond the 'rationale of utility and profitability' of themed shopping malls and contribute to the transparency of scenographic agency, 'specifying the scope and scale of what one can realistically make claims of impact about' (Bala 2018: 197). As it reflects on the past, it explains the global expansion of themed shopping malls since the end of the 1990s, following the success of strategies established in Las Vegas, and points out the close link between the deployment of commercial scenography and changes in the market.

The third chapter, 'Themed Malls as a Global Trend', presents four different scenographic approaches to themed malls to illustrate the global implications of this phenomenon: aesthetic (Montecasino, Johannesburg), educational (the Ibn Battuta Mall, Dubai), aquatic (the Villaggio Mall, Doha) and transitional (Terminal 21, Bangkok). Using these four examples, it addresses visual appropriation by means of ageing techniques, explores the educational aspects of permanent themed exhibitions, considers the use of water for an additional kinaesthetic experience, such as a boat ride along an indoor canal, and examines the travels imagined in the aesthetics of an airport terminal. The description of the case studies, supported by visuals, analyses different branding strategies, showing how stylistic architectural references are combined and rearranged to transform places lacking any significance into tourist destinations meant for mass consumption. A detailed examination of their theatrical features provides a base for further discussion on how commercial scenographed spaces correspond to tensions between the local and the global. Thus, beyond following the evolution of scenography in enclosed marketplaces around the world, and its relationship to profits, this section discusses how theatricality is used to draw consumers into a mass spectacle, dissolving the boundaries between life, consumption and theatre.

The fourth chapter, 'Producing Experience', investigates the transformation of early scenographic strategies based on distance and visual allure, which left room for interpretation and imagination, into a more intimate seduction through tactility and body movement. In this context, the chapter explores the persuasive power and sensual seduction of symbolic scenographic imagery and exposes the conflict between the perception of space and its function. In this respect, it reviews the tradition of performativity driven by technology and a spectacular scenographic atmosphere delivered by mechanics and machinery. It facilitates a thorough scrutiny of the interdependent relationship between scenography and technology and the resulting manifestation of perception and attention in places of mass consumption. Finally, the analysis of the technology behind theatricality in shopping malls includes the latest developments in the implementation of elaborate water displays. The extensive use of water as a leitmotif in shopping malls has inspired additional amusement and recreational offers, entertaining visitors with fountain shows, projections, enormous waterfalls, large-scale aquariums with walk-through tunnels, gondola rides along indoor canals, snow towns and indoor ski slopes. Bearing in mind all these different environments, we can examine the connection between the materiality and performativity of scenographic spaces in themed malls, the mimicry in which they are grounded, and how they absorb consumers into their own tangible worlds.

The fifth chapter, 'Consuming Experience', delves further into these imagined worlds, which intensify the senses and emphasise feelings of 'otherness'. The discourse on this topic presents different views of shoppers: some critics see them as passive, while others regard them as active participants. Consequently, this section explores the controversial issue of freedom in meticulously planned, organised and controlled places of commerce and trade, trying to pinpoint the degree of involvement and impact of spatial design. It looks specifically at the semiotics of places of consumption with the perception of pedestrians as 'flâneurs'.[8] A critical analysis of ornamentation and symbols in themed environments from a scenographic and performative angle offers additional insights and contributes a contemporary perspective to the discussion of symbols' dominance over form. Within the broader topic of theming and globalisation, we can observe the complicity of scenography in the appropriation of space as a commodity, which influenced the creation of a universal language of signs at the cost of detachment from the local and regional. In this context, the exchange of stimuli, both sensory and cognitive, activated through our participation in the activities on offer, frames our reality within the imaginary worlds that, according to Schechner, constitute the essence of theatre. This chapter thus weighs the impact of idealised scenographic worlds on consumers' senses. It considers the question of sociopolitical responsibility with regard to the manipulation of sensory experience, which is inherent in the creation of a parallel universe seemingly free of the complexities of the real world outside the mall.

The sixth chapter of the book, 'The Deceitful Charm of Scenography', offers a critical overview of the current scenographic approach to themed architecture while also pointing out its unused potential. As the medium for the stimulation of human needs and desires, themed scenography only reflects the sociocultural impulses of the society in which we live. The capacity of scenography to interpret consumers' societally established wants and needs makes it a perfect tool, easy to exploit for the purpose of profit. To demonstrate its potential, this chapter covers the historical, aesthetic, social and political implications of themed spatial design, addresses its immersive impact on consumers and rethinks the dynamics of the spectacle in environmental settings. By considering all these various aspects, it highlights the relevance, cultural impact and responsibility of scenographic interventions that command the engagement of all our senses in commercial urban spaces. It breaks down the traditional divide between architecture and scenography that associates one discipline with meeting permanent social requirements and the other with satisfying temporary human desires, one with providing a shelter and the other a backdrop for entertainment, thus bringing the need for collaboration between the two to a deeper and more meaningful level. The performative aspects of spatial design have pushed the architecture of themed environments beyond the traditional architectural parameters of a building's function, structure and materiality, reaching instead into the scenographic and ephemeral, and blurring the line between functional and fictional. The transplant of theatricality into open urban spaces went from using existing city architecture as the set to creating designated permanent facilities to serve as scenography. In light of this phenomenon, this chapter reflects on scenographic techniques, their consumption in themed shopping malls and, more generally, the perception of the physical scenographic environment within the ideological framework dictated by economic modes of production, distribution and reception (Haslett 2000: 36).

The closing chapter, 'Spatial Flexibility: A Yearning', summarises the observations presented in the book's earlier sections. While doing so, it highlights the 'unmediated relationship' with economics of both the scenography and the architecture of themed shopping malls, which reverberates through inseparable ties to commissions and land values (Jameson 1991: 5). In Postmodernity, no discussion of culture can escape the economic context in which it is steeped; it is actually impossible to 'talk about culture without simultaneously discussing economics and vice versa' (Haslett 2000: 113–14). The result is an attempt 'to articulate ideology's repressed preconditions, to articulate its unconsciousness, the things it cannot say in order to exist' (2000: 68). Consequently, *Consuming Scenography* asks how we can use scenographic knowledge to better understand scenography's ideological context within a system, thereby making change possible[9]. In the contemporary era of digital and increasingly immaterial scenography in the theatre, commercial entertainment and themed areas offer a background for study that the classic theatrical stage cannot currently provide. Considering the influence of digital media on human perception and the developments they have initiated in the way we perceive our environment, my hope in this book is to shed some light on the role played by scenographic architecture in our experience of the world.

Opposing a common misconception of scenographic architecture that thinks of it as external, descriptive and disguising, I argue that, by discrediting its theatricality as superficial and untrue, we are missing a chance to go beyond what meets the eye. Doing so, on the other hand, allows us to better grasp the notion of belonging that scenographic practice as 'intervention with place' can provide (Hann 2019: 119). At a time when the 'distant' senses of vision and hearing dominate our awareness, *Consuming Scenography* looks at the relevance and cultural impact of scenographic performativity, which continuously expands its sensory effect in architectural places. As scenographic discourse moves away from the question *what is scenography?* (Howard 2008) towards its expanded agency (Hann 2019; McKinney and Palmer 2017), my aim is to reach beyond a simple understanding how themed shopping malls could help us both comprehend neo-traditional nostalgia, as a simulation of the principles of new urbanism,[10] and to justify the human need to step out of reality into places of fantasy and imagination. Following Kathleen Irwin's discussion of scenographic agency in its showing-doing, its responsibility in this regard, and Juliet Rufford's enquiry into the relationship between architecture and theatre (Irwin 2017: 111–23; Rufford 2015: 46), this book offers an exploration of what scenography *does* in themed shopping malls and what it might *enable*.

1

Staging Consumer Seduction: A Brief History

1.1 The market enclosure as a scenographic principle

Ever since mankind first began trading, the market has been about more than simply buying and selling goods. It was also a place to socialise, to be seduced by the mystical and exotic, to be entertained and to witness demonstrations of political power.[1] Historically, traders' attention-seeking competitiveness in the pursuit of profits targeted all the consumer's senses, thus intertwining the exchange of goods and performativity, and making the latter an inherent feature of the marketplace (Wiles 2003: 85). The temporal abolition of established rules and norms, often associated with liminality,[2] created a transitional space among permanent settlements. Spreading 'the intoxicating energy of the crowd channelled within the confined public space', the traditional marketplace introduced theatricality into everyday life (Goss 1993: 27). While the architecture of urban settlements provided a static backdrop, goods laid out on mats and in improvised stalls morphed according to ever-changing multitudes, weather and seasons: the marketplace internalised the very essence of theatrical temporality visually conveyed through this special kind of environmental scenography.

The confluence of economy, society, politics and theatre grew even more compelling when outdoor market stalls were gathered into inner-city constructions and topped with roofs (Lepik et al. 2016: 6). Shops grouped together in shaded pedestrian streets, covered walkways and colonnaded porticos can be traced back to the stoa[3] of Attalos, Trajan's Market, and medieval European enclosed markets; and qaysariyya, khans, wakalas, souks and bazaars spread across North Africa and Southwest Asia.[4] Swapping the adaptability of their outdoor counterparts for a permanent setting within architectural complexes, roofed markets advanced the process of seduction and persuasion, cultivating an atmosphere that influenced their patrons' behaviour and decision-making.[5] They created the conditions for customers to take their time purchasing goods, to enjoy the setting, to engage in conversation, price negotiations and entertainment, independent of the weather conditions and other activities happening in the agora, forum or medieval town square at the same time. So, drawing outdoor stalls into the unified urban structures of inner cities, early enclosed markets set the scene for a unique ambiance to develop in places of trade through their architecture and displayed commodities. Colonnaded porticos and arcades directed the way light entered trading spaces, elevating the staged quality not only of the goods being presented but also of the market's atmosphere.

Some unique examples from the classical civilisations give us an idea of the seductive effects of roofed markets at their very beginnings. The stoas in ancient Greece evolved from simple colonnaded buildings not meant for any purpose more specific than to offer shelter and serve as gathering places to spaces where trade mingled with the entertainment provided by jugglers and sword-swallowers, philosophical discussions, exhibitions of art (Stoa Poikile) and simple relaxation.[6] The Stoa of Attalos in the agora of Athens (150 BCE) hosted forty-two shops on two levels under a single roof (McK. Camp 2015). In addition to the scenographic staging of goods meant for sale,[7] common in places of trade, the Stoa's double-colonnaded portico created dramatic shadows that moved with the sun, introducing an extra layer of visual seduction to the market space. In ancient Rome, the concrete grain vault in the central hallway of Trajan's Market (112 CE) shows innovation in how its incorporated arches were designed to conduct the movement of light through the space. During the day the rays of light played with the place's atmosphere. The sun created strong contrasts between light and shadows, highlighting some surfaces while toning down others. Today, the remains of coloured marble ornaments, columns, mosaic floors with different patterns for each shop and the vaulted ceiling along the curved alleys in this 170-room multi-storey complex give us a hint of the visual appeal that Trajan's Market had on Roman citizens and visitors alike (Becker 2018). On the upper floors, circular arched walkways opened a view to the city and its surroundings.

The image of the city was still present in this particular setting of ancient roofed markets, but in a different way than in the open squares of the Athens agora or the Roman Forum. In both cases, especially in Trajan's Market, the city itself became scenography, a backdrop, a distant image that one could observe only between the columns of the colonnaded porticos and from the walkway galleries. The enclosure of the marketplace, though embedded in the urban matrices of Athens and Rome as part of the agora or forum complex, created a physical divide between the market and its surroundings. Perhaps counterintuitively, the very withdrawal from open spaces into enclosed buildings opened the door for a scenographic way of thinking about the use of space in places of commerce. In this context, a scenographic approach included appropriating existing spatial conditions and the physicality of the architecture in order to elevate the appeal and enhance the drama that unfolded in the action of trade. We can well imagine how the architecture of hallways and market alleys, the goods displayed on the counters set up in shop entrances and stored within the shops themselves, and the scent of food and drink all contributed to the scenographic atmosphere of the first roofed markets. Development from this point was not, of course, a straightforward process.

Early medieval enclosed markets in Europe were incorporated into the open, arcaded ground floors below town hall and guild offices (Coleman 2006: 20). They enabled the fluid use of space in town squares for trade businesses. Partially roofed and partially open to the elements, market stalls were surrounded with the architecture of the existing urban settlements, a panoramic image that changed unremittingly as medieval towns expanded their reach with both public and private buildings, gradually enveloping the town squares. Over time, this architectural typology saw many variations. In some European towns, the separation of businesses led to independent building units; in others, ground floors remained part of the town hall.[8] Depictions of the medieval marketplace in frescos in the courtyard of Issogne castle (Aosta valley, Italy) suggest how scenographic interventions might have been implemented. Individual elements such as stalls set up between columns, merchandise arranged skilfully around them and goods displayed behind the merchants on the wall across the colonnade are framed by the architecture of the marketplace. Although artistic expression has to be taken into account, the frescos portray products set out on counters, shelves in the background and wooden constructions specially made to hold tools and weapons. The way medieval shops and stalls were equipped clearly reflects the aesthetic approach to exhibiting textiles, shoes, food and tools. Another source, a fifteenth-century French engraving,[9] presents a scene from a covered market with a counter positioned between the columns of an inner arched colonnade, set on a pedestal and draped with cloth onto which shoemakers, goldsmiths, crockery and textile merchants lay out their wares. The image shows shelves and cabinets behind the merchants that contain attractive arrangements of goods.

In the sixteenth century, evolving trade, bank and credit systems influenced the emergence of a new architectural typology (Coleman 2006: 25). The inward orientation of these buildings blended out the city as scenography, leaving only the facades of the courtyards and atriums to visually dominate places for trade. Stock exchange markets in Antwerp, Amsterdam and London introduced buildings with an enclosed atrium boasting a colonnaded courtyard on the ground floor and rows of stalls in the gallery of the first floor that provided market space for luxury items (Coleman 2006: 25–6).[10] Offices, shops and stalls encircled the courtyard between the colonnade and the facade. Peter Coleman confirms that extending buildings to include ground floors with a colonnade to protect shops from the weather was also characteristic of the first shopping streets established in Italy during the sixteenth century and in northern Europe in the seventeenth century (2006: 26–8). Lewis Mumford emphasises the importance of the physical protection for stalls and booths, because until the seventeenth century, when they were gradually 'put behind glass', the active life of citizens took place outdoors (1996: 56). Merchants presented their goods on counters and in front of the open shopfronts, merging the architecture of the medieval towns with their own arrangements. The shoppers' visual field was thus bordered by the shopfronts on one side and the immediate urban surroundings behind the colonnade on the other. Contrary to exchange markets, early shopping streets opened towards the city's atmosphere. Because trading still took place in front of the shops (Coleman 2006: 28), the architecture of the streets provided its environmental scenography. Occasional temporary withdrawal from the streets into a more intimate and visually controlled environment started in the late seventeenth century with the first glass shop windows. These helped move counters out of entrances and into the shops themselves, opening their interiors to the public (Coleman 2006: 28). As Clare Welsh's study of the design of early eighteenth-century London goldsmiths' shows, the 'theatre of consumption' at the time was also reflected in highly skilful and sophisticated strategies of display (1995: 96–111; Berry 2002: 384). Until plate-glass technology enabled the production of large shop windows in the mid-nineteenth century, grids of small glass panels prevailed. While interior design and scenographic arrangements facilitated a more individual approach to the perusal and purchase of merchandise, they also faded out the architecture of the towns as soon as buyers were tempted inside.

    Late eighteenth- and early nineteenth-century buildings for markets and fairs continued to merge shopping, leisure and entertainment. Shops and stalls organised into open courtyards surrounded by a colonnade on the ground floor and a gallery above (Hungerford Market, London) and later fully enclosed within market buildings (Les Halles, Paris) were increasingly oriented inwards, continuing the practice of physical separation from the surrounding urban environment (Coleman 2006: 28–9). In some cases, this tendency offered a fruitful playground for new theatrical forms to unfold. The annual fairs of St Germain and St Laurent contributed to the emergence of musical theatre, especially *comédie en vaudevilles*. Even though different forms of marketplace existed simultaneously throughout medieval Europe, the transition from early open-air market stalls to later enclosed shopping areas paved the way for the architectural typologies that followed. As a result, the conditions were prepared for scenographic interventions gradually to develop their influence over commercial spaces.

In North Africa and Southwest Asia, as in Europe, adding roofs to the market served not only to protect merchants and patrons from the climate but also to shield particular goods and high-quality fabrics like silk (Hmood 2017: 265). Mixing trade with other functions within larger building complexes was characteristic for the region since ancient times. Qaysariyya, khans and wakalas combined the market with lodgings and the storage of goods and, in some cases, with a water supply and a school,[11] while souks and bazaars, though predominantly oriented towards trade businesses, were embedded in the functional versatility of inner-city structures.[12] Made at first of improvised constructions covered with mats, fabrics and wooden planks, souks and bazaars transitioned into solid architectural buildings with cross-shaped vaulted ceilings and domes, which started to emerge in the late Middle Ages. Their inward orientation blanked out the surrounding distractions of lively city streets, while openings in the vaulted ceilings allowed the goods on display to be illuminated by daylight in a theatrical manner. The familiar image of souks and bazaars that we have today, with lushly decorated shops surrounded by a wealth of exotic goods that scenographically overwhelm the architecture itself, does not exactly recapture the oriental market's origins. As Walter M. Weiss points out, one of the most famous oriental bazaars, Kapali Carsi in Istanbul (1461), did not feature attention-seeking merchants calling out prices (1994: 171–2). Tradespeople sat quietly in their alcoves, letting their wares do the talking. Weiss emphasises that at Kapali Carsi's beginnings, there were no vitrines in front of the shops, no lettering to advertise what was for sale; discreet wall paintings were the only ornament (1994: 172). The architecture of the place, its form and materiality, brick and wood patterns, grill decorations, light that entered the space vertically (Isfahan Bazaar, Bokhara Bazaar) or diagonally (the Grand Bazaar, Istanbul) from above through the vaulted and domed ceilings[13] played the major role in using atmospheric flair to provide visitors with a visual experience. It was not all left to the architecture, though. From the beginning, arranging goods in an attractive way inside their shops was a subtle scenographic art practised by the merchants, who were aware of the relevance of visual appeal to running a successful business. At the peak of Kapali Carsi's splendour in the nineteenth century, the fine tactility of draped fabrics such as velour, silk and muslin, the glittering reflections of stained glass, weapons and jewellery, and the intense colour spectrum of spices added to the overall scenography of the place. Furthermore, as Weiss highlights, the variety of high-quality products exceeded by far the offer one could find in the shopping arcades of London or Paris at the time.

Examples of markets from the classical civilisations, medieval Europe and the Orient suggest that the early stages of scenographic interventions in enclosed marketplaces present more a story of fragmented highlights than the continuous evolution of the visual appropriation of an architectural typology (Coleman 2006: 51–4, 57). Viewed from the perspective of the market's theatricality, however, even this initial, haphazard history points towards the presence of scenographics in the marketplace over several centuries. The continuation of this story in the next chapters will show how scenography further expanded its influence in a specific type of marketplace, which laid the foundations for simulations of spatial reality and the establishment of a tradition that is still practised today. Through all the historical forms of the enclosed marketplace, a single scenographic principle shines through: the need to find an adequate means of compensating for what got lost in the transition – the atmosphere of the city.

1.2 Industrialising pleasure: Shopping arcades and department stores

Architecture's contribution to 'pleasure'[14] and the scenographic in Western commercial spaces was introduced with the advent of shopping arcades in the late eighteenth and early nineteenth centuries. A long way from the unpaved, muddy market streets of days gone by, the first arcades in Paris and London propelled the unique use of scenography into places for trade, spreading the practice across Europe and overseas to her colonies. Tracing the origins of modern consumerism, Colin Campbell calls attention to the preoccupation with pleasure, 'envisioned as a potential quality of all experience', which focused 'on the meanings and images which can be imputed to a product' (2005: 463). Taking its cue from daydreams and fantasy, the scenographic approach to the manipulation of space and introduction of illusion in shop-window displays set in motion the individual substitution of 'illusory for real stimuli' (2005: 463). The dreamy worlds of shopping arcades thus seduced consumers, encouraging them to create their 'own pleasurable environment', and established the modern approach to consumerism 'by creating and manipulating illusions and hence the emotive dimension of consciousness' (2005: 463).

The three- to fifteen-metre-wide passages that connected inner-city streets and the facades of alleys in enclosed blocks presented exterior architecture in semi-interior spaces,[15] giving them a theatrical and aesthetical character.

Offering a stylish interpretation of the outside world, stained-glass roofs flooded tiled floors and shop windows with light, placing the objects in the windows and the people gazing at them centre stage. Arcades were among the first public spaces to experiment with gas and later electrical lightning,[16] so it is easy to imagine the advantage during night hours of their lanterns, chandeliers and console lamps among the sparsely lit city streets of the nineteenth century (Geist 1982: 28). As Walter Benjamin puts it, 'The arcades are *the scene* of the first gas lighting' (1999: 3). Apart from the use of light and floors luxuriously designed with tiles and mosaics, decoration also extended to facades adorned with clocks, figures, colourful stained-glass windows and mirrors, all of which added to the visual opulence of the arcades and created a strong contrast to the city streets. Luxury goods were skilfully arranged as objects of desire that, by means of packaging, presentation and advertisement, should find their way to the consumer. 'The arcade is a street of lascivious commerce only,' Benjamin notes. 'It is wholly adapted to arousing desires' (1999: 828). In this newly conceived setting, shop windows established a special kind of communication between consumers and commodities. Jean Baudrillard writes: 'That specific space which is the shop-window – neither inside nor outside, neither private nor wholly public, and which is already the street while maintaining, behind the transparency of its glass, the distance, the opaque status of the commodity – is also the site of a specific social relation' (1998: 166). Signs, painted boards, display cases, posters and lettering on shop windows spoke to the overall atmosphere of visual seduction (Geist 1982: 267). Furthermore, the scent of freshly ground coffee, truffles, pastries, tobacco, exotic plants, lemons and oranges extended the sensory allure of the place (Benjamin 1999: 46; Geist 1982: 266). The objects in the windows, set up 'in a glorious *mise-en-scène*', reinforced what Baudrillard calls the 'consensus operation' – a speechless 'communication and exchange of values' (1998: 166). The showcased commodities, he continues, 'aped by the objects themselves on their stage-set, this symbolic, silent exchange between the proffered object and the gaze, is clearly an invitation to real, economic exchange inside the shop' (1998: 166).

Adhering to the pleasure principle, the architecture of nineteenth-century shopping arcades formed the next stage of the journey of roofed markets and bazaars as scenographic places of commerce. Besides shops, arcades housed restaurants, reading rooms, baths, clubs, hotels, theatres, vaudevilles, cabarets and even scenographic installations such as panoramas, dioramas and cosmoramas, which served, in some arcades, as attractions to draw in more visitors.[17] One of the earliest arcades, the Passage des Panoramas in Paris, built in 1800, had two rotundas to the left and right of its entrance. In 1805, a third was added, with realistically painted city landscapes on the circular canvas.[18] In the first half of the nineteenth century, this popular scenographic invention offered an 'optic spectacle', using theatrical effects to introduce life, movement and the passage of time into painted cityscapes. Attempts in paintings to imitate transformation included 'the changing daylight in the landscape, the rising of the moon, the rush of waterfalls' (Benjamin 1999: 5). Until 1831, the year in which the rotundas of the Passage des Panoramas were demolished, the painter Pierre Prévost manufactured with his apprentices eighteen panorama paintings that depicted diverse topics and landscapes (Geist 1982: 264).

Throughout the nineteenth century, scenography and the theatre were closely connected to a variety of different amusements on offer in shopping arcades. The Royal Opera Arcades (1818) in London were originally an extension of the King's Theatre (now Her Majesty's Theatre). In 1884, the Brussels Théâtre du Vaudeville was inaugurated in Les Galeries Royales Saint-Hubert (1846). The Passage des Panoramas hosted the Théâtre des Variétés and the Children's Theatre of M. Comte. The Gymnase-Enfantin was situated in the Passage de l'Opéra, 'where later on, around 1896, the commentating naturalist theater of Chirac housed the Théâtre de Vérité, in which one-act plays were performed by a nude couple' (Benjamin 1999: 831). According to Benjamin, 'it was the custom to name fancy-goods shops after the most successful vaudevilles of the season. And since such shops, by and large, made up the most elegant part of the arcades, the gallery was, in places, like the mockup of a theater' (1999: 831). The influence of the theatre on the visual seduction of consumers made the shopping arcades a place not only to do business and to be entertained but also for social encounters based on the very essence of theatre, namely directing attention. The theatrical side of the arcades thus shaped consumers' identity as active players in bourgeois society. As Marvin Carlson noted, the theatres of the eighteenth and nineteenth centuries, like the arcades and passages, 'became the favoured gathering places of the new monied classes. [T]heir public spaces became a kind of indoor parade ground not only for the gathering of fashionable society, but even more important, for its display' (Carlson 1989: 151).

The emergence of the scenographic in places of commerce came hand in hand with the rapid modernisation of the time and the tendency under industrial capitalism to clamour for attention for new products in order to maximise profits (Crary 2001: 14). According to Jonathan Crary, the second half of the nineteenth century brought a shift, a liberation, in understandings of perception. Increasing awareness of the impact of external stimuli opened the door to a 'dramatic expansion of the possibilities of aesthetic experience' (2001: 13). Scenographic inventions in commercial settings demonstrated the seductive and manipulative aspects of perception, shaking the common understanding of vision as a simple sense that was a certain and necessary component for the acquisition of knowledge. Drawing upon Guy Debord's

Society of Spectacle and Michel Foucault's *Discipline and Punish*, Crary's historical analyses present 'attention' as a process of selection and exclusion (2001: 24), established in the late nineteenth century, that 'has little to do with the visual contents ... and far more with a larger strategy of the individual' (2001: 74). 'Spectacle', he continues, 'is not primarily concerned with *looking at* images but rather with the construction of conditions that individuate, immobilize, and separate subjects, even within a world in which mobility and circulation are ubiquitous' (2001: 74). Crary's argument is rooted in his analysis of Georges Seurat's painting *Parade de cirque* (1888) and of one of his unfinished drawings, *A Shop and Two Figures* (1882), where the 'scenic' and 'spectacular' are introduced with scenographed shop windows and seductive architecture in shopping arcades. The art implies that both the scenography and the architecture of such places supported the illusion of choice while serving capitalist forms of power as a method to fix the gaze and so manage attention (2001: 75). This point of view shifts the focus away from the products themselves to the techniques of their presentation. 'In this way', Crary explains, 'attention becomes key to the operation of noncoercive forms of power' (2001: 74). Towards the end of the nineteenth century, the notion of perception as a passive process entirely dependent on external stimuli shifted to accommodate an understanding that the perceiver actively contributes to visual experience of the world 'through a layered complex of sensory and cognitive processes, of higher and lower cerebral centers' (2001: 95).

Even though earlier forms of roofed marketplace, such as the Oriental bazaar, do bear some similarity to shopping arcades and passages, Johann Friedrich Geist's historical overview clearly demonstrates the uniqueness of this type of building. As privately owned and developed public spaces, the advent of arcades corresponded with the rise of high capitalism and a search for new ways to present and sell luxury merchandise. After a period of continental blockade (1806–13), a liberal economic system and capitalist production methods were restored (Geist 1982: 97). The consequent accumulation of goods introduced scenography into commercial spaces, using Eclecticism as a stylistic background to unleash its power. Between 1820 and 1840, no fewer than fifteen new shopping arcades were built in Paris alone, spreading this new architectural structure across wealthy, industrialised European cities and their provinces, as well as America (e.g. Philadelphia, New York, Cleveland, Atlanta) and, later, Australia (e.g. Adelaide, Melbourne, Sydney).[19] Industrial production made it possible to manufacture bigger glass sheets, which, in turn, influenced how goods were pulled back into shop interiors and arranged behind glass, eventually creating the conditions for a new profession to emerge: shop-window designer. Scenographic signs in the shape of products, boards, graphics and displays obstructed the narrow passages to the extent that,[20] in 1847, police in Paris released a decree restricting how much space retailers were permitted to use in front of their shops for presentation and advertisement (Geist 1982: 29). Development over the next forty years culminated in a rise in iron and glass production, which facilitated the construction of more monumental and majestic shopping structures, such as Milan's Galleria Vittorio Emanuele II (1865–77).[21] Iron could now be embossed and ornamented, while larger sheets of glass could be incorporated into roofs and shop windows. Thanks largely to these innovations, the scenographic and theatrical approach reached a peak during the last decades of the nineteenth century.

Meanwhile, the merciless conquest and exploitation of colonies brought unprecedented wealth to imperialist Europe, and the architecture of arcades entered the decadent phase of the Belle Époque (Geist 1982: 106). During this period, the eclectic facades of shopping arcades typified its over-decorated and theatrical aesthetic with their exaggerated sense of scale and proportion (1982: 106). Some examples include the Galleria Umberto I in Naples (1887–91), the Upper Trading Rows in Moscow (1888–93) and the Cleveland Arcade in Cleveland (1888–90).[22] Thus, during the nineteenth century, establishing scenography in shopping arcades and passages went hand in hand with the confluence of theatre and commerce in spectacular urban settings and the intensified use of land in central city districts (Coleman 2006: 30).

An increased awareness of the monetary value of scenography on the capitalist market came as a logical consequence of the Industrial Revolution, a phenomenon that contributed heavily to the burgeoning development of scenographic elements and attractions in places of commerce. Yet, shopping arcades and passages were not the only commercial places that acknowledged its power. Department stores, which evolved from the *magasins de nouveautés* (novelty shops) in Paris and the London markets, began to emerge in the mid-nineteenth century (Coleman 2006: 33; Whitaker 2013: 18). This had an effect on the slow decline of the shopping arcades. According to Benjamin, there were several factors that brought about the end of the arcade era, including 'widened sidewalks, electric light, ban on prostitution, culture of the open air' (1999: 88). Threatened by a lack of public interest, the Paris arcades had started to close by the end of the nineteenth century.[23] Attempts to revitalise them by introducing music events to enhance their theatricality did not prove successful (Benjamin 1999: 204). Very few arcades were built after 1900 and the concept was eventually abandoned in the 1920s.[24] Nonetheless, shopping arcades had already profoundly influenced how theatricality was applied to marketing.

Department stores picked up where the arcades had left off, going even further by allowing consumers into their vast spaces and into close proximity with the items for sale. They eliminated the 'outside' perspective of the consumers, of the *flâneurs* who admired the luxury items from behind the glass of shop windows. Contrary to most arcades and passages,[25] department stores were arranged vertically, offering more possibilities for staged and theatrical presentations of the goods (Brune et al. 2011: 9). Elaborate decorations, galleries overlooking the shop floor, impressive staircases, mirrors and atriums covered with glass roofs that offered dramatic interior lighting set new standards for places of commerce. Once inside the department stores, the opulence and scale of the architectural space, with the 'grandness and finery of metal balustrading, elegant bridges and flying staircases', and the smell of perfume that filled the air seduced customers by appealing to all their senses, keeping them in the shopping mood for as long as possible (Coleman 2006: 34; Ritzer 2005: 65; Whitaker 2013: 155). Apart from making quality products affordable for the middle classes (Brune et al. 2011: 9), indulging the consumer became the primary goal of department stores, which led to more elaborate efforts such as the creation of attractive displays of the goods for sale. These lavish interiors, enhanced with scenographic installations of presented merchandise, provided the setting for 'a special experience set apart from everyday life', like the theatre (Carlson 1989: 164). Traditionally, says Marvin Carlson, the theatre has offered 'an experience not restricted to the actual performance but extending to the entire event structure of which the performance is a part, and the location of that event structure has often carried forward that image by displaying the symbols of elegance, pleasure, and high culture' (1989: 164). Similarly, Jan Whitaker notes that using the same approach to design department stores elevated their importance and value. They were presented as a special kind of landmark and tourist attraction, placed in the same category as museums, churches and castles (Rooch 2009: 21; Whitaker 2013: 155).

Attention to commodities and their presentation in a way that heightened the pleasure experience rather than the purchase was further cultivated through world exhibitions. With their themed environments, Mark Gottdiener argues, the exhibitions incorporated a 'sign system as a way of communicating to onlookers the meaning of buildings' (1997: 32). Especially influential in both Europe and America, the World Fairs presented a multitude of items but did not offer them for sale. It is believed that the art of presenting exhibits at World Fairs inspired William Whitely to establish London's first department store (Gottdiener 1997: 37–8; Whitaker 2013: 12). Sharing 'a common rudimentary form which had its origins on the marketplace of old' (den Oudsten 2017: 2), it was perhaps inevitable that theatre and exhibition should meet in department stores. Lessons learned from exhibitions elevated ordinary products made for sale into exhibits, equating shopping with a cultural activity. According to Whitaker, by the turn of the twentieth century, department stores had transformed the necessary act of shopping into the pursuit of pleasure and recreational enjoyment (2013: 7). She also points out that the advent of department stores established new conditions that allowed consumers to take their time to look around, to touch the products and to engage with sales personnel without being pressured to purchase the goods (2013: 64). The aim was to create a public place with a pleasant flair, with the result that shopping became an almost incidental occurrence (2013: 64). The new politics of department stores encouraged spatial solutions that allowed customers to walk around as freely as they would when visiting an exhibition. In doing so, they reintroduced and remade the concept of the consumer as a *flâneur*, an idea previously established by the arcades.

This modified approach to shopping was supported by additional elements. A lavishly decorated reading room, a place where visitors to the department store could relax, read a newspaper or even leave someone a note, was first introduced by the Bon Marché in Paris in 1870. The idea spread quickly and became an integral part of big department stores across Europe at the beginning of the twentieth century (Whitaker 2013: 229). As the majority of those visitors were, at the time, women, the relaxation areas were carefully adorned in a traditionally feminine manner, with flower arrangements, live music and fountains, all of which was designed to keep them happy and ready to shop (2013: 229). These areas soon became places where consumers would meet to socialise, thus joining the social, entertainment and consumer aspects of city life. At the beginning of the twentieth century, roof terraces were very popular, and some department stores transformed them into pleasant environments. In 1907, Mitsukoshi in Tokyo opened its Sky Garden, which included a pond, fountain, shrubs, bonsai plants and a telescope to enjoy panoramic views of the city (MacPherson 2016: 160). During the 1920s department stores across Japan expanded the entertainment on their rooftops to include shrines, teahouses, playgrounds, ice rinks and even a zoo (Whitaker 2013: 236). Drawing on Paul Nystrom's observations, Whitaker indicates that, by the 1920s, the department store was a place that equally served both shopping and amusement (2013: 224).

The profession of window 'trimmers' or 'dressers', originally introduced in the shopping arcades, was tied to the developing capitalist market, and its ultimate goal was to increase profits. Yet this artistic practice nevertheless incorporated theatrical influences. In addition to the explicit theatricality of shop-window displays designed by renowned theatre artists like Frederick Kiesler (Saks Fifth Avenue) and Norman Bel Geddes (Franklin Simon) in the late 1920s and throughout the 1930s, William L. Bird's historical overview highlights the theatrical background of many other window dressers as well. Landy R. Hales, the commercial artist responsible for Macy's Christmas displays at the beginning of the twentieth century, was also involved in the production of stage props for Morris Gest's musical *Parade of the Wooden*

Soldiers (2007: 16–17). George Harold Messmore, an influential designer of mechanical installations and animated animal figures during the 1920s, started out in set-painting and props. In the course of his long career, when demand for window displays began to decline, Messmore redirected his company's activities towards production design for feature films and television soap operas (2007: 49, 136). James Albert Bliss, an animation artist whose reputation spread across the United States in the years following the Second World War, grew up among vaudevilles and gained early theatrical experience as a child actor (2007: 62). According to Bird, Bliss acknowledged his theatrical inspiration, describing his window sets as 'larger versions of the theatrical models that he had once made' (2007: 62). This became especially evident with his Bell Windows installation, which introduced atmospheric and emotionally charged scenography for shop windows without merchandise. Mark Gottdiener notes that '[department] stores used the theatrical techniques of staging, lighting, and posing to great effect' when promoting and displaying commodities and so boosted their sales (1997: 35).

In his *Arcades Project*, Benjamin also acknowledges the entertaining theatricality of early department stores: 'The circus-like and theatrical element of commerce is quite extraordinarily heightened' (1999: 43). He mentions the trend, around 1880, of draping tapestries over staircase balustrades (1999: 48, 59). This kind of scenographic intervention that prominently featured a specific theme was visible in the considered arrangement and design of shop windows and interiors, which became an occasional focus in department stores in the second half of the nineteenth century. The initial elaborate effort to stage products and decorate the stores' vast spaces according to a particular theme for a special seasonal occasion such as Christmas soon became a regular habit. It also became an indispensable routine during periods of weaker sales and led to the phenomenon known as White Week, when rather boring white household goods and clothing items were presented in extraordinary scenographic compositions. Aristide Boucicaut, founder of the Bon Marché department store, is credited as its inventor (Cucheval-Clarigny 1894: 32; Whitaker 2013: 76–7). In addition to other innovations, he organised exhibitions and concerts and introduced monthly changes among the in-house arrangements. February was reserved for household linens and gloves, March for spring novelties and fashion, May for the summer collection, September for carpets and furniture, October for winter clothing and December for toys and gifts (Cucheval-Clarigny 1894: 16, 32). As in the case of White Week, this sales strategy included an opulent snowy landscape with white bears and penguins lining the staircase of the Bon Marché (1926), a massive all-white installation, including a pyramidal construction decorated with ornaments, lights and crystalline forms, and a giant papier-mâché bird in the Tietz department store (1926), and white gondolas in extravagant light fixtures, strings of pearls and translucent drapes hanging from the ceiling in the atrium of KaDeWe (1929) (Rooch 2009: 18; Whitaker 2013: 76–7).[26] Artistically arranged shop windows with geometric compositions of white towels complemented such exceptional efforts to attract consumers.[27]

Staging products thus accompanied sales, special offers and exhibitions, subsequently turning the shopping experience into a show (Whitaker 2013: 74). Earlier, the goal had been to address all of the consumer's senses; the focus now was an emotional appeal and the impression that they were taking part in something very special (Bird 2007: 17; Whitaker 2013: 74). Early themed settings involved an exhibition of wild animals with a 'walk-through jungle of live trees, shrubbery and artificial rocks, and a one-ring circus with professional performers, including clowns, acrobats, performing dogs, ponies, and other animals' on the fourth floor at the Siegel-Cooper & Company in Chicago (1910), the Headquarters of Father Christmas and His Treasure Caves, arranged as grottoes with tanks of subtropical fish at Selfridges in London (1930), and Cozy Cloud Cottage (1948), where reindeer rested around the stove in the kitchen and Santa reclined in his living room, by John Moss at Marshall Field & Co (Bird 2007: 25–6, 121–3). These walk-in settings immersed consumers in scenographed environments, merging artistic craftsmanship and commerce and transforming a visit to a department store into a trip to see a spectacle.

Exhibitions had, of course, been a regular attraction at department stores since the early days and, in some cases, attracted an impressive number of visitors (Whitaker 2013: 250). The aircraft exhibitions that started at the beginning of the twentieth century and continued after the First World War were, from the scenographic point of view, perhaps the most interesting (2013: 249). According to Whitaker, these exhibitions included the first aeroplane to fly over the English Channel in 1909, the one that landed on the River Thames in 1926 and the one that flew over Mount Everest in 1933 (2013: 249). According to archival images, exhibited aeroplanes, such as the glider hung in the atrium of the Tietz department store in Berlin (1929), were also used for advertising purposes, in this case for the famous Astoria variety theatre in Bremen. Themes of consumerism, however, Gottdiener explains, were usually limited to 'exoticism (such as the sale of imported commodities like silk) and opulence (for perfumes, home furnishings, fashions, and the like) within the new marketing structure' (1997: 35). Nevertheless, he argues that by stimulating consumers' desires, themed scenographic displays and images exercised an influence not only on shoppers' perceptions but also on culture more generally (1997: 35).

At the very start of the department stores' era and especially during the building boom at the end of the nineteenth and beginning of the twentieth centuries, their cultural influence went beyond impressive interiors to encompass the exteriors as well. Many could easily be mistaken for public buildings (Whitaker 2013: 102). Because of height and safety restrictions in Europe, the buildings sometimes stretched up to 244 metres along the boulevards, as in the case of Hermann Tietz (1911) in Berlin,[28] or took over whole blocks, as did the Bon Marché in Paris (2013: 102). The first step was to wow shoppers and capture their attention using the shop windows and the store's exterior (2013: 101). However, the facades were not only eye-catching because of their architecture but they were also used for advertisements and promotions. The oversized dimensions of scenographics covered large parts of the facades, allowing them to overshadow the buildings' architecture, especially at night. The logotypes, gigantic lettering spanning two floors, large-scale billboards and imaginative light installations created for White Week sales by the Berlin department stores KaDeWe, Jandorf, F. V. Grünfeld and Tietz were common practice in the late 1920s. In 1930, the whole facade of Hermann Tietz on the Alexanderplatz was covered with a light installation showing a bird of paradise with 'White Week' emblazoned in huge letters and framed by open wings.[29] Christmas was another opportunity for scenographic interventions on facades. The transformation of the Grands Magasins du Louvre in Paris for Christmas 1927 included a light installation that stretched over eight storeys of the huge building, depicting a winter landscape with moving figures building a snowman (2013: 155).

The seductive allure of such fantastic scenographic solutions, which began as subtle suggestions in the shopping arcades and then grew to greater heights in the department stores, went hand in hand with new insights into perception and attention. The combination of these factors laid the crucial foundations for the marketing strategies developed in the second half of the twentieth century. When it came to the newly emerging typology of the shopping mall, which started to dominate the market from the 1950s, commercial scenographic interventions had to adjust. Some tactics, such as the occasional amplification of shopping-mall interiors and exteriors using scenographic means during the holiday season and festivities, continued. But, as the enclosure of the marketplace got bigger, due in part to the rapid development of technology, demand for a corresponding expansion of scenographic approaches followed.

1.3 Post-war functionalism: Shopping malls

After the Second World War, an increase in the production of goods brought about substantial changes in how department stores were designed. Although their architecture is frequently criticised (Brune 2011: 14–15), it can still be considered inherently innovative. Transparent glass facades on the ground floor connected the interiors with their city surroundings, leaving visitors with the impression that, by entering, they were simply continuing their walk through the city. Large open spaces offered more possibilities for displaying the steadily growing amounts of merchandise, and see-through structures of stairs and elevators enabled easier orientation while their central positions allowed more light to come in (Brune 2011: 14). Even though scenographic interventions were still visible in department stores after the war, their impact was more subtle and less opulent than before. The ostentatious facades and fanciful shop-window displays, which had previously served as the main forces pulling consumers inside, were exchanged for functional architecture and design solutions that focused their attention on a more profitable use of space (Whitaker 2013: 130). The new strategy prioritised the most effective way to lead customers through the store, exposing them to as many products as possible and directing light sources to highlight the items for sale, rather than distracting visitors with impressive decorative elements. Walter Brune explains that the conceptual changes in the architectural planning of department stores in the first decades after the war placed 'the emphasis on showcasing brands, accessibility by car and spatial economy', which led to 'large solitary buildings' (2011: 11–16).

The same period saw affluent city inhabitants from all over the United States migrate in droves to the suburbs. Along with the rising number of chain stores near satellite neighbourhoods, this threatened the existence of department stores in downtown areas.[30] The new concept of the shopping mall, established in America by private investors from the early 1950s, was a successful avenue and provided the department store with the opportunity to regain its reputation (Longstreth 2016: 53).[31] Some early examples of grouping multiple shops together into one unified entity, outside the pattern of nineteenth-century American cities, suggest that the concept of the shopping mall dates back to 1870.[32] Even so, enclosed shopping environments that aspired neither to connect with the city nor to expand its urban sprawl with new residential areas began in the 1950s. Following the Second World War, city centres across the United States started to lose their appeal as desirable residential locations for the rising middle classes (Oc et al. 1997: 8).[33] As opposed to the Western European tendency to keep inner-city rents and living standards high in neighbourhoods that then remained affordable only for a wealthy middle class, conditions in American city centres deteriorated. Socioeconomic inequality deepened among their inhabitants, caused by disadvantageous positions and limited opportunities for new immigrants, seniors and minorities. Meanwhile, an increase in the number of cars on the roads, and the ensuing traffic jams, did nothing to improve inner-city life. As a result, prosperous citizens started to migrate to the suburbs. Restructuring the marketplace, as Lizabeth Cohen explains, was also influenced by government support for building highways and for the construction and purchase of new homes during a period marked by a shortage of urban housing. The suburban population consequently rose 43 per cent between 1947 and 1953 (Cohen 1996: 1051).

Correspondingly, shopping malls, which housed specialised and affordable chain stores under one roof, sprang up in suburban areas on important traffic junctions that were easily accessible not only for the inhabitants of those suburbs but also from the city (König 2008: 75; Whitaker 2013: 22, 24). Using Samuel and Lois Pratt's consumer surveys of Bergen County in the late 1950s and early 1960s, Cohen points out that 80 per cent of the inhabitants had stopped shopping in New York City by 1959 after the Garden State Plaza (1957) and Bergen Mall (1957) opened in Paramus, New Jersey (1996: 1061). Following the decline of downtown shopping, department stores became legitimate contributors to the malls' success.[34] According to Richard Longstreth and Barbara Hahn's historical overviews, more than forty regional malls were built in the United States between 1948 and 1956 (Hahn 2002: 33; Longstreth 2016: 53).[35] There were so many that it is difficult now to talk about a single initiator of this architectural concept (Bader in Lepik et al. 2016: 12–13).[36] Still, among the multitudes, scholars agree that Victor Gruen stands out as the designer of the first fully enclosed and air-conditioned shopping centre, Southdale in Edina, Minnesota, which opened in 1956. He can be considered the architect who set and developed the typology of the shopping mall as we know it today.[37]

Although Gruen established the conceptual connection between architecture, graphic design and art, his theatrical background did not shine through in Southdale. His involvement in political cabaret (*Politisches Kabarett*) in Vienna and the Viennese Theatre Group in New York[38] was noticeable in his earlier work as retail designer at Lederer de Paris (1939) and Grayson's in New York (1939–40),[39] but his efforts in Southdale were more concerned with urban development, architecture and the building's interior logistics (Gruen et al. 2014: 149, 153; Lepik et al. 2016: 13). Gruen explained his initial idea as a reaction to the very long shopping streets in Los Angeles that could only be managed by car. In his first article on the topic, published in *Architectural Forum* in 1943, he suggested displacing shopping from the main central streets into a unifying building that would enable a more economical approach, with garden-like pedestrian walkways and without any traffic or parking restrictions (Gruen et al. 2014: 166). Climate control throughout the enclosed pedestrian areas in Southdale came about as a result of Gruen's observation of the seasons in Minneapolis: harsh winters, very hot summers and rainy springs and autumns (2014: 211). Drawing inspiration from Oriental bazaars and European passages and galleries, he aimed to create contemporary public spaces, sheltered from the weather conditions by the roof and by air-conditioning that simulated a European city centre (Brune 2011: 17). To do this within the limits of the budget, the initial idea, which incorporated direct entrances to the individual shops from the parking lot, was changed. In the revised concept, all the shops within the shopping centre could only be entered from inside the building, which significantly reduced costs (2014: 212). The final plans for Southdale were the result of an economically led decision-making process. The intention to connect all the shops under a single roof and create a microclimate inside the building was responsible for the inward orientation of this new architectural typology. Air-conditioning also enabled the building's interior 'to expand to the point that the exterior is no longer necessary'.[40] As a result, the interior was separated from its surroundings and became a self-sufficient, 'introverted' world of its own (2014: 213).

Despite some harsh criticism,[41] the financial success of the Southdale concept established this architectural typology as a universal model whose triumph could potentially be repeated almost anywhere. It moved away from the earlier architecture of arcades and department stores, which strove to seduce passers-by with decorative facades and shop windows, and focused instead on the interior, sealing off the surroundings with plain and minimalistic exteriors. Its location on a traffic junction in a suburban area, where it could only be reached by car, also enhanced the circumstances for self-sufficiency (Brune 2011: 17). In this special environment, the theatricality that had been played up by scenographic interventions in shop interiors in the arcades and department stores transitioned into a spacious inner court and indoor shopping streets, supporting promotions, contests, events and festivities. Decorated with art works, fountains, trees, tropical plants and a huge birdcage, Southdale, shortly after it was opened, offered a place to stroll around and take part in the consumption of theatre even when the shops were closed (Teaford 2016: 108).[42] Even if the new concept of the shopping mall seemed, in its first decades, to scale down the scenographic extravagance established in department stores, the appropriation of the latter's use of scenography for the purpose of entertainment continued to evolve over time. Towards the end of the twentieth century, when theming as a branding strategy entered shopping malls, and especially at the beginning of the twenty-first century, a time when theming became a global phenomenon, scenography reclaimed its relevance as a highly successful and influential marketing strategy. Themed malls, developed along the guidelines set by Gruen in Southdale, would reach a level of excess that cast a shadow over even the most daring scenographic interventions in earlier market typologies. Overall, as Cohen argues, Southdale laid the foundations not only for the development of urban planning in the American suburbs but also for cultural conditioning through the 'expansion of mass consumer society' on a global scale (1996: 1051).

2

Framing Consumption in Late Capitalism

2.1 Entertainment, please!

In the post-war period, during the late 1950s and 1960s, tax breaks for trade businesses encouraged developers to invest in the construction of shopping malls. This prompted high market values and made them easy to sell after only a few years of operation, and so the number of new malls across the United States multiplied. As a consequence, Barbara Hahn's analysis shows, the market had already started to reach saturation point by the 1970s (2002: 44).[1] In the meantime, experience revealed that, in order to keep up with changing demographics and customer preferences, shopping malls needed some improvements after seven years and more extensive renovations after twenty-five. Yet these alterations would not necessarily be rewarded by an increase in shoppers' spending.[2] This limited developers' freedom to make other investments (2002: 43). The allure of the shopping mall, which had been present in the early decades, started to wane (2002: 45).

Even though statistics published by the International Council of Shopping Centres show that 16,000 new malls were built between 1980 and 1990, the new tax regulations that came into effect in the 1980s made this type of construction hard to finance (Coleman 2006: 78; Hahn 2002: 34, 43). As a result, different tactics were implemented to keep the business going. In addition to a variety of specialised shopping malls that were developed in answer to the crisis, including the Factory Outlet Center, the Value Center and the Power Center, entertainment and theming were also explored as a new approach. According to the Urban Land Institute, 'overbuilding, aging facilities, loss of traditional tenants, competition from value-orientated retailers' were some of the reasons to embark on the adventure of developing entertainment-oriented shopping destinations (Beyard et al. 2001: 15). During the 1980s, the first urban entertainment centres, commonly referred to nowadays as 'retail entertainment destinations' (Beyard et al. 2001; Coleman 2006: 217), began to appear. These centres offered a wider range of entertainment venues and facilities to accompany the retail aspect, aiming to attract customers from beyond their regional reach (Coleman 2006: 78; Hahn 2002: 115).

The move towards centres that combined retail and recreation was also a reaction to market competition and a symptom of their developers' wish to differentiate their offers from outlet malls and budget suppliers (Hahn 2002: 115). According to Peter Coleman, 'entertainment or lifestyle retailing' was established as a new way of shopping, and was based on three main principles: 'the mix of merchandise, the importance of the environment in forming the character of the place and the complementary nature of catering and retail' (2006: 217). Retail entertainment destinations located either downtown or in suburban areas encouraged people to spend time with friends and family; entertainment became the priority, while shopping was almost coincidental and related to the purchase of goods that were not really necessary.[3] With the introduction of water parks, ice rinks, cinemas and food courts, retail entertainment destinations shifted the focus towards shopping as an experience and other recreational activities. One increasingly popular strategy for giving this new type of mall a strong visual identity was theming. Themed parks, themed restaurants and themed hotel rooms accompanied an already familiar selection of retailers and services. It is important to note, however, that scenographic techniques in early retail entertainment destinations were implemented only in the specific parts of the mall designated for entertainment and in select shopping and catering areas. The rest of the space was designed in a traditional manner without any stylistic connection to the theme. Nevertheless, theming and scenography had a profound influence on the design of shopping-mall interiors. Regional shopping and leisure centres such as the West Edmonton Mall in Alberta, Canada, and the Mall of America in Bloomington, Minnesota, were the forerunners of the grand North American retail entertainment destination. They used scenography to complement the new standards being set in design and construction and, in doing so, reflected how theming began to unfold on a grand scale in the 1980s.

With theming as a visual brand identity, theatricality has become an inseparable part of a retail experience that bridges the gap between shopping mall and amusement park. Pioneering steps in this direction started with the Triple Five Group, the development corporation behind the West Edmonton Mall in 1982 and its American counterpart, the Mall of America, which opened in 1992. Its impressive size, capacity and vast variety of options for both shopping and entertainment have allowed this special type of mall to become a landmark similar to the department store of the turn of the twentieth century. Travel agencies offer trips to the West Edmonton Mall and the Mall of America, describing them as a 'vacation experience like no other' with optional overnight stays in the malls' hotels.[4] With the help of scenographic techniques, parts of these mega-structures are organised into themed areas, giving each section a unified appearance. To understand the theatrical nature of the scenographed spaces made for these ambitious entertainment destinations, where theming has become more holistic and expanded its cultural dimension, it is necessary to take a detailed look at their design.

In the West Edmonton Mall, which was conceived by Maurice Sunderland, themed entertainment areas[5] on the first floor follow one after the other, in addition to the themed alleys, Europa Boulevard and China Town, on the second floor. Theming, as a fragmentation of 'conventional geographical space and historical time' (Shields 1989: 5), extends to 120 rooms in the Fantasyland Hotel, also housed within the mall, which are decorated according to Polynesian, Roman, Space, Hollywood, Western, Arabian, African and Imperial subjects.[6] A closer look at some of these themed areas offers an impression of the overall scale and influence of scenography in the West Edmonton Mall. The Galaxyland Amusement Park, for example, covers 37,100 square metres.[7] It is designed with the overall theme of outer space, depicting references to space ships, advanced technologies and unfamiliar vegetation, though stylistic eclecticism still shines through. Throughout the 'space-age', scenographed ride machineries, a nineteenth-century-style carousel, the Dragon Wagon, the Fun House and the Haunted Castle, whose facades resemble the walls of a medieval fortress, are also to be found. While Galaxyland is extensively scenographed, the World Waterpark, on the other hand, includes only occasional scenographic interventions. The entrance is designed as a giant wave, with fish coming out of the water and a shark on a surfboard at the top. Sporadic murals throughout the World Waterpark theatrically extend the view into imaginary landscapes, as painted sets and backdrops have done for centuries. The entrance to Marine Life is similar, though more extravagant – a giant fish holding the staircase in its open mouth. It leads the visitors to the lower level, where the aquariums and pools are located. The walls, ceiling, tanks and benches of the Marine Life zone are decorated with rustic stone surfaces, vegetation and even some forgotten 'treasures' from the sea's depths. Apart from Marine Life, the mall's Deep Sea Adventure section incorporates an indoor lake, with a replica of Christopher Columbus's flagship the Santa Maria parked in the lagoon.[8]

In addition to these themed entertainment areas, the West Edmonton Mall also introduced themed shopping alleys and holistically designed retail spaces.[9] Combining recognisable architectural elements, layouts and colourful neon signs,

BRBN St. on the mall's first level features bars and restaurants that reference the famous Bourbon Street in the French Quarter of New Orleans. The West Edmonton Mall's second themed street is the elaborately designed Europa Boulevard, which aspires to invoke the flair of European inner-city streets. A Postmodern simplification of architectural allusions to different historical styles primarily recalls the revival movements of the nineteenth century. However, what appears to blend highly stylised Neo-Renaissance, Neo-Baroque, Neoclassicist, Empire, Biedermeier, Napoleon III and Victorian references, among others, does not actually correspond to any specific European style or city. Rather, the design of Europa Boulevard is based on imaginative eclecticism, inspired by the past but daringly mixing elements in a generalised and playful way that would be hard to find in nineteenth-century Europe. Nevertheless, the barrel-vaulted ceiling of the glass roof inevitably evokes associations with late nineteenth-century shopping arcades. Skilful scaling is used to enhance the effect: the upper floors of the buildings are scaled down in relation to the shops on the first level, making the facades seem taller from the *flâneurs'* perspective. This old scenographic technique, taken from the theatrical stage, was also applied in department-store design at the end of the nineteenth century (Whitaker 2013: 101). In both cases, the aim was to make the architecture look even bigger and more impressive than it really was.

The Mall of America, designed by Jon Jerde, is a bit different. The overarching theme is reflected in the symbolic use of colours and elements from the American flag, such as stars and stripes, leaving interpretations of the theme open and serving simply 'as a consummate mass-marketing device' (Gottdiener 1997: 85). Considering the annual number of visitors and comparing revenues from the West Edmonton Mall's amusement parks with those of its stores, developers opted to change the West Edmonton Mall's balance of 60 per cent retail and 40 per cent entertainment to just 25 per cent retail and 75 per cent entertainment in the Mall of America (Shields 1989: 5). Rob Shields points to the 1986 interview with the president of Sears Canada, R. Shape, who claimed that the majority of tourists were interested in entertainment rather than shops, which appealed predominantly to locals (1989: 5). The Mall of America is organised around an indoor theme park, which is its main attraction: the Nickelodeon Universe[10] spreads over 28,322 square metres.[11] Brightly lit by sunlight streaming through the glass ceiling, the scenography of the vast entertainment area follows the themes of different rides. It encompasses rocky landscapes with vegetation, trees, cascades and waterfalls, ponds and animal animatronics. Characters such as SpongeBob SquarePants, the Ninja Turtles and Dora the Explorer are incorporated into the themed rides as oversized sculptures embedded into environments associated with their cartoon surroundings. The loops of rollercoaster tracks and their supports, the El Circulo del Cielo Ferris wheel, the curved slides and rope-climbing structure of the Dutchman's Deck Adventure Course, and the lavishly designed Guppy Bubbler gondolas in the shape of sea shells spinning high above the ground fill the enormous space that stretches vertically over three of the mall's levels. They all contribute to the theme park's colourful appeal.

Apart from the variety of rides, the Nickelodeon Universe also offers immersive experiences such as flight simulation in the FlyOver America flying theatre, experience stores[12] and a 91-metre acrylic tunnel through the Sea Life Aquarium. Unlike in the West Edmonton Mall, the theming here does not extend into the mall's retail sections. Still, over the years, the Mall of America has expanded the scenographic strategies first set by its predecessor. Its visual identity has been altered and enriched in order to keep up with the expectations of contemporary audiences to stimulate more than just their visual or kinaesthetic senses. Robotic technology combined with digital projections in FlyOver America offers a more contemplative encounter, as opposed to the adrenaline rush of rollercoaster rides. Synchronising the progress of the ride with images on the quarter-dome projection screen and the strategic use of fog, water sprays and scent activates visitors' senses of movement, touch and smell, going beyond the traditional scenographic impact based on hearing and vision. Visitors to the Sea Life Aquarium go through unusual visual sensations as they advance through the glass tunnel, observing sea creatures from a perspective that suggests walking on the ocean floor while remaining dry. At the same time, the curved acrylic glass in the tunnel makes the aquarium's inhabitants appear about 20 per cent smaller, prompting an additional shift in perception inside the aquatic environment.

By reinterpreting environmental, site-specific and immersive theatre, where the divide between spectatorship and performance is hard to distinguish, the West Edmonton Mall and the Mall of America introduced consumers to 'a maze of entertainment and commerce' (Aronson 2014). They established parameters that pull together consumption, entertainment and theming, tying theatricality to trade predominantly by means of spatial design. Alongside the architecture, scenography has here become a co-creator of ambience, a feature highly effective in boosting the number of visitors. In these places where capital is realised, where selling goods and services is the primary goal, theming has thus been used as a marketing strategy to shift focus away from the space's main function (Gottdiener 1997: 74). The inclusion of cultural, geographical or historical design references, Alan Bryman notes, elevates the malls' value to the level of 'must-see' locations and tourist attractions (2004: 45). The place is wrapped in a colourful setting, tied with a ribbon of entertainment, and offered to patrons as a complimentary souvenir, its purpose transformed into a consumable product. In the midst of the obvious cultural emptiness of the act of shopping, designers used a theme to create the illusion of additional content, 'mediating materialist relations of mass consumption and disguising the identity and rootedness of the shopping centre in the contemporary capitalist social order' (Goss 1993: 19). Cloaking the ordinary in a theme had other interesting effects from the scenographic point of view as well. It exposed consumers to different perceptions of architectural styles, scale and history, brought them into close contact with scenographic materiality, and involved their bodies in an experience of theatricality, highlighting embodiment through entertainment in these commercial settings.

2.2 Theming the identity of consumption

Themed shopping initially began as an open-air adventure. The Country Club Plaza in Kansas City (1923), developed by Jesse Clyde Nichols, is still considered a forerunner of the North American shopping mall.[13] The Plaza is also one of the earliest examples of a themed urban concept applied to a shopping district. Edward Buehler Delk and George E. Kessler designed it in the Spanish-Revival style, using the highly decorative architecture of the city of Seville as the inspiration behind the Plaza's stucco facades, bell towers, ironwork, bricks, ceramic tiles, mosaics and tiled roofs.[14] Artwork, such as figurative sculptures, and a cinema were also incorporated into the complex, creating a stylish and fashionable environment that attracted both existing downtown stores and new shops (Coleman 2006: 41). A site map from the district's early development between 1920 and 1940 shows some fifteen blocks of shopping facilities and parking spaces along the Ward Parkway Boulevard, Alameda Road and Forty-Seventh Street.[15] Over the years, this area was continuously extended with additional buildings and apartment blocks.

A unique example of an early shopping mall, the Plaza was constructed in an open urban space outside Kansas City's business centre. By referencing the architectural style of Seville, whose origins go back to the eighth century BCE, Delk and Kessler gave a strong visual identity to an area built on 'land from various run-down plots and swamp land', providing a sense of urban history where there previously was none (Coleman 2006: 41). This appropriation process introduced 'applied artificiality' into shopping environments, which laid the foundations for simulation and the idealisation of 'otherness'.[16] The shopping district's visual identity was strengthened through the adaptation of stylistic references to somewhere else, which set it apart from its competitors. Although truly progressive for its time in terms of design, theming and location, the Country Club Plaza, during the early years of modernism, also applied a very old urban technique characteristic of European cities. As it developed residential areas around the shopping district, the Plaza aimed to extend the city around the marketplace.

Another noteworthy case is the high-end community centre Highland Park Village (1931), designed by Marion Fooshee and James Cheek, north of Dallas, Texas. Twenty years in the making,[17] it followed in the Country Club Plaza's footsteps, and was intended to serve as both a shopping centre and a town square. The Village was presented as a set of buildings whose shops were oriented inwards towards the inner court. Another similarity between the Village and the Plaza was the architectural theme, namely the Spanish Revival. The inspiration for the visual style came as a result of the developer's research trips to Spain, Mexico and California. The aesthetics were thus a combination of domestic elements with features imitative of traditional Spanish architecture, with arched shop windows, wooden balconies on the first floor, exposed stone textures, trefoil arches, merlons with pointed arches, alcoves and tiled roofs. The design of the relief ornamentation on the facades, arches and merlons was drawn from the *mudéjar* style,[18] as well as from the Spanish Renaissance. In 1935, a luxury film theatre was added to the existing complex, but it took until 1951 for the infrastructure of Highland Park Village to look the way it does today. By that time, the loading zones were arranged behind the shops, so the pleasure of strolling through the inner court on a shopping excursion was not interrupted by deliveries. This feature of the Village's original plan would become one of the main organisational adjustments in the shopping malls that subsequently started to emerge.

The concept of the themed shopping mall, as imagined in the pioneering examples of the Country Club Plaza and Highland Park Village, had to wait more than half a century to be introduced again. Starting in the mid-1990s, the McArthurGlen development and management company revived the idea by establishing a number of designer outlet malls in the UK, Europe and North America. Throughout its various manifestations, from the Country Club Plaza to McArthurGlen, the use of historical architectural styles to present a unified visual identity was an attempt to give the mall's shopping streets the quality of an urban environment. This included a sense of history and an opportunity to wander and explore, all of which added emotional content to enhance the shopping experience (Underhill 2004: 484). As this new type of mall was designed to occupy an outdoor space, theming was applied to the architecture of the whole complex, giving it the characteristics of scenography and so transforming it into a theatrical setting. Besides disguising the basic 'relation of money for a commodity as another relation between commercial place and the consumer' (Gottdiener 1997: 74), the notion of theming supported a further exchange of roles between scenography and architecture. The simulated reality of the themed environment positioned consumers in a situation where a privately owned, commercial public space meant for trade became 'a site of performance and participatory spectatorship united through scenography' (Aronson 2014). As a result, the conditions were created for a special kind of environmental theatre to occur, where the distinction between stage and auditorium became difficult to grasp (Aronson 2014). In scenographed shopping spaces and landscapes, cultural geographer John Urry recognises, we consume not only food, clothing or retail items but also experiences. The objective in giving places of consumption an identity is grounded in the observation that more money will be spent if the purchase has an additional experience or deeper meaning attached to it.

The idea that consumption 'takes place', first introduced by human geographers, looks at how it occurs in certain locations and 'how it recreates and transforms those places' (Jones 2012: 79–80). This process is supported by the phenomenon called 'imaginative geographies', a tendency to 'attach attributes to specific places that we consume' (2012: 79–80). The bias towards a 'consumption of place', Andrew Jones explains, results from a global growth in tourism where 'places are packaged up as things [or "commodified"] to be consumed' (2012: 81). According to Jones, visitors do this by gazing at famous landmarks or by experiencing the atmosphere of certain neighbourhoods in the cities they enter as tourists (2012: 81). When they are themed, places that lack any distinctive characteristics are branded with an identity and differentiated from their competition; their appeal is advanced as they become destinations people want to visit in order to gain a novel shopping experience. For this purpose, themed shopping malls produce stylised, consumable geographies as (hyper)realistic versions of existing or imaginary places (2012: 80). Alan Bryman compares it with a kind of rerun of well-known cultural references, recycling 'iconic representations of these places that are part of popular culture' (2004: 143). Annual visitor numbers indicate that theming is highly effective at boosting the purchase of products and services that lack anything unique or meaningful behind their function. Neville Wakefield refers to this additional effect as 'adjacent attraction': the strategy of 'placing otherwise unremarkable goods or services for sale in an environment that is interesting or conveys messages beyond those provided by the goods or services themselves renders them more attractive and hence more likely to be purchased' (Bryman 2004: 34). The goal of staging scenographic interventions in themed shopping malls is to enable consumers' full participation in the experience of fantasy. However, in order actually to become full participants, Bryman argues, they need to consume. Therefore, 'in part, the consumer in a themed setting is consuming that setting as much as the goods or services themselves when making a purchase' (2004: 34).

By involving performative space in the consumption, themed malls place consumers in a play where reality and fantasy overlap. Disguising familiar brands behind the dollhouse facades of Main Street in Disneyland, Umberto Eco observes, encourages obsessive buying, persuading visitors that shopping is part of the game (Eco 1986: 43; Bryman 2004: 59). But attempts to make the products in themed environments look appealing by integrating them into a theatrical setting appear to be more a suggestion and an endeavour to 'stir the consumer's imagination' (Hosoya et al. 2001: 560). Hiromi Hosoya and Markus Schaefer call this strategy 'added-value' – 'an essential dimension of productivity that can be increased and consumed almost without limits' (2001: 560). Eco, on the other hand, points out that if theme parks such as Disneyland are trying to reproduce anything absolutely, it is, in fact, not reality but fantasy. In *The Experience Economy: Work Is Theatre & Every Business a Stage* (1999), B. Joseph Pine II and James H. Gilmore argue that in order 'to stage compelling esthetic experiences, designers must acknowledge that any environment designed to create an experience is *not* real', instead of trying to sell the unreal as reality (1999: 37). As a result, hyperrealistic scenography can be seen not as an effort to make shopping alleys look like city streets but as a bid to accentuate the artificiality of the fantasy, an alternative to existing urban constructs. Still, labelling it all a 'fantasy' perhaps does not do justice to the true nature of themed scenography in the shopping mall; the real manifestation actually effects real action and produces real outcomes (Jones 2012: 77; Driver 2014: 234–48, cited in Cloke et al. 2014).

Even if globalisation has encouraged re-creation of 'the same' in very different social environments and thus increased the similarity between them, Jones emphasises, it has not made all human societies homogeneous (2012: 29). Rather, scenographic agency in theme parks or themed malls uses 'imaginative geographies'[19] to dilute differences. Drawing upon Gaston Bachelard's poetics of space, Edward Said notes the emotional and poetic aspects that convert distance 'into meaning for us here' (1979: 55). According to Said, 'imaginative geography and history help the mind to intensify its own sense of itself by dramatizing the distance and difference between what is close to it and what is far away' (1979: 55). The scenographic conversion of original sources into 'imaginative geographies' in themed shopping malls represents other cultures not as they are but as they are assumed or imagined to be. It reinforces an oversimplification of otherness in order to be more easily received by consumers and avoid any resistance to 'untreated strangeness' (Said 1979: 67). In other words, scenography undergoes schematisation, a process with a very long tradition in both theatrical and commercial contexts.[20] Mock facades do not aspire to be an accurate reconstruction of the real world but instead 'reflect and sustain how people imagine that world and have real effects' on consumers (Jones 2012: 77). Consequently, they strive for the creation of something new, something that does not exist anywhere else. Set up for play, they try to emphasise, dramatise and enhance the feeling of otherness.

A focus on malls' interiors, an inheritance from developments after the Second World War led by Gruen and his concept for Southdale, accordingly puts aesthetic experience ahead of functional objectivity, intensifying the visual attraction in order to draw consumers into a mass spectacle. The consumption of experience through scenography, however, functions beyond its visual impact. Scenographic performances, Stephen di Benedetto explains, 'are more than the visible, constructed elements on stage; scenography also is constructed as a part of the audience's embodied experience' (2017: 166). 'A scenographer', he points out, 'not only creates a stage design but stimulates [an] experiential journey' (2017: 166). While the effect of scenographic stimuli in the experience of themed malls builds upon our own embodied memories of how certain materials feel against our skin, the 'presentation of materiality' in such a setting leads to predictable consumer behaviour (Böhme G. 1995: 62; Hosoya et al. 2001: 560). Despite the fact that the experience economy revolves around materials' aesthetic and atmospheric characteristics (Böhme G. 1995: 63), some developers have set the materials themselves as thematic cornerstones. In response to a notable trend in the mid-1990s that showed a decrease in both the time and money consumers spent in shopping malls (Coleman 2006: 106), Park Meadows Mall in Lone Tree, Colorado (1996), and Flatlron Crossing in Broomfield, Colorado (2000), introduced theming built around natural materials. As a result, these malls offer new ambiences to inspire visitors to linger, reaching into the realm of retail resorts (2006: 106).

Surrounded by the landscape of the Rocky Mountains, Park Meadows Mall uses wood and stone to convey the cosiness of a mountain lodge. The mall's interior, designed by Anthony Belluschi, has created 'a unique sense of place with a synergy to this particular location' (Coleman 2006: 106). The use of traditional building materials in both Park Meadows and Flatlron Crossing delivers a sensory impact through the architecture, placing solid materiality against the dematerialisation of surface aesthetics, and letting both substantial and ephemeral characteristics contribute to theming the space. Scenographic interventions, for example, the oversized fireplace in the Park Meadows' food court or the artistically shaped hearth encircled by living-room-style seating arrangements in the spacious hall in Flatlron Crossing, are only accents in an atmosphere already established by architectural means – the organisation of space, the choice of materials, a warm colour scheme, natural light. As they avoid scenographic gimmicks, which elsewhere include imitating one material by painting the surface of another (for example, painting wood to simulate marble), Park Meadows and Flatlron Crossing take a more upscale, organic approach in accordance with their Rocky Mountain environment. Instead of unabashedly calling to the masses, they aim for the comfort and luxury that will expand their target consumer groups to include more mature and affluent customers (2006: 110).

In order to deal with the issue of spatial identity, developers and designers have tested different theming strategies over time. Apart from establishing destinations that combine retail, dining and entertainment in a unique way, their goal has been to craft a place that is 'entertaining in itself' (Beyard et al. 2001: 96). They have thereby advanced the way in which cultural, historical and geographical references are interpreted scenographically. The simulation of place through theming that started in nineteenth-century department stores has developed into even more holistically scenographed spaces in shopping malls. Those original Christmas-themed villages and home interiors told visitors about Santa's character, activities and interests (Bird 2007: 109), and elicited an emotional response by embedding shoppers in walk-through settings. Since then, placing the accent on materiality has broadened the effect to include consumers' haptic and kinaesthetic senses, while it also aims to convey more about the place itself. Now, thanks to the rapid development of digital technologies currently underway in the first decades of the twenty-first century, aspirations to 'sense the place' are caught between the physical encounter and media images delivered in advance, which challenge our perception and our experience of the 'real' place (Ritzer 2005: 104). The imitation of reality with which we are confronted today can be traced back to the opening of the Circus Circus Hotel & Resort (1968) in Las Vegas. As Ritzer explains, this resort on the Strip marked a turning point in design, where occasional references to a theme's inspirational sources became insufficient to make 'otherness' believable (2005: 106, 108). Instead, the copies became more detailed and objective, introducing a new trend in theming, namely the creation of other realities, which started to flourish in Las Vegas during the 1990s (2005: 106, 108). From there, efforts to establish the identity of the simulated place have grown in size, opulence and attention to detail.

In 1992, the same year that marked the opening of the Mall of America, the luxury hotel and casino Caesars Palace in Las Vegas presented the next phase in themed mall design with The Forum Shops. Dougall Design Associates was responsible for the interior design of the extended wing of the hotel and casino complex in which the mall is situated. Maintaining the high quality of services at Caesars Palace, luxury brands and gourmet restaurants are integrated into the mall's main theme: ancient Rome. Allusions to this period include an *impluvium*, a water basin with fountains surrounded by columns in the centre of the entrance hall, characteristic of the residences (*domus*) of wealthy Roman citizens, the marble finishing on Ionic and Corinthian columns, coffer ceilings, arches and the dome, the geometry of the railing baluster and window grilles, murals on the walls, ceilings and caryatide pedestals, and mouldings, ornaments and consoles. Some parts of the mall are devised with extended architectural references to later periods, mostly the Italian Renaissance and Baroque. These are, however, combined with Postmodern design interventions that suggest ancient Rome in a rather loose and exaggerated way: oversized caryatides and columns that stretch over two of the mall's levels, fantastic capital, shaft and pedestal designs for some of the columns in the entrance hall, chairs in the form of Roman busts, tables and benches constructed as cannelured column segments, spiral escalators framed with coffered walls, amphora-shaped rubbish bins, and canapé benches inspired by the ancient Roman folding chair known as a curule seat (*sella curulis*). In some areas, the Forum introduces a new element: a sky ceiling that imitates the transitions between night and day (Bryman 2004: 33). These changes from sunlight to dusk to darkness recall nineteenth-century panoramas and further contribute to the overall visual impression instilled by the themed shopping alleys. By adding these active sky murals to the ceilings, The Forum Shops has created a completely enclosed environment, separated from any external influences, in the same way scenography does in the theatre. As Alan Bryman has noted, the lack of windows (and clocks) encourages visitors' total immersion in an overwhelmingly themed milieu and causes them to become disoriented, losing any connection to the outside world and sense of time (2004: 33).

In 1999, The Venetian hotel and casino in Las Vegas introduced Grand Canal Shoppes. Designed by WATG of Nevada – Wimberly, Allison, Tong and Goo – this upscale shopping mall set a new standard for the concept of themed design. Following the resort complex's Venetian motif, it represented, at the time of its construction, the most ambitious approach to themed shopping to date. Rearranged on the Las Vegas Strip, replicas of Doge's Palace, Rialto Bridge, the Campanile di San Marco and St. Mark's Clocktower, and the Ca' d'Oro palace announce a special kind of shopping adventure, inviting all passers-by to visit. Crossing over the 'Rialto Bridge' and traversing the Great Hall, visitors enter Grand Canal Shoppes. Recalling Venetian architecture, the shopping mall is paved with dark cobbled tiles and opulently scenographed with Renaissance facades, arched passageways and even a scaled-down version of St. Mark's Square. Retail shops and restaurants are skilfully incorporated into the theme, organically combining history and the present day. As in the Forum at Caesars, the sky mural on the ceiling encloses the shopping space in its themed artificiality, helping to create a world of its own. Lanterns, light sconces and shop windows illuminate the streets, while their reflections on the shiny floor double the effect. Supplementary light sources brighten the sky ceiling, and lights behind the windows in the building facades conjure life within. In the middle of the shopping street, a canal stretches a quarter of a mile, crossed by a number of bridges that mimic the aspect of Venetian alleys. On the canal, gondolas take visitors for a ride while a gondolier sings a song from the Italian classical repertoire. To complement the overall shopping experience, visitors' audio sensations are accompanied by the sound of birdsong. Live performances are given by singers, actors and musicians throughout the mall.

In the enclosed spaces within Las Vegas's extravagantly themed resort and hotel complexes, consumption of place is not based exclusively on the surface cosmetics of their 'imaginative geographies'. Aiming to entertain, their design reaches beyond mere visual schematisation. By combining traditional scenographic techniques with emerging technologies, developers have here expanded traditional theming strategies to include the simulation of weather conditions. In some cases, a painted sky combined with an artificial lighting system enacts the time of day or night. In others, the simulation extends to staging a rainstorm, as in Miracle Mile Shops (previously Desert Passage), a shopping mall that still incorporates sections of its former interior inspired by the ancient spice route.[21] Such scenography, which enhances the themed experience and heightens the thrill while keeping patrons dry, has opened the door to the more complex experiments that we are beginning to witness today. Beyond temporary effects delivered in the controlled environment of indoor malls like Miracle Mile Shops, developers are announcing climate simulations in open-air setups as well. Katara Plaza in Doha is being marketed as the first air-conditioned outdoor themed shopping mall.[22] While temperatures in Qatar's subtropical summer reach over 40 degrees Celsius, the two-stage Air2O air-conditioning system claims to cool the air up to a height of two metres.[23] Profound interventions of this kind not only change the sense of place by simulating a different climate and then immersing the consumer's whole body within it, but they also evince the contemporary ambition to establish a strong and recognisable themed identity.

Throughout the 1990s, Las Vegas's elaborately devised shopping malls, especially The Forum Shops and Grand Canal Shoppes, enjoyed increasing levels of success. At the end of the decade, for the first time since Las Vegas was established as a home for gambling, the annual revenues generated by non-gaming services in the city's casino resorts exceeded their income from gaming.[24] These results indicated a change in tourists' spending behaviour that was to continue for the next years: in 2016, of the 42.9 million people who visited Las Vegas, 29 million went to The Forum Shops.[25] Following the prosperity of the themed shopping experience in Las Vegas, the concept went global, becoming increasingly visible around the world. As the gap between gaming and non-gaming revenues continued to widen in the first decades of the twenty-first century, stories of the financial success enjoyed by the themed malls travelled fast. Consequently, developers in countries with newfound wealth followed the example set by Las Vegas and adopted the idea of themed shopping in their own way. Some of them even outshone their inspiration in concept, scale and extravagance. Even if it can be assumed that not all visitors to these places make a purchase, the statistics undeniably reveal the vast numbers of people who are exposed to their atmosphere every year and how far-reaching their cultural impact is.

Looking back at some prominent examples developed in the twentieth century, from the Country Club Plaza to the shopping extravaganzas of Las Vegas, it is evident that themed consumption evolved gradually over time, claiming its market share with 'imaginative geographies' embedded in everyday culture. While scenographic strategies were constantly adjusted and modified, oscillating between Baroque theatricality and more subtle approaches, they all reflect, as Tracy C. Davis observes, the unifying theme of consumer materialism (1991: 11). In such environments, where visitors are surrounded by 360-degree 'performances of the theme' (1991: 12), exposure to a dramatised hyperreality saturates the shopping with a new identity and erases any reminders of what the place is actually about. Oblivion of this kind is a costly endeavour, with a tendency to demand additional future investments as a result of consumers' rising expectations, and without any guarantees that the concept will provide capital returns (Bryman 2004: 17). The unstoppable progress of technology, which supports the vicious circle of an experience economy, places simulated environments at permanent risk of becoming outdated if they are not constantly improved (2004: 17).[26] Consequently, as one of the driving forces behind the creation of a shopping identity, scenography in commercial themed settings is tied to capital with very restricted possibilities to change its conditioning.

2.3 Drama on sale

Even though the connection between the theatre and the marketplace goes far back in history, as a brief recap of past practices demonstrates, the conscious introduction of scenographic techniques into commercial settings began in earnest during the Industrial Revolution. In her article 'Theatrical Antecedents of the Mall That Ate Downtown', Tracy C. Davis uses the example of the West Edmonton Mall to examine the theatrical roots of early entertainment centres. Among these is the Exeter Exchange, a mixed-use marketplace in which trade and entertainment were combined under one roof. This building on the north side of the Strand in London (1773–1829) exhibited exotic animals, wax works and one-person performances on the first floor, above an arcade with forty-eight stalls occupied by merchants (Altick 1978: 38; Davis 1991: 7). Although it alters the scene according to the artist's impression, a plate by Thomas Rowlandson of the Exchange's Royal Menagerie shows a mural painting on the wall behind animal dens: a recreation of a foreign forest used as scenography.[27] Davis also mentions the panoramic paintings and art exhibitions set up in commercial spaces in the Lowther Arcade, Cosmorama Rooms and Royal Bazaar, which all took up this aspect of the Exeter 'Change (1991: 7).

This tendency to place the exotic in a commercial context, Davis points out, was propelled forwards by eighteenth- and nineteenth-century colonialism. The theatrical experience of the exotic as scenography was, at the time, reflected in panoramas and dioramas as a way to encounter the unknown through images. The principal motifs of Prévost included, in addition to the panoramic landscape of Paris, representations of Toulon, Rome, Naples, Amsterdam, Tilsit, Wagram, Calais, Antwerp, London, Florence, Jerusalem and Athens (Benjamin 1999: 528). Remembering the Exeter 'Change, Davis suggests that its displays of the exotic (animals) were a representation of political superiority (of the British Empire) over the colonies, enabling the working class to participate 'in the glory of domination' for just a few pence (1991: 8). Drawing on such historical examples, Davis explains the political aspect of universal dominance expressed by today's malls in the same manner, as they capture and classify animals in aquariums and cages (1991: 8). As well as the popular sea life exhibitions, exotic birds are also on display. What started with a single birdcage in Southdale Mall has evolved into bird and wildlife parks such as the one in Johannesburg's Montecasino, a leisure and entertainment complex, situated directly beside its themed shopping mall. Over sixty species of exotic birds can be seen in the themed setting. Thanks to the role it plays in the creation and design of these environments, scenography is complicit in the experience.

The stylistic approach has naturally evolved over time as technology has developed, but its purpose has stayed the same. The traditional scenographic techniques used in the West Edmonton Mall, shaping an entrance into the open mouth of an oversized fish, for example or simulating an underwater cavern with 'rocky' walls decorated with corals, are still in use. The theming in Montecasino's Bird Gardens also runs along conventional lines in its Italy-inspired setting. Yet, in the last few decades, shopping malls have favoured more sophisticated strategy, combining a visual experience with kinaesthetic involvement. In the Mall of America and the Dubai Mall, for instance, visitors are wrapped in underwater scenery as they walk through acrylic tunnels that cut through gigantic aquariums. Supported by current technological possibilities, scenography serves to deepen an immersion into the exotic whose genesis goes back to the Exeter 'Change. Davis sets this fascination with the alien against a backdrop of ennui with all that is well known and familiar; the encounter carries a certain detachment, neglecting 'sentimentality and associative guilt' and opening the door to escapism.[28] This argument suggests that, by enhancing the embodiment of the unfamiliar, scenography in a commercial context creates a break between reality and fantasy. While supporting the intensity of new experiences, it dissociates us from reality, forcing us to embrace the spectacle as an alternative way to encounter life.

The conjunction of theatricality and commerce used to 'relocate' consumers from their daily routines to spectacular surroundings in today's shopping malls is a continuation of a long process consciously advanced by nineteenth-century department stores. In those environments, the stimulus to buy came not from merchant pressure but from the urge 'to gaze and admire' (Rufford 2015: 3). In addition to the items' aesthetic and monetary worth, the emergence of another factor can also be recognised, as its dominance spread widely in the second half of the twentieth century. This third measure has been described as 'staged value' (*szenischer Wert der Ware*) (Böhme G. 1995: 46).[29] In other words, the early department stores set in motion the metamorphosis of locations of capital realisation into stages. The experience and adventure that we witness today evolved from this point, adding their influence to the goal of stimulating buying behaviour (Haug 2009: 105–11). Capitalist market changes thus combined effectively with theatricality to create a new atmosphere, provoking the imagination by delivering spectacular narratives. Together, these two elements altered the physical marketplace into an ephemeral scenographic space that extended visitors the possibility of transformation through consumption. This approach prioritised fantasy over reality and gave free range to the beautification of commerce that turned it into a show.

The use of mirrors in early department stores, seen previously in arcades and shopping passages, added to the illusionist flare by multiplying the products and making the interiors look bigger than they were. At the same time, they allowed consumers to view a reflected image of their future selves as well as of others. As a result, shoppers became voyeurs (Brune et al. 2011: 10). Likewise, of course, the stage was never the only object of interest for theatregoers or opera enthusiasts, especially in the past: it was also an excuse for social interaction and observation. Between the late sixteenth and mid-nineteenth centuries, acknowledging the presence of other attendees, showing off, talking and flirting were as important a part of the show as the play itself (Rufford 2015: 5). Even in the later spatial setup dominated by a proscenium stage and darkened auditorium, a trend established by the Bayreuter Festspielhaus in the late nineteenth century that focused audience attention on the stage (2015: 5), socialising remained an integral aspect of attending cultural events. It happened before and after the auditorium lights were dimmed, as well as in the foyers between acts, as it does today.

Erika Fischer-Lichte points out that the habits established in the nineteenth century reappeared after the Second World War. In her 'Policies of Spatial Appropriation', Fischer-Lichte discusses spatial displacement in Western theatrical practice and its transition from theatre buildings to appropriated spaces during the 1960s. She looks at how spaces were conquered that were not primarily meant to serve as performance sites, a movement that emerged as a result of the critique of theatre as a bourgeois institution, the inadequacy of theatre buildings, and developing spatial relations between the audience and performance (2013: 219–39). Close ties were consequently forged between the theatre and other aspects of life (2013: 219–39); everyday places became potential locations where theatre could be enacted. The notion to appropriate a piece of land such as a town periphery and use it as scenography was not a new one. In the nineteenth century, as Fischer-Lichte mentions, Richard Wagner had the idea of setting up a temporary theatre as a festival. He considered turning some free space into a fairground, where attendees were guests rather than paying customers, in order to create an event accessible to everyone (2013: 219–39). The practice of using a city and its architecture as scenography was also common in pageants such as those organised by Louis Napoleon Parker in England at the beginning of the twentieth century. These were an attempt to bring a collective spirit back to communities through historical drama with musical numbers and parades (2013: 219–39). The third example that Fischer-Lichte gives in her history of spatial appropriation is Max Reinhardt's democratisation of the theatre. He used exhibition halls, circuses, marketplaces, churches, gardens, parks, streets and city squares as scenography (Aronson 2018: 44–7; Fischer-Lichte et al. 2013: 219–39). In this way, Reinhardt's 'Theatre of the Five Thousand' aimed to change the social conditioning of theatregoers, leaving the theatre building as a symbol of the bourgeoisie while moving theatre itself to include a wider spectrum of the population. Although these three cases are all rooted in different ideological contexts, Fischer-Lichte acknowledges their common basis. She sees the appropriation of existing urban spaces for theatrical purposes not only as an attempt to modernise theatre but also as a reaction to the modernisation of society (2013: 219–39). Turning familiar and recognisable environments from everyday life or popular culture into scenography enhanced the feeling of community and participation, as Parker desired, because it facilitated the involvement of both performers and audience.

The transformation of commercial spaces such as shopping malls into theatrical settings demonstrates the endurance of the processes laid out in Fischer-Lichte's historical examples. After the Second World War, Disney's amusement parks introduced theming as a way to apply theatrical terms in everyday places, designating public and restricted areas as 'onstage' and 'backstage', employees as 'cast members', and crowds as the 'audience' (Bryman 2004: 11). Unlike these environments, however, which employ the whole site as a stage for a production put on by costumed animators, themed shopping malls are not designed to be used for any specific performance. Still, consumers' expectations correspond with the expectations of a theatre audience: to be entertained and to be exposed to new experiences (2004: 16). As in the theatre, little here is left to chance: occasional performances by acrobats, clowns or 'street' musicians, a custom well established in urban entertainment centres (Hahn 2002: 120), are choreographed to deliver the feeling of spontaneity and serendipity associated with city life. Appropriation in themed shopping malls happens by way of a scenographic approach to interior and spatial design, which sets the stage for any kind of drama that might occur in a controlled public space where people come together to work, stroll, shop or socialise. This displacement of scenography from the theatre into themed shopping malls is led by the intention to displace consumers into unfamiliar surroundings. Their attention is held by theatrical means: they are sold a promise of becoming someone else, as in a play.

Thus, Wagner's vision of a periphery as a performance site, Parker's attempt to recapture the spirit of community and history through a city's architecture, and Reinhardt's removal of the stage into a variety of urban settings all continue to be reflected in the cultural performance of themed shopping malls. Special events and festivities, including band performances, circus and acrobatic appearances, puppeteers, beauty pageants, arts exhibitions and shows for children have been an inseparable part of shopping malls' theatricality since the first 'open-air' shopping mall Shopper's World (1951) opened in Framingham, Massachusetts (Erben 2016: 38). The Garden State Plaza (1957) and Bergen Mall (1957) in Paramus, New Jersey, hosted 'evening concerts and plays, ethnic entertainment, dances and classes for teenagers, campaign appearances by electoral candidates, and community outreach for local charities' (Cohen 1996: 1058). Attracting the suburban population with their variety of programmes, shopping malls were regarded as a new type of community centre. As Cohen reports, Willowbrook Mall (1969) had, in the 1970s, up to forty-five weeks a year of activities (1996: 1063). This tradition of festivities, established in the early decades of shopping-mall culture, is still present today. Atmosphere and 'the institution of dynamic and energetic bodies' (Fischer-Lichte et al. 2013: 219–39), the essence of interlinking theatricality and festivity, are delivered in themed shopping malls by scenographic elements both physical and intangible. The constant movement of consumers through these settings contributes to the feeling of participation and sense of community. As a result, the shopping mall is made into a social and cultural phenomenon with distinguishing theatrical features. By drawing consumers into the 'scenographic frame' of the 'stage' and involving them kinaesthetically, allowing a physical exploration of the performance space (Aronson 2018: 8–9), themed shopping malls have come to establish themselves as a special kind of environmental theatre.

A cultural activity located between festivals, rituals and entertainment, theatre strives to transform its participants (Carlson in Fischer-Lichte et al. 2013: 15–30; Schechner 1990: 69). In themed shopping malls, the consumption of goods and services transforms consumers. Here, a layout devised for spatial mobility and entirely scenographed surroundings substantially supports the theatrical modification of public life. Dietrich Erben notes that consumers 'act against the backdrop of the world of commodities', as on a stage, and sales personnel are 'expected to present themselves to their best advantage' (2016: 25). Shoppers are enveloped in the theatrical illusion in order to distract them from everyday mundanities (Schechner 1990: 70). Speaking about the theatre, Richard Schechner mentions the audience's expectation to experience a 'healing' effect (1990: 71). This is echoed in visitors' trips to themed parks and shopping malls: they expect to go through the experience and come out a 'different' person, with a new identity carved from a combination of consumed goods, services and atmosphere. Shopping, as Wade Graham puts it, is 'irresistible – because it promises not just new shoes or clothes, but the possibility of a new identity' (2017). Writing about the relation between production and consumption, Tim Ingold describes production as 'a becoming of the environment', while consumption is 'a becoming of persons' (1992: 51). 'Like perception', he notes, 'consumption is an ongoing process and its outcome is not the utility but a new state of the consumer him or herself' (1992: 51). Alan Bryman argues that the willingness to consume is backed by the conviction 'that goods bestow meaning and are a source of identity' (2004: 159). The process of consumption is not seen as a result of seduction by advertisements and packaging, therefore, but as an active search for meaning (Bryman 2004: 159; Twitchell 1999: 22).

In this context, scenography plays a similar role in shopping malls as it does in performances because it sets the stage for consumers' transformation by theatrical means: it allows the possibility of advancing one's social identity through the consumption not only of status goods but also of the theatrical atmosphere. Here, scenography also promotes participation in the shared experience as a kind of modern-day initiation rite (Schechner 1990: 237). According to Mark Gottdiener, scenographed environments actually trigger the process of constructing the consumer self (1997: 128); the scenography of themed areas, set against the wider social milieu, encourages self-realisation through consumption (Gottdiener 1997: 128; Pimlott 2007: 278, 292). Focusing on the recreation of identity by predominantly younger consumers in postcolonial shopping malls in India, Rohit Varman and Russel W. Belk argue that adapting to the circumstances of the shopping mall happens through costuming and masking prior to the consumption itself, for example, as visitors put on nice clothes, change the way they address the retailers and lower their voices (2012: 76). These efforts serve 'as a necessary precondition for young consumers to participate in the shopping malls' by counteracting the reality of their lower-middle-class identities (Varman et al. 2012: 76). Referring to the transformation as a masquerade,

Varman and Belk explain this phenomenon as the consumers' awareness of entering a scene where their performance will be watched and judged, and their acceptance of the price they have to pay in order to participate.

Scholars have acknowledged that public spaces can acquire performative characteristics and have the potential to become an event, even where actual theatrical production does not take place. This idea is repeatedly addressed in the theoretical discourses of diverse academic disciplines, including theatre, architecture and social studies, each of which highlight particular aspects from different angles. Alongside flagship stores, such as the Hard Rock Café, the Rainforest Café and Nike Town, themed shopping malls are just one of the many contemporary manifestations of stages on which 'cultures both assert and question themselves' (Kozinets et al. 2008: 87–118; Harvie et al., cited in Rufford 2015: vii). If we draw out Schechner's binary relation between the agency of the ritual and the entertainment of theatre (1990: 102), scenography emerges as the tool with which to stage situations in the cultural practice of theming commercial urban environments. In this role, it mixes the spontaneity of a shopping experience with the artificiality of theatre (Schechner 1990: 103) and, in doing so, creates the circumstances for 'aesthetic drama'. According to Schechner, 'aesthetic drama' has a function similar to that of 'social drama': it provides a space and shows the way for an aesthetic transformation of consumers (1990: 136–7). As Schechner explains further, 'aesthetic drama' forces spectators to reflect upon how they see and experience life by exposing them to the world and occurrences that are more extreme than those of their normal routines (1990: 137). 'Social drama', however, is lived in the breaks between shopping, for example, by socialising in a restaurant in the mall's food court. This is a practice that corresponds to social encounters in theatre cafés and canteens during the intermission or after the play ends, and it goes back to a primal human habit rooted in prehistoric ceremonial gatherings (1990: 140). In themed malls, the 'social drama' involves the metamorphosis undergone by all participants, performers and spectators alike, which is reflected in their 'restored behaviour', a sociocultural phenomenon connected to taking part in an event, performance or festivity. By converting a common environment into a fantasy land, scenography in this setting unleashes the possibility of adopting what Schechner calls an 'other self', 'the special kind of behaviour "expected" of someone participating in a traditional ritual' (1990: 160). Schechner specifically emphasises the presence of restored behaviour in themed parks such as Disneyland and heritage village museums, acknowledging them as forms of environmental theatre (1990: 193). As he points out, even though consumers register that the new environment is only an illusion (1990: 194), it still triggers a different kind of behaviour in line with the design concept. This response is strengthened as the divide between the stage and the auditorium disappears in favour of a shared space (1990: 197). In themed malls, the invitation to interact with the set, for example, to take a gondola ride, deepens the involvement. The scenographed environment thus acts as a catalyst, prompting a fluid exchange between the roles of spectator and performer, staged and everyday realities become intertwined, and a space is opened for the 'unreal' to become 'real' for as long as we agree to play the game.[30]

Many scholars agree that the influence of themed theatricality also happens on a more profound, invisible level, tapping into our subconscious. The theatrical quality of the shopping mall, and its staged approach to the social activity of purchasing goods, reaches further than a simple ambition to entertain: it aims to provide shoppers with a totally new emotional encounter (Böhme, G. 1995: 39). This is accomplished by providing a scenographed experience of participation and immersion in order to maximise productivity. The effect is more than skin-deep, directly influencing visitors' moods and feelings (1995: 39). Even if it operates as an invisible force, our senses detect the scenographic atmosphere intensely as it reaches deep into the unconscious (1995: 39). 'We feel the influence of the mall', Nicholas Jewell observes, 'and perceive its identity, far beyond the limitations of its physical structure' (2001: 330). A systematic review of forty years of research on shopping malls reveals that, in order to create this emotive power, 'ambience décor' is highlighted alongside design and architecture (Gomes et al. 2016: 14). Colin Campbell recognises the change in modern hedonism (consumption) from sensations to emotions, emphasising that 'an emotion links mental images with physical stimuli' (2005: 161). The design of themed areas must, therefore, Antje Böhme underlines, incorporate the potential to deliver an enduring emotional impact that stays with visitors long after they have left the shopping mall. As such, it is a central focus of marketing such facilities, because returning visitors secure the malls' financial stability (2012: 30). What remains puzzling, however, is that the representation[31] of atmosphere to provoke an emotional response, as in themed shopping malls, still draws on old-fashioned scenographic techniques that started to disappear from the theatrical stage at the beginning of the twentieth century. In the theatre, the Modernist generation of scenographers exchanged a literal stylistic representation of the drama's location for the power of suggestion. Edward Gordon Craig claimed that this was a more appropriate way 'to create the atmosphere of mystery that was considered most conducive to the perception and revelation of Truth and Beauty' (Eynat-Confino 1987: 25). Suggestion, in other words, is better suited to mystical and spiritual discovery, and better able to help spectators visualise 'the inexpressible in things' (1987: 25). The symbolism, Craig describes, however, targeted the intellectual and artistic elite (1987: 25), while the use of symbols in themed shopping malls reaches out to a mass audience rather than aiming solely to modify the look of the space. Nevertheless, representation and mimicry still seem oddly out of place for our times.

The appropriation of inadequate theatricality from the past in order to serve today's audiences has prompted a lot of criticism and added to the already-heated debate on the problematic of shopping malls. The architectural discourse echoes with aloof hostility towards a theatrical approach to the topic, reducing it to the level of harmlessness.[32] Interestingly, the discussion about the consumption of the city as theatre, although it began in architecture, has been taken over by other disciplines, which have developed it further. Acknowledging the transformation of consumption into play (Bryman 2004: 1), which makes the spectacle an inseparable part of the shopping mall (Debord 1970: 29; Ritzer 2005: 95), necessarily implies the complexity of the subject and the importance of taking the theatrical point of view into account. As we saw in the historical overview, the very core of shopping-mall evolution, namely, the enclosure of the city into indoor environments, is based on economics and politics but also has theatrical roots. Different forms of environmental theatre, practised on city squares and in open markets, are still around today. However, since the theatre entered courts and palaces during the Renaissance and subsequently developed its own institutional framework, mainstream theatrical practice has been orientated inwards. As a result, it has shut out not only nature and the city but also, as Carlson explains, all the ones who were not 'invited' or who were not privileged enough to experience it (Carlson 1989: 61). Themed shopping malls, functioning as theatrical places, similarly exclude both their surroundings and any disadvantaged would-be visitors. Even though they do not charge an entrance fee, as themed amusement parks do, and are in theory open to everyone, they can truly be experienced only through the act of consumption.

Furthering the likeness with theatre, almost every shopping mall is also a site where architecture and theatricality are intertwined through the use of space for various kinds of events and performances. In the late 1990s, unique theatre venues emerged as an integral part of retail, leisure and hotel complexes, just as theatres were incorporated into nineteenth-century arcades and passages. For now, they remain the privilege of affluent cities and famous tourist destinations such as Las Vegas, Macau and Dubai, but, due to their successful operation, the concept is likely to prevail. The O theatre in the Bellagio (Las Vegas), Le Rêve theatre in the Wynn (Las Vegas), theKá theatre in the MGM Grand (Las Vegas), The House of Dancing Water theatre in the City of Dreams (Macau) and La Perle theatre in Al Habtoor City (Dubai) are some examples of specially conceived theatres within larger mixed-use complexes. They all feature high-end spectacles and aquatic shows created specifically for each location. The theatre in Montecasino (Johannesburg) features musicals, ballet, opera concerts and one-person shows, as well as various additional performances. Other, smaller theatres in shopping malls situated in less exclusive tourist destinations include The Barnyard Theatre franchise.[33]

Looking at these examples and others like them, it becomes clear that merging the architectural and theatrical discourses on the topic of the shopping mall is necessary if we want to understand how theatricality works within an ever-changing perception of the city, and what we can do to steer future developments in the right direction. In this regard, the global propagation of theming in shopping malls offers us a solid base. Exploring this phenomenon will allow us to gain a better grasp not only of how different cultures have encountered and adapted the theatricality of shopping first introduced in North America but also of how scenographic means have been mobilised to boost the consumption of experience around the world. To discover how scenographic techniques are used to create atmosphere, and to demonstrate how a melange of historical architectural references can transform ordinary places of commerce into exotic tourist attractions, a city into a theatre, a descriptive study is required before we attempt an in-depth analytical discussion. Therefore, in addition to providing visual documentation, the next chapters offer a detailed examination of four different approaches to themed malls in South Africa, the Gulf region and Southeast Asia.

3

Themed Malls as a Global Trend

3.1 Make me look older: Montecasino

Montecasino, an upscale leisure, entertainment and business complex in Johannesburg, was completed in December 2000. Its infrastructure encompasses three hotels, a casino, a shopping mall, multiple entertainment venues, an outdoor piazza, The Pivot (a business centre) and Bird Gardens (an aviary and wildlife park). It was developed by Tsogo Sun, a leading hotel, gaming and entertainment group in South Africa, while Dougal Design, appointed as concept architects, worked together with Bentel on its realisation.[1] Eduardo Robles and Thanu Boonyawatana of Creative Kingdom Incorporated were responsible for the design. In fact, Montecasino is one of several projects in South Africa conceived by Creative Kingdom, which made a name for itself with themed designs for hotels, casinos and entertainment resorts, including Suncoast in Durban and The Ridge Casino in Emalahleni.

Italy serves as the inspiration behind the plan for Montecasino. The theme is primarily wrapped around Tuscan architecture, though this is combined with broader references to the Italian Renaissance and Baroque. According to Dougal Design, extensive research including sample collection was carried out on location in Italy 'to ensure the authenticity of the original architecture'.[2] Covering a 38-hectare site, the compound is enclosed by gates and protective walls based on medieval Tuscan cities and villages.[3] Upon passing through the main gate and driving along Palazzo Lane, visitors are drawn into the themed environment as they head towards the clock tower, which acts as a visual reference point in front of them. The characteristic architectural style of this distinguished signifier establishes an immediate association with Italy

IMAGE 1 *Montecasino, Johannesburg, South Africa. © Image Philip Mostert.*

and announces the themed setting, which radically sets itself apart from the rest of its surroundings.[4] The square at the entrance to the Montecasino complex is organised around a fountain and enclosed with buildings, walls and vegetation designed in the spirit of medieval Italian towns. Before visitors even go inside a building, any reference to the city of Johannesburg is out of visual reach. Contrary to the other case study examples we will look at, where the themed experience starts by entering a shopping-mall interior, with scarce or totally non-existent references to the theme on the buildings' outside facades, Montecasino extends the design concept across the whole compound, introducing visitors to the thematic setting more gradually.

Although the Creative Kingdom Herald, the firm's in-house publication, acknowledges specific inspirational references for the design of some buildings, such as the Apostolic Palace of Castel Gandolfo for The Palazzo Hotel, the connection is often loose and sometimes even hardly noticeable.[5] Although the use of the classical orders recalls the Italian originals, the design of the shafts, bases and capitals in some buildings on the premises goes beyond the Tuscan vocabulary, mixing fantasy with historical associations. Baroque architectural elements are treated similarly. The materials of the exterior facades – stone, brick and plaster accompanied by artificial traces of time – vary from naturalistic to Disneyesque, which often appear side by side. The Postmodern clash is illustrated in this combination of influences that can occur within a single building, for example, in the Teatro and in The Pivot conference centre, which both comprise a 'broken' historical outer shell ringing a contemporary facade. Situated in a mix of classic architectural features and their imaginary interpretations, Montecasino is arranged around the main casino, which draws a parallel to the Las Vegas resorts and distinguishes it from themed malls purposely built to serve only as shopping centres. Here, on the other hand, the shopping mall is more of a support for the dominant 8,500-square-metre MGM Grand Casino and the entertainment venues containing the Nu Metro and Il Grande movie theatres,[6] the Madame Zingara show, the Pieter Toerien Theatre and a ballroom. A daily bird show, 'Flights of Fantasy', at the Bird Gardens and performances at the Teatro supplement the entertainment.

Despite not being the main attraction at Montecasino, however, the shopping mall nevertheless demonstrates a distinctive visual approach to themed shopping that sets it apart from the other examples discussed in this book. The way architectural and stylistic details are combined in the interior of the complex is inherently theatrical, fluidly exchanging allusions to inside and outside as visitors move through it. One of the entrances to the Montecasino shopping mall leads through a hall with

IMAGE 2 *Montecasino, Johannesburg, South Africa.* © *Image Philip Mostert.*

a coffered dome ceiling. While the hall displays the indoor character of an Italian Renaissance building, the Via Siena and Via Amore shopping alleys conduct visitors further into a scenographed milieu that evokes the outdoor streets of a Tuscan village. Just the first few steps inside prompt the experience of a spatial crossover, interior to exterior, commercial to residential architecture, day to night – back and forth depending on the direction in which one moves. The use of a scenographic approach to suggest otherness in this context fills the interior with contradictory visual references, confronting spatial and atmospheric relations in a theatrical manner. Labyrinthine indoor alleys continue to conjure the outside world. Paved with different types and patterns of cobblestones, they house retail stores, cafés and restaurants that connote the flair of medieval Italy. Shops line up under the sky-painted ceiling. Its appearance changes throughout the mall and casino area from day to night. As one approaches the casino section, the light blue sky gradually tapers out in some places or ends abruptly in others, transitioning into a cloudless deep blue ceiling.[7] In spite of the spaciousness that the sky ceiling brings to the themed interior, shadows cast upon it by the rooftops of the upper floors and a lost helium balloon stuck to its surface break the spell, exposing the limits of the trompe-l'œil seduction.

One- and two-storey facades are occasionally interrupted by a third floor or by annexes that reach to the ceiling, suggesting an imaginary extension of the 'city' beyond the shop fronts. In contrast to the bright, wide and well-lit shopping streets generally encountered in malls, Montecasino offers the dim glow of narrow curved alleys, which helps to hide the otherwise-obvious deceit, at least at first glance. It invites visitors to embark on a discovery of the place or to take a break in the restaurants on the small piazzas and immerse themselves in the staged surroundings, all in order to experience the Tuscan village's intimate atmosphere. The Italian theme is also reflected in the mall's earthy colour palette of beiges, yellows and reds, light and shade. The shopping alleys are punctuated with the arched galleries of upper floors, small piazzas surrounding a fountain or an obelisk, and an atrium. Meanwhile, the facades are dynamically arranged: instead of following a straight line, they form an irregular row both horizontally and vertically, leaving some parts of the construction to function solely as scenography. Artificial trees and plants support the irregularity of the walkways, giving the street fronts a dynamic rhythm. The theming extends to both the cinema and the casino area. The subtle divide between the mall and the casino is facilitated by a meandering canal, adorned with small fountains and fake birds, across which bridges lead visitors towards slot machines and card tables.

IMAGE 3 *Montecasino, Johannesburg, South Africa. © Image Philip Mostert.*

Unique among our other examples for another reason, Montecasino is the only complex discussed here in which scenographic techniques of ageing are applied.[8] This technique of sculpting and painting, which is used on stage, film and television sets, applies patina, cracks, stains and damage to the newly built flats of facades with the purpose of making them look old. It adds another layer to stylistic elements inspired by past times and endeavours to give the themed setting more credibility. While some buildings show heavy patina, as those in Sun Square Montecasino,[9] others demonstrate a more subtle approach to ageing, as in The Palazzo InterContinental and Southern Sun hotels. In both cases, there is a visible effort to make buildings appear more authentic by marking them with the traces of time. An ambition to imbue the mock facades with a sense of time and history emphasises the effort to transport visitors into another world. Like the outside areas, the interior surfaces here are also aged, moving away from the polished look of historical references common to such places.

Another specific feature of the mall's scenography is the open windows and balcony doors on the upper floor, which allow a peek behind the facades. Dressed with framed pictures, clothing items, posters, sports trophys, display mannequins and rugs spread over the balcony railings, they suggest the existence of imaginary tenants. The facades are embellished with creeping ivy, as well as with other elements not usually encountered in themed malls, such as rain gutters, exposed electrical installations on damaged building fronts, storks in nests on the rooftops and chimneys, and birds on the window sills. Rather conspicuously, fantastic effects, including a sculpture of a winged dragon climbing along one facade, also have a place. In addition, props like a parked old-timer, bicycles leaning against a wall, strung washing lines and a fake shop window with antique books all aim to breathe life into a static background. Occasional live performances of 'street' musicians in this setting are supposed to underline the feeling of an accessible urban environment.

Such detail-orientated design introduces an additional level of meaning into the overall narrative, providing visitors with a lot of visual information that calls for attention. Still, even in this ambitious attempt at authenticity, the missing connection to real city streets is evident. It is not reflected only through the extension of materiality and content with prints attached to doors and windows or the exclusion of anything so aesthetically unpleasing as a dumpster. It also concerns the absence of the less fortunate city inhabitants, who are visible as soon as one steps out of the complex's gates. In a place troubled with high crime rates, where open windows are not a matter of course, Montecasino offers the idea of safety. What brings it back to its staged reality is that it is one without real life behind those open windows.

3.2 Shopping for education: The Ibn Battuta Mall

Designed by Dewan Architects and Engineers, the premises of the Ibn Battuta Mall (2005) in Dubai fill 350,000 square metres, spreading along more than 1.3 kilometres of themed retail streets.[10] Inspired by the travels of fourteenth-century Moroccan explorer and scholar Ibn Battuta, the mall is divided into six courts: Andalusia, Tunisia, Egypt, Persia, India and China. Representing the important stops along the scholar's twenty-four-year journey, the themed design ambitiously aspires to connect education with entertainment, dining and a special kind of retail experience.

From the southwest entrance, the Andalusian court opens the themed adventure. Here, in the centre of the mall's smallest themed area, stands a fountain that references the fourteenth-century Fountain of Lions in the Court of the Lions in Alhambra.[11] The court's entire ceiling is covered with dark wooden beams and slats that resemble those found in early Middle Age Islamic mosques and palaces. In particular, the Grand Mosque of Cordoba served as the inspiration behind the arch reliefs, ornaments and mixed materials that adorn the court's four sides. The ornate chandeliers and lamps hanging from the high ceiling contribute further to the place's Andalusian spirit. In the small transitional atrium that leads to the next area, the Tunisian court, visitors encounter the first scenographic installation meant for educational purposes. Sunlight streams through a roof window screened with a geometrical wooden grille, and a figure of Abbas Bin Firnas with the first 'flying machine' is suspended in the air among models of modern-day hang gliders, taking visitors back to the first attempt at flight in the ninth century. Underneath the installation, a vitrine display shows a model of the flying machine backed by an image of Cordoba and an information board with a story of Abbas bin Firnas's attempt at flight.

Moving farther towards the northeast doors, visitors enter the Tunisian section of the mall. Grouped in triangular and trapezoidal blocks, the shops form a dynamic pattern along the alleys. From the brightly sunlit Andalusian area, whose large arched windows allow daylight to flood its central court, visitors now enter streets with sky-painted ceilings, illuminated entirely by artificial light. A combination of lanterns, sconces, shop windows, spotlights, oriental lamps and occasional backlit windows in mock facades together accentuate the atmosphere of the theme and enhance the illusion. The lack of a direct connection with the outside world further increases visitors' immersion in an environment that references architecture from the Tunisian Middle Ages. Paved in geometrical patterns with cobblestones and tiles, the court's streets and alleys bring together the fronts of different types of building: the battlement walls of Islamic fortresses, arched city gates with double columns, towers and staggered facades inspired by medieval Tunisia.[12] One of the alleys is covered with a vaulted ceiling, decorated with embossed geometrical ornaments, and

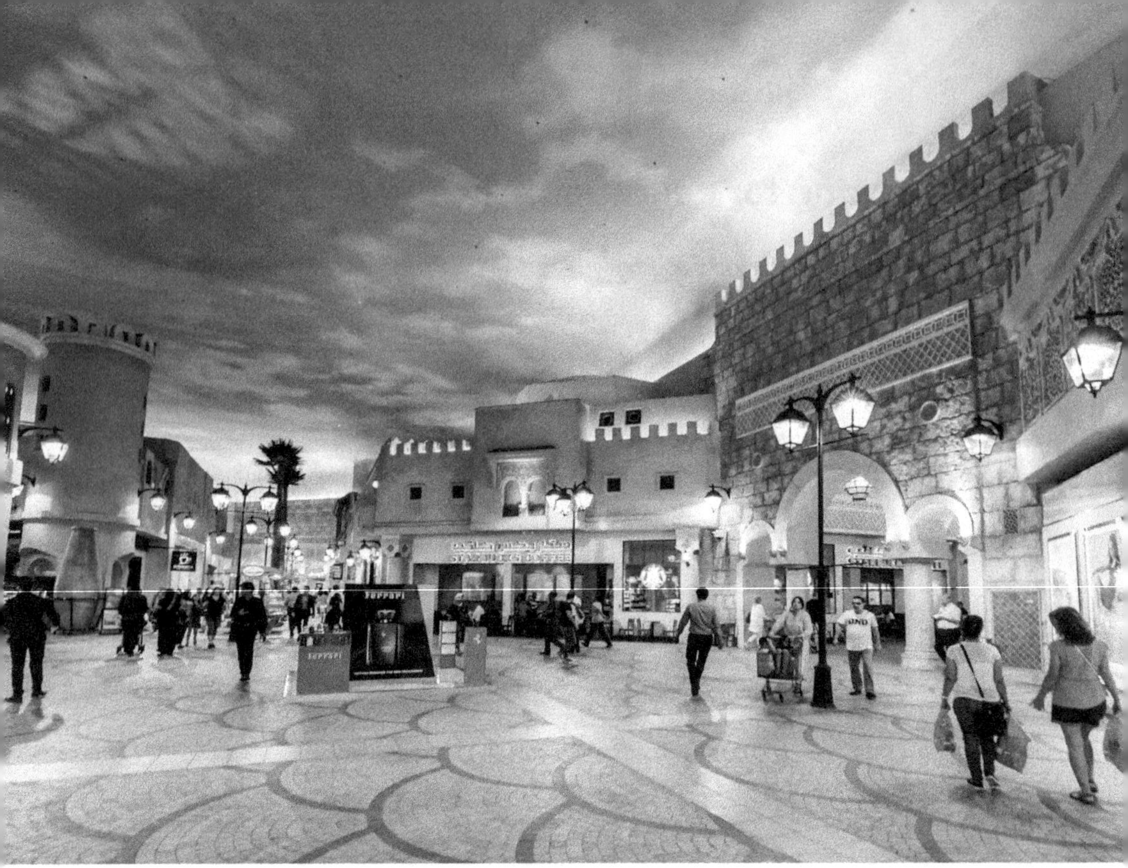

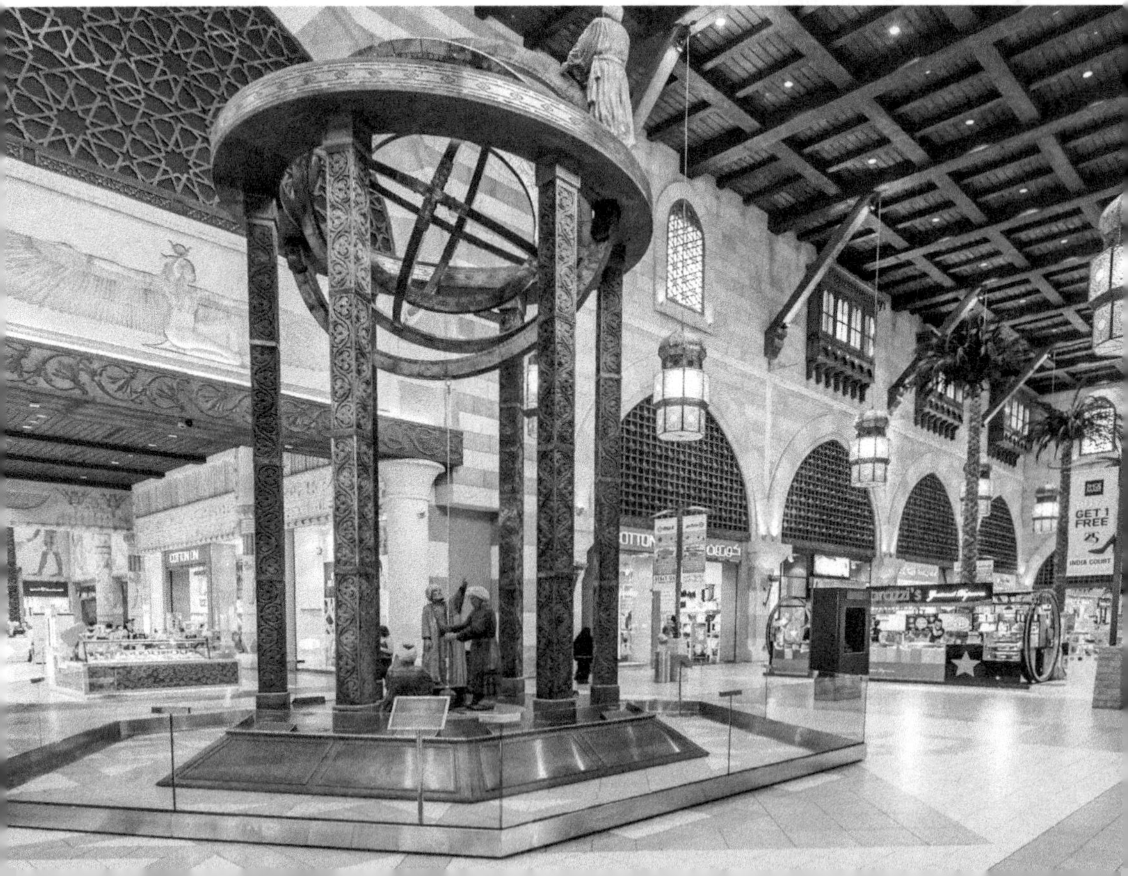
GET 1 FREE
INDIA COURT

lit by two rows of hanging oriental lamps that recall souks and bazaars. To add to a sense of the external world, palm trees are positioned along the shopping streets, reaching high up to the painted ceiling.

The journey continues through the Egyptian court with its references to medieval North African architecture. Pointed arches, two-coloured sandstone facades, merlons, wooden grilles with geometrical patterns and various ornaments follow the Mumluk architectural style, which originated in the building techniques set out by Fatimidian caliphs. These are combined with elements from ancient Egyptian architecture such as columns and pilasters with palm and papyrus capitals, decoratively painted walls and ceiling,[13] and curved reliefs. Elaborate brass lanterns hang from the high wooden ceilings of the alleys and from the walls, adding accents and associations with the ornamental Islamic arts of early medieval Egypt. In addition to the artificial lighting, sunlight enters through the upper windows, enhancing the height and spaciousness associated with Egyptian temples. Complementing some sections that give the illusion of outdoor streets and building exteriors, and contradicting others that offer an impression of interior spaces, high palm trees elongate the court's verticality. The educational aspect of this section is supported by a sculpture of an observational armillary sphere held by six carved columns, with figures of astronomers manipulating a spherical framework of rings and noting measurements. Two of them are positioned on a small revolving stage underneath the sphere, turning the central scenographic composition in slow circles. Plates with original notations of measurements are inserted into the sides of the hexagonal pedestal.

The Persian court occupies the central position in the mall. The walls of the Persian court are lavishly decorated with colourful tiled segments framed by brick finishings: ornamented tiles in blue, turquoise and beige are embedded in recessed sections. Such niches as well as vaulted passageways and windows are often home to pointed arches, a leitmotif of the Persian theme. Although this theme remains unified throughout the court, each of its sections is imbued with a slightly different atmosphere by the way the shopping streets are constructed and illuminated. This ranges from spaces with high ceilings and big upper windows above the vaulted passageways to narrow alleys with sky-painted ceilings to the extravagant heart of the court, where the enormous central dome over the lounge and restaurant area is adorned with arabesque patterns and hand-painted florals. Light from oversised brass chandeliers and lamps is intensified by strong high-key lighting in the shop windows, and by reflectors mounted on the walls and ceilings. Display vitrines are positioned around the central dome. Exhibiting images, artefacts, maps and texts, they give more

IMAGE 4 *Ibn Battuta Mall, Tunisia court, Dubai, UAE.* © *Manowar 1973, Dreamstime.com.*

IMAGE 5 *Ibn Battuta Mall, Egypt court, Dubai, UAE.* © *Manowar 1973, Dreamstime.com.*

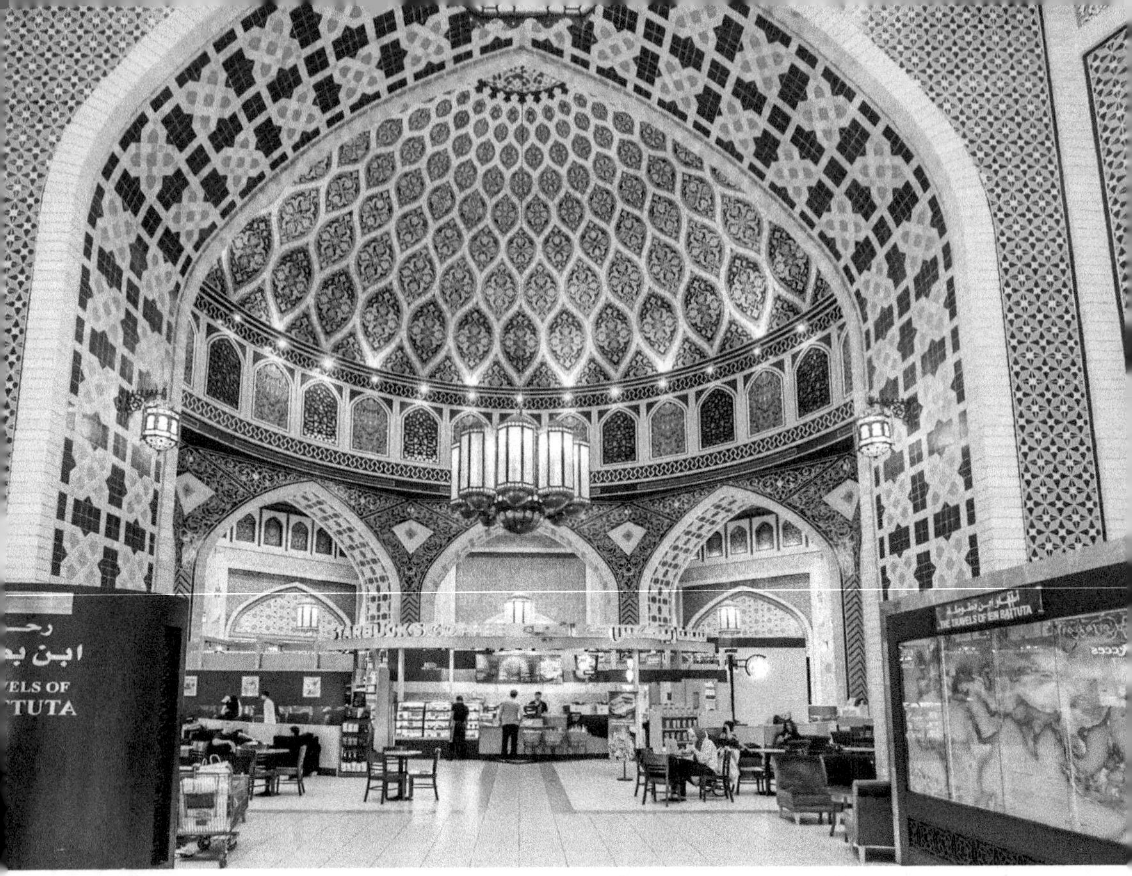
THE TRAVELS OF IBN BATTUTA

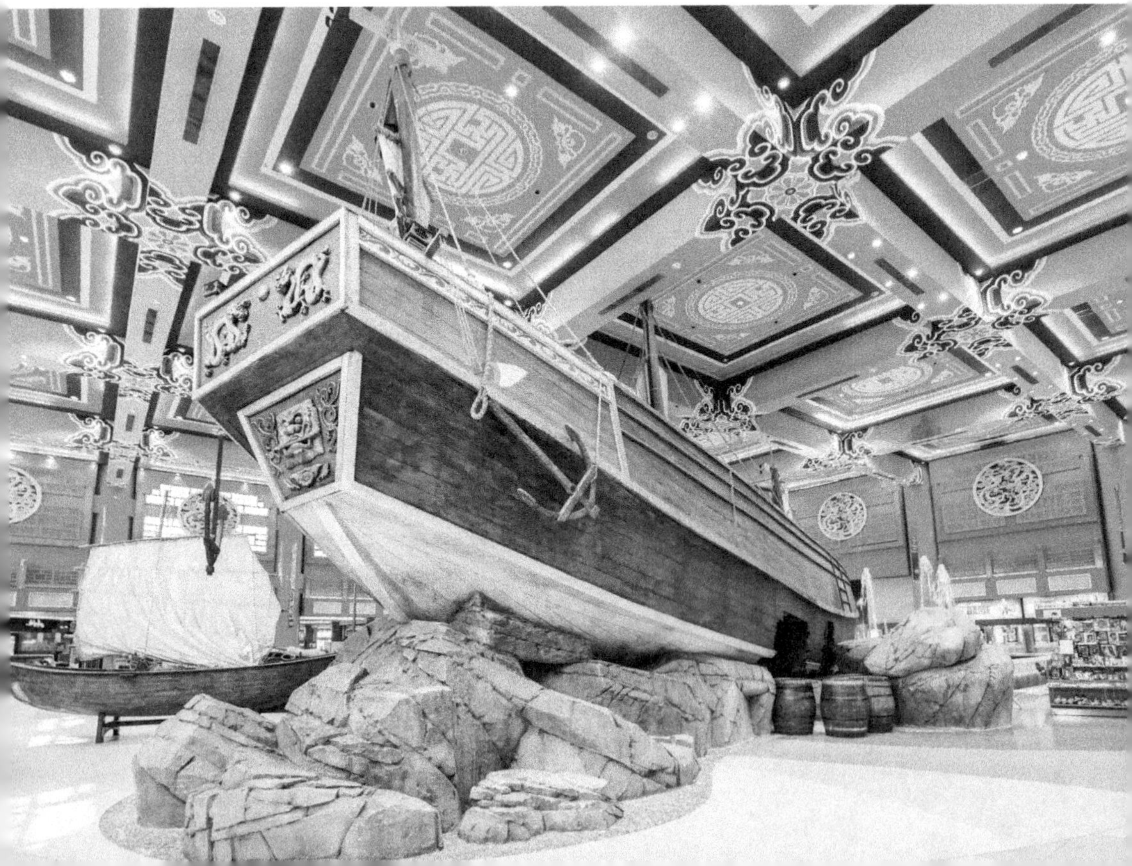

information about Ibn Battuta's journey and his time, tackling topics such as quality of life, trade, mathematics, music and mysticism in the Middle Ages.

The Indian court is the fifth theme in the Ibn Battuta Mall. An almost entirely monochromatic visual impact in white and beige is solely interrupted in the shopping alleys that reference Indo-Islamic architecture.[14] The walls of the hall are extravagantly decorated with reliefs, mouldings, niches, bay windows, arches and pilasters. The surfaces are painted to give the illusion of a marble finishing, as used in India. Unlike the themed courts described earlier, which are based on references either to Ibn Battuta's time or to earlier periods, the Indian court draws inspiration from the architecture of the later medieval period.[15] A sculpture of an elephant clock in the central court not only adds to the rich design and the mall's educational facet but also brings to mind the layers of meaning inherent in the clock's machinery. This elephant clock is a life-sized model of the medieval weight-powered water clock invented by Al-Jazari in the thirteenth century. It draws attention to the superior engineering visible in Islamic cultures in the early Middle Ages, as well as to the importance of time in Islamic faith and the rhythm of daily prayer. Alongside the impressive mechanical system, animated elements of Al-Jazari's clock symbolise how knowledge is gathered from different cultures: figures riding the elephant stand for the Muslim world, the elephant itself for India, dragon-like serpents for China, a phoenix for ancient Egypt.

The final themed area in the mall is the Chinese court. As opposed to the monochromatic concept of the Indian court, this section stands out due to its extensive use of bold colours.[16] Massive red columns on large bases support the beams of the coffered ceiling, suggesting the spacious interiors of the buildings and temples of medieval Imperial China. Between them, painted motifs symbolising prosperity and happiness fill the central hall's twenty-five red ceiling panels. In some shopping alleys, the ceiling is further embellished with interlocking wooden brackets (*dougong*), resembling the traditional roofs of Chinese temples. In addition to both direct and indirect artificial light, the court's central hall is lit on two sides through continuous windows, which are masked with the orthogonal patterns of red Chinese lattices and oversized medallions decorated with dragons. The court's main attraction is a life-sized model of a Chinese junk, an ancient sailing ship used for ocean voyages, whose sails reach up to the ceiling from the central fountain. The composition stages the ship as it hits the rocks on the shore, positioning the stranded junk in one corner of the fountain. The broken central part of the hull reveals its construction and creates a see-through tunnel to the other side of the hall. This 'coastal' corner is scenographed with imitation rocks, smaller sailing boats, barrels and anchors. The hull's bow and stern are painted blue and decorated with ornamental reliefs and dragon motifs.

IMAGE 6 *Ibn Battuta Mall, Persia court, Dubai, UAE.* © Manowar 1973, *Dreamstime.com.*

IMAGE 7 *Ibn Battuta Mall, China court, Dubai, UAE.* © Manowar 1973, *Dreamstime.com.*

Overall, the number of architectural and decorative references to six regions and, occasionally, to different eras, the juxtaposition of interior and exterior stylistic elements, and the ever-changing colour schemes in the Ibn Battuta Mall combine to draw patrons into a visually overwhelming conglomerate of imaginative history. By embedding the exhibited replicas, artefacts and models of the time of Ibn Battuta's journey into the main narrative, the mall ambitiously connects theming with education, forging stronger ties between shopping, entertainment and culture using scenographic interventions. Abbas Bin Firnas's 'flying machine', the observational armillary sphere, Al-Jazari's elephant clock, the Chinese junk and display vitrines all signal to shoppers that they are in a place where Islamic culture and history are revisited and celebrated.

3.3 A boat trip to fantasy land: The Villaggio Mall

The Villaggio is a themed shopping mall in the Aspire Zone in Doha, Qatar. It was developed by Gondolania Entertainment and designed by F+A Architects. The mall opened in 2006 and was extended in 2013 with a new wing, currently covering a vast area of 183,000 square metres. Following the example set by Grand Canal Shoppes in Las Vegas, the Villaggio's developers and designers adopted the meandering canals of Venice as their primary inspiration as well, albeit extending the theme introduced by the mall's Vegas predecessor. Located near the Doha Sports City complex, the mall's exterior combines diverse architectural characteristics from the Italian Renaissance, breaking the huge monolithic facade into smaller segments. In contrast to Grand Canal Shoppes, the Villaggio does not hold any exact copies of famous Venetian buildings. Features such as porticos, arched colonnades, octagonal rooftops, towers, and fake and blind windows are combined into one entity in a truly Postmodern manner. Nevertheless, even though the facades do not directly mirror any specific Venetian buildings, surface finishings in brick and stone optics as well as a colour palette dominated by beige, dark red and ochre increase associations with Venetian architecture. Simplified versions of Venetian street lanterns along the walkways and in the parking lot continue the theme in front of the mall.

Six entrances lead to five shopping streets: Carrefour Street, Veneto Street, Canal Street, Sportif Street and Via Domo. Although the shops themselves

IMAGE 8 *Villaggio Mall, Doha, Qatar.* © *Wing Travelling, Dreamstime.com.*
IMAGE 9 *Villaggio Mall, Doha, Qatar.* © *Wing Travelling, Dreamstime.com.*

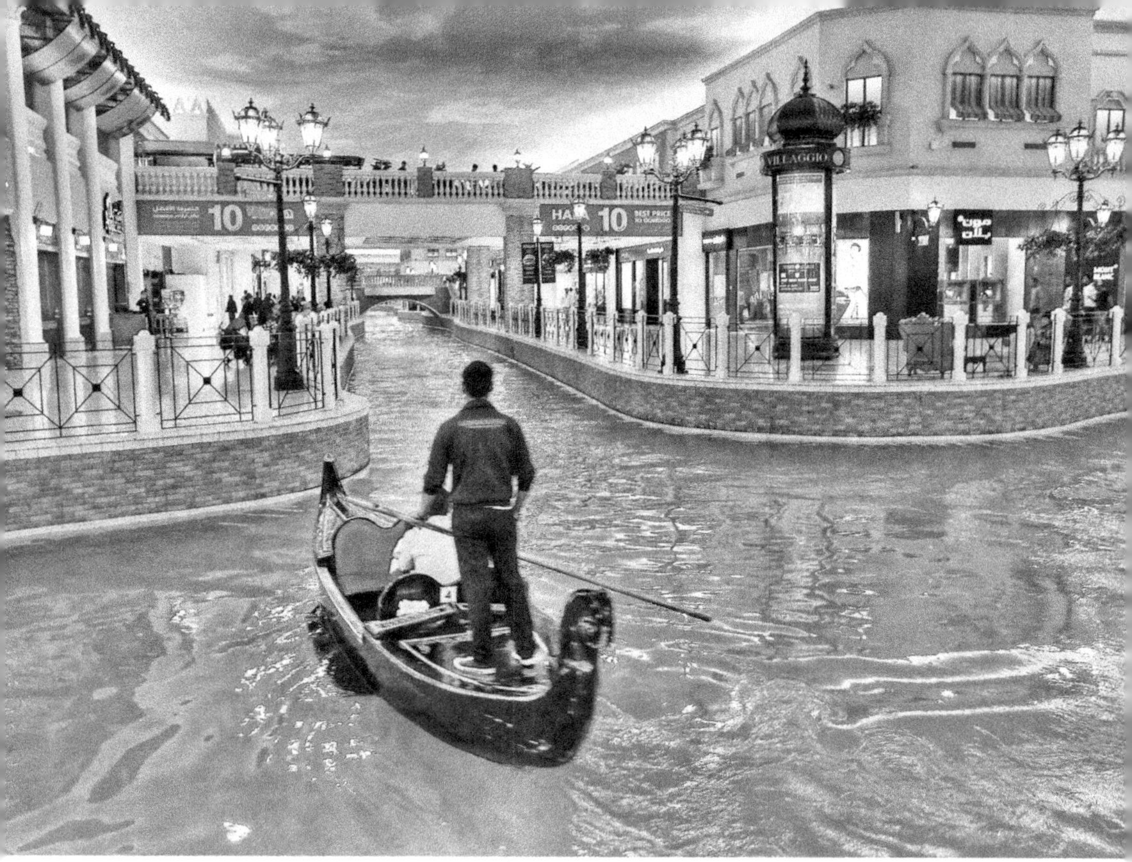
VILLAGGIO

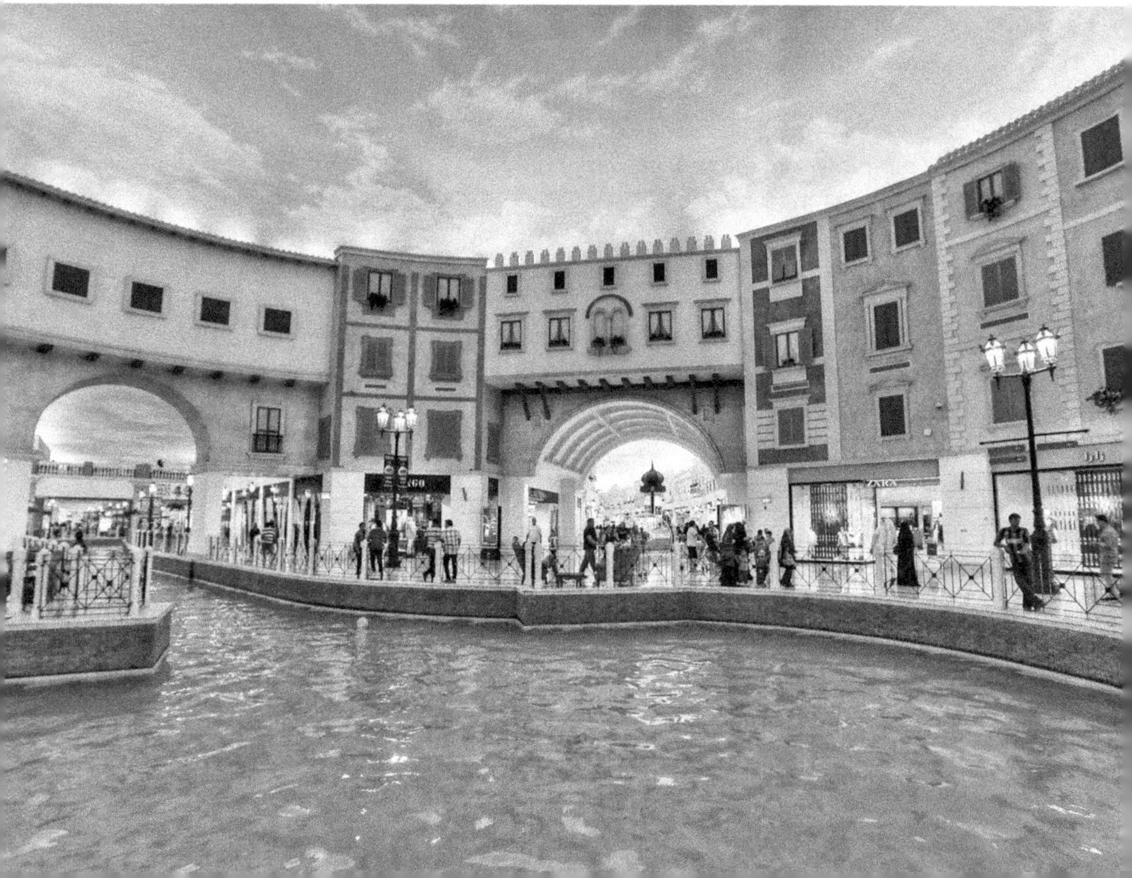

occupy only the ground floor, high ceilings leave enough space for mock facades that, in some parts of the mall, suggest higher buildings with up to three additional floors. Carrefour Street sets itself apart from the mall's other shopping alleys. Contrary to the mall's general stylistic direction, which encompasses the Italian Renaissance and Baroque eras, Carrefour Street picks up some earlier historical references, mostly from ancient Rome and ancient Egypt. The redesign and scale of the vaulted coffered ceiling and cornices, oversized denticles and characteristic wall mouldings break away from being exact copies of their ancient Roman origins, yet still stay clearly recognisable. The proto-doric cannelured pilasters and their capitals draw inspiration from ancient Egyptian columns, even though their use as pilasters started later, in ancient Rome. Painted leaves on the capitals recall motifs from Egyptian faience tiles in the shape of lotus flowers. Interestingly enough, the colours used on the capitals correspond with the practice in ancient Rome, in which doric capitals were painted blue and red. Although beige dominates, bright yellow sections of the walls and ceiling highlight the street.

Similar in their visual appeal, Veneto and Sportif Street evoke comparisons with imaginary Italian city streets. Underneath the sky-painted ceiling, residential facades that extend above the shop fronts for an additional level are occasionally interrupted by segments of representational architecture. Semi-circular arches around the food court in Sportif Street, arched city gates and passages with decorative bifora mullions, consoles and merlons in Veneto Street are inserted into facades that otherwise reference domestic architecture. Despite the lack of archetypes, some references to famous buildings like the Palazzo Venezia remain discernible. They are decorated with randomly positioned ivy garlands that aim to breathe life into overall artificiality. Light behind the windows and balcony doors of mock facades connect imaginary upper floors with bright shop windows, merging the existing retail space with a non-existent city. A variety of pointed, curved, open and broken pediments above the windows, sunshades and balustraded balconies give a dynamic rhythm to the shopping streets. The fronts imitate the materiality of brick, stone and concrete. Their earthy colour palette of ochre, yellow, dark red, dark pink and beige underpins the Italian theme.

In Canal Street, the highlight of the mall, the Venetian theme is executed in a more elaborate way. From the main entrance to the Villaggio, where Carrefour, Veneto, Canal and Sportif Streets meet, to the food court and the top of Via Domo, a 150-metre-long indoor canal winds along the shopping street. Battery-operated gondolas with gondoliers stand ready for a ride into the Italy-inspired fantasy. Unlike their Las Vegas counterparts, the gondolas are not rowed, nor can visitors hear any Italian opera arias; the gondoliers merely assist the passengers as they enter and exit the boats. Still, the boat ride offers an additional dimension to the shopping experience, allowing visitors a different kind of interaction with the space. As well as the chance to encounter the imaginative setting from another perspective, the effect is amplified as the shoppers themselves become part of the scenography. The water basin with its parked gondolas in the middle of the circular hall, facades that simulate three additional levels with arched gates and jetty upper stories, the street lanterns and the ceiling painted to recall a summer sky all aspire to transmit an impression of the outside world. Along the canal, five pedestrian bridges connect both sides of the shopping street. Schematic copies and fragments of famous Venetian buildings such as Doge's Palace are inserted into the street fronts. Balconies, pilasters and decorative pediments inspired by Byzantine and Moorish influences frame the windows on the imaginary first floors, making them look bigger and so suggesting the high ceilings and spacious upper storeys characteristic of Venetian Gothic and Renaissance architecture.

In the city of Venice, weather conditions and the safety and prosperity of the region contributed to the emergence of a specific type of architecture, a patrician palace facing the Grand Canal, as early as before the twelfth century (Ajzinberg et al. 2010: 187–8). These palaces comprised huge windows with loggias and decorative pilasters on the upper storeys, where the reception (on the first floor) and living area (on the second floor) were situated, while the ground floor was reserved for business and storage space (2010: 187–8). In this regard, the design of the shopping streets in the Villaggio follows the source of its inspiration, at least visually and conceptually. It is interesting to note that the first-floor facade segments in Canal Street are not scaled down, as is often the case in themed shopping malls. On the contrary, they even give the impression of having been scaled up. Contributing further to the visual impact, one pedestrian bridge is incorporated into a restaurant that, unlike the Villaggio's other services, occupies the first floor and uses the bridge as a terrace.

The walk or boat ride along Canal Street ends in the food court, with an ice rink and Gondolania, an indoor theme park, on one side, and Via Domo, on the other. Crowning this special shopping journey, the street fronts in Via Domo mimic sixteenth- and seventeenth-century Italian architecture. Above the exclusive, high-end shops hosted in this section of the mall, the facades are sculpted to imply two additional storeys.[17] On the ground floor, shop fronts are framed by ionic pilasters that hold a continuous frieze topped with arched wall mouldings, emphasising the shops and visually defining the height of the ground floor.[18] The windows are opulently encased with balustrade railings and curved, ornamented Baroque pediments. The balconies and windows are all randomly decorated with artificial plants. In some sections, jetty facade segments break the monotony of the decorated surfaces. They include bay windows on the first level and balustraded balconies on

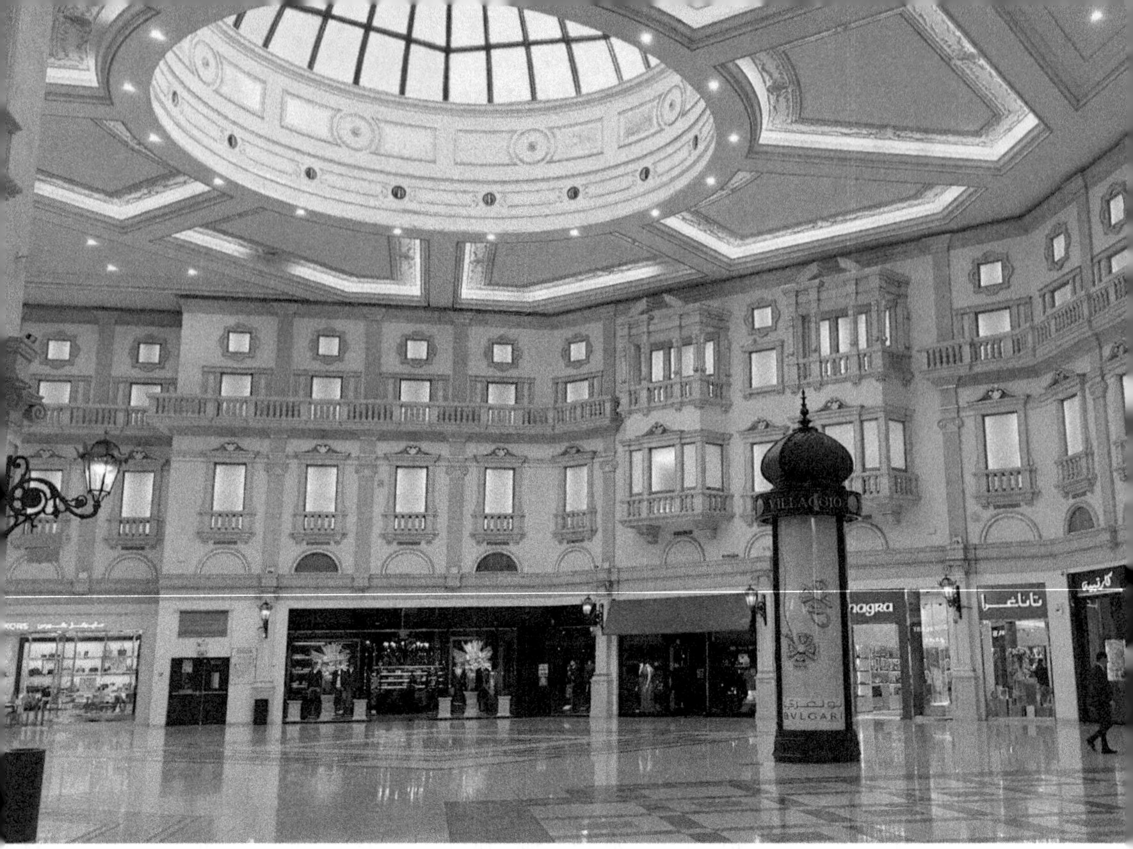
VILLAGGIO
nagra
تاناغرا
BVLGARI

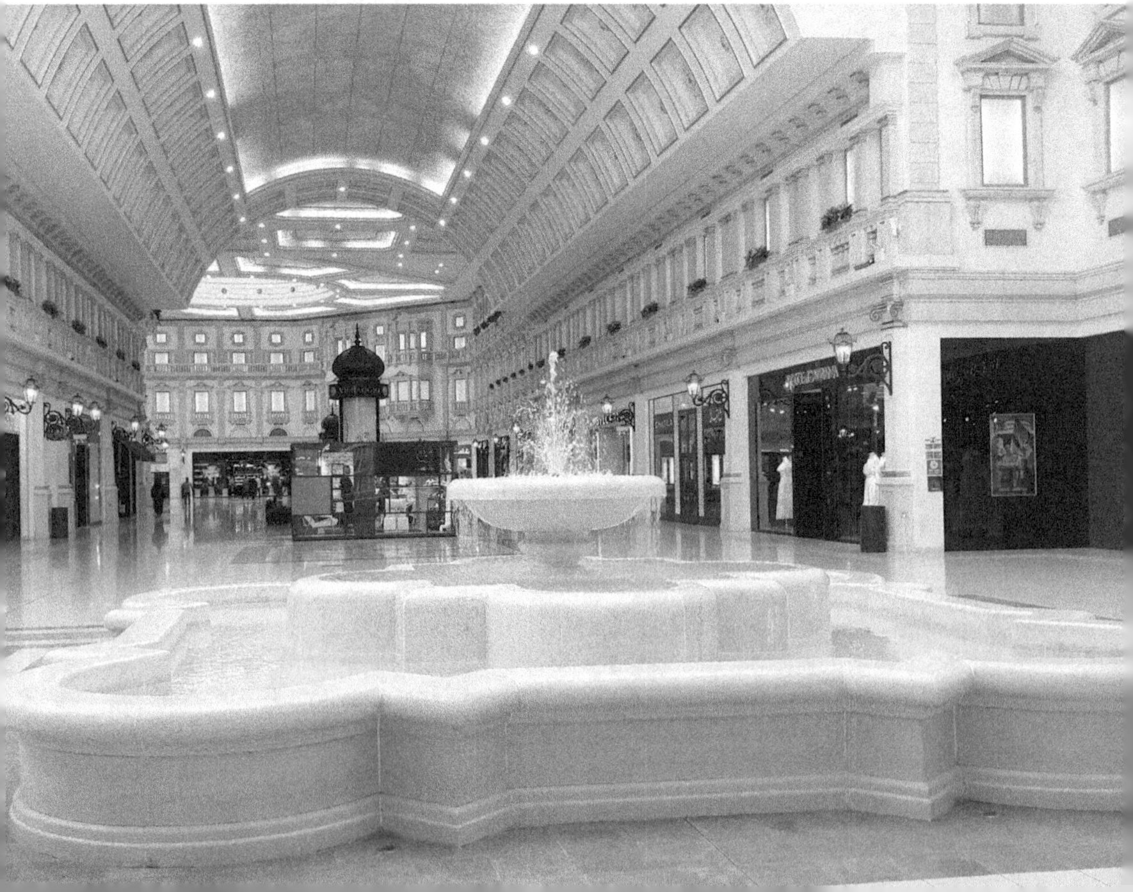

the second, capped with free-standing broken pediments. A Baroque-style coffered ceiling, partially vaulted, opens the shopping street to natural light, with two domes inserted into the construction. These let the sunlight brighten parts of the shopping street from above in the manner of Roman atriums. A fountain underneath one of the domes brings water, the leitmotif of the Venetian theme, into this area of the mall. The central parts of the vaulted ceiling imitate additional roof windows. Behind painted ornaments that replicate decorative iron grids, the sky depicted on the ceiling shines through. Via Domo ends with a restaurant, whose fake facade features a balustraded balcony with four pairs of ionic pilasters topped with a cornice. The colourful palette of the other shopping streets is tuned down, giving Via Domo an almost-monochromatic visual appeal.[19] Only some parts of the ceiling, ornaments and capitals are highlighted with gold. As opposed to Carrefour Street, which has the character of an interior space, the facades in Via Domo clash with the mall's ceilings. References to both interiors and exteriors are juxtaposed, thus merging inside and outside into one entity. Baroque elements add to the opulence of this section of the mall, elevating its visual appeal to match its high-end stores.

Overall, then, it is evident that although the Villaggio Mall in Doha closely resembles Las Vegas' Grand Canal Shoppes, it also moves on from the concept that inspired its design. It does so by expanding upon the Venetian theme, referencing ancient Egypt and the Baroque period to escape monotony in the larger space, and by providing additional offers of entertainment. The scenographic interventions present in the mall affirm the effort put into the stylistic details and their imaginative interpretations. Via Domo, especially, aspires to achieve the atmospheric 'wow' effect of the Forum Shoppes, underlining the separation between the aquatically themed interior and the desert landscapes that start just a few blocks west of the mall. Mirroring its Las Vegas precursor, the Villaggio is an oasis, though it lacks any of the regional references that seem obligatory in global strategies for themed franchises such as Disneyland (König 2008: 208). Tracy C. Davis's comment regarding West Edmonton Mall still applies to the themed malls that succeeded it: Grand Canal Shoppes and the Villaggio are conceived as vacation resorts, providing an 'escape from ordinary life while structuring how the body and mind are recharged, presenting a local identity that caters more to fantasy than indigenous geography or custom' (Davis 1991: 1–15). In both cases, the city of Venice, with its long and rich history, is an equally distant, fantastic destination.

IMAGE 10 *Villaggio Mall, Doha, Qatar.* © *Hakan Can Yalcin, Dreamstime.com.*
IMAGE 11 *Villaggio Mall, Doha, Qatar.* © *Hakan Can Yalcin, Dreamstime.com.*

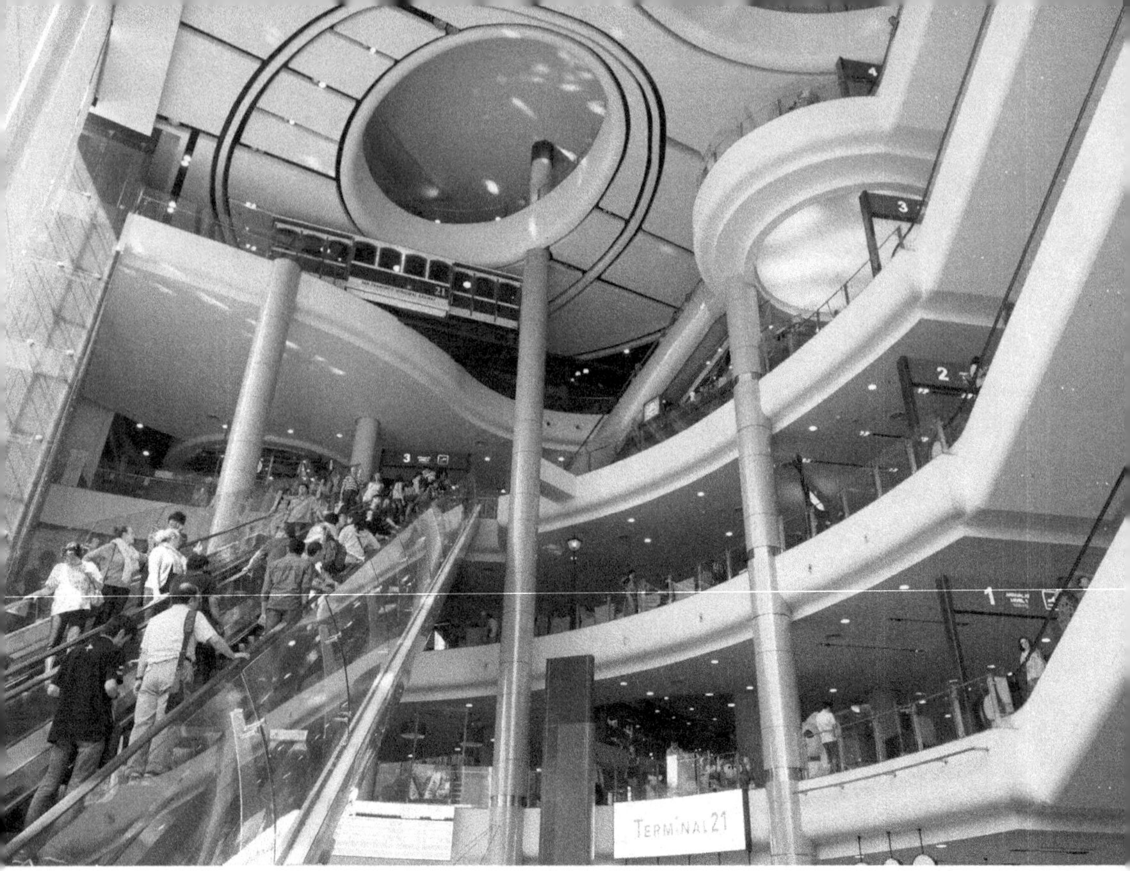
TERMINAL21

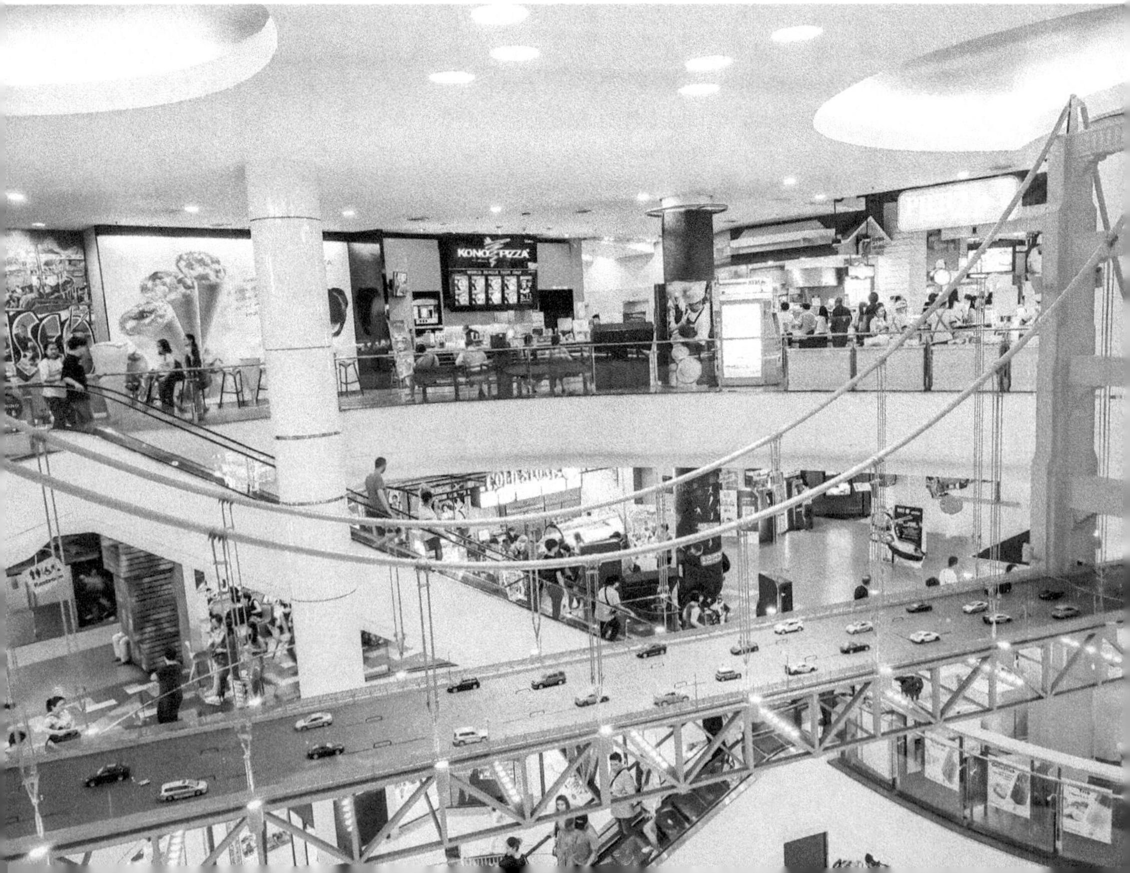
KONO PIZZA

3.4 Have a safe flight: Terminal 21

Terminal 21 opened in 2011 in the Asoke district of Bangkok, Thailand, is developed by LH Mall & Hotel Co. Ltd., designed by Palmer & Turner (Thailand) Co. Ltd., and RDG Planning & Design. The mall is part of a mixed-use building complex that incorporates a hotel. Reinterpreting the idea of a transport hub, the concept chosen for the visual brand of Terminal 21's interior is an airport terminal with gates leading to different destinations around the world. Entering the mall via a door marked with a gate sign, visitors go through a metal detector, pass a security guard dressed in a theme costume and come into the main hall, where several clocks indicate the time zone of each of the cities included in the themed design. Huge LED displays, similar to those that show airport arrivals and departures, announce special features and offers for the day as well as upcoming events, with their date, time, location and status (on board/coming up). 'Check-in' touchscreens can be found throughout the mall, enabling visitors to navigate their journey around the space. If additional information is needed, an employee in a cabin crew uniform is ready to help.

At first glance, the curved, reflective surfaces and staggered levels connected dynamically by an escalator stretching over three storeys together create an interior that could easily be mistaken for the futuristic film sets of William Cameron Menzies's *Things to Come*. But as soon as visitors start wandering around the mall, the initial visual impact fades, giving way instead to themed references to specific places implanted in the contemporary environment. Terminal 21 consists of nine floors, each of which depicts its own theme. The number of themed references varies from one level to another: the range goes from scarce acknowledgements of the chosen concept in some areas to more elaborate and detailed associations with city or regional landmarks in others.

In addition to a scale model of a lighthouse, a recognisable Caribbean reference that extends over two of the mall's levels, visual connections to the theme on the lower ground floor can be found throughout the area,[20] even in the restrooms. The walkway to the restroom ends with an oversized strap coming out of the wall bearing a large medallion: its coat of arms resembles that belonging to the House of Stuart, recalling the British colonial conquest of the Caribbean islands and the famous pirate stories of that time. The bathroom walls and cubicle doors are covered with seventeenth-century maps of the region. Slanted wooden walls, historical lanterns, a sail canvas stretched over the ceiling, washbowls standing on base columns and mirror frames shaped as rudders also all allude to seventeenth-century ships and seafaring. The Caribbean theme shines through in the colourful facades of surrounding shops, hints of upper balconies decorated with flowers, a floor printed with a

IMAGE 12 *Terminal 21, Bangkok, Thailand.* © *Biserko, Dreamstime.com.*
IMAGE 13 *Terminal 21, Bangkok, Thailand.* © *Chingyunsong, Dreamstime.com.*

cobbled pavement, and a signpost with directions to an imaginary beach and bay. Between the escalators, a giant anchor lies in a small artificial pond. A palm tree stands beside it with signs and directions on nailed wooden boards, further contributing to the scenographed corner.

The design is more holistic on the ground floor, where it features associations with Rome. The shiny surfaces of the central area are interrupted by an arched colonnade, and parts of the walls are tiled in beige stone reminiscent of ancient Roman architecture. Inscriptions on the walls in Roman letters, statutes with consoles, street signs, relief images, mural paintings on sections of the ceiling and even a fountain with a statue of Nike of Samothrace are brought together to support the allusion to the Italian capital. In a Postmodern fashion, columns on this level are partially covered with simplified versions of cannelured Roman-Corinthian column shafts that crumble at two-thirds of the height, letting their contemporary counterparts out of their shell to meet the ceiling. In a similar way, the benches and seats are designed as ionic capitals and curved chunks of a cannelured column. Additional props are scattered around, including a Vespa scooter parked in the corner. As on the lower ground floor, the themed design here also extends to the restrooms, with further references to ancient Roman monuments.[21]

The mezzanine is designed to evoke Paris, with shop fronts that look like simplified houses. Their uniformity is disrupted by the use of a pastel colour spectrum, signs and awnings, which give each shop an individual character. Dollhouse facades have their upper portions scaled down, with irregular dwarf windows on the 'first floor'. Lanterns, advertising columns, street signs and tree crowns (without trunks), which are incorporated into the ceiling between the lights, accent the attempt to give this level an outdoor feeling and simulate a Parisian shopping street. Decorative props, such as a bicycle leaning against a street lamp, reinforce the theme. On this floor, however, that theme does not extend to the restrooms, which bear more of a resemblance to the ones found in airport terminals. Indeed, a stripe inspired by a boarding pass printed on the cubicle walls comes back to the mall's overall theme.

The first floor is inspired by the city of Tokyo. At the entrance to this level stands a giant *maneki-neko*, a famous Japanese figure of a cat beckoning with an upright paw, which is believed to bring good fortune. The fronts of the shopping alleys are framed with light wooden constructions. Their graphic geometry, patterns and repetitiveness resemble elements of traditional Japanese architecture, though in a simplified way. Above the shop entrances, bright pop art draws inspiration from woodblock prints, manga comics and floral arrangements. Countless paper lanterns inscribed with Japanese characters hang from the ceiling of the narrow alleys. Further scenographic elements include scaled-down *torii*, traditional gate constructions usually found at the entrances of Shinto shrines, suggestions of porch roofs, figures of sumo wrestlers and a geisha, and *noren*, an exterior fabric used by shops and restaurants printed with logos and signs. *Noren* are also used in front of the restroom area to indicate entrances for men and women. The design of the restrooms continues the Tokyo theme by incorporating door grilles inspired by the sliding panels typical in traditional Japanese houses, the use of bamboo stalks as pipes from which multiple taps protrude and high-tech toilet bowls with multiple functions.

Terminal 21's second floor is based on the streets of London. In order to boost associations with the British capital, the shops on this floor imitate its brick facades and timber shop fronts. Stall risers, pilasters, capitals, mullions, friezes, cornices and signs all have a place. Simplified arches bridging narrow alleys imitate the iron roofs of shopping arcades, while street lamps on iron stands offer a hint of nineteenth-century London. Additional décor includes characteristic icons of the city. As they wander around, visitors will come across a red telephone booth, a double-decker bus, a figure of a Buckingham Palace Guard, a sculpture of a street policeman sitting on a bench, another bench painted with a Union Jack, an oversized letterbox, signs for streets and underground stations, and a shop in a tube carriage. The iconography of the London Underground seems, in fact, to have provided the main stimulus for the design of this part of the mall. As on the lower levels, the restrooms are included in the theme.[22]

The third floor is reserved for Istanbul. Nods to Islamic architecture include a dome-shaped wooden ceiling, pointed and Moorish arches, geometric and floral patterns on the floor, pilasters, tiled columns and upper shop fronts, draped awnings diagonally supported by decorative poles suggesting tent constructions, wooden grille panels, and colourful brass lamps hanging in groups or alone along the shopping alleys. Further references to Turkey consist of fabric stretched between the shop fronts, recalling the covered walkways of the souks. The sculpted figures of two whirling dervishes, dancing back to back on a column, and of a musician in traditional Turkish costume, sitting on a bench and playing a *bağlama* guitar, add to the themed iconography of this level of the mall. The restroom area is designated by lettering and signs incorporated into a decoratively perforated brass frame. The interior of the restroom continues to call upon Islamic architecture and artisanry, including an arched alcove, a chandelier, lamps, the imitation of a stone wall, Moorish arches framing the mirrors, painted glass, brass taps, sculpted basins in marble optic, tiled walls and wooden grilles.

The fourth and fifth levels of the mall are linked under a San Franciscan theme.[23] The fourth floor uses references to the city and the fifth to Fisherman's Wharf. A huge model of the Golden Gate Bridge, with miniature cars 'driving' from one side to the other, stretches over the atrium. Its pillars rise up to the fifth-floor ceiling, connecting the two levels into a single unified whole. The restaurants are designed to follow the iconography and architecture of the city

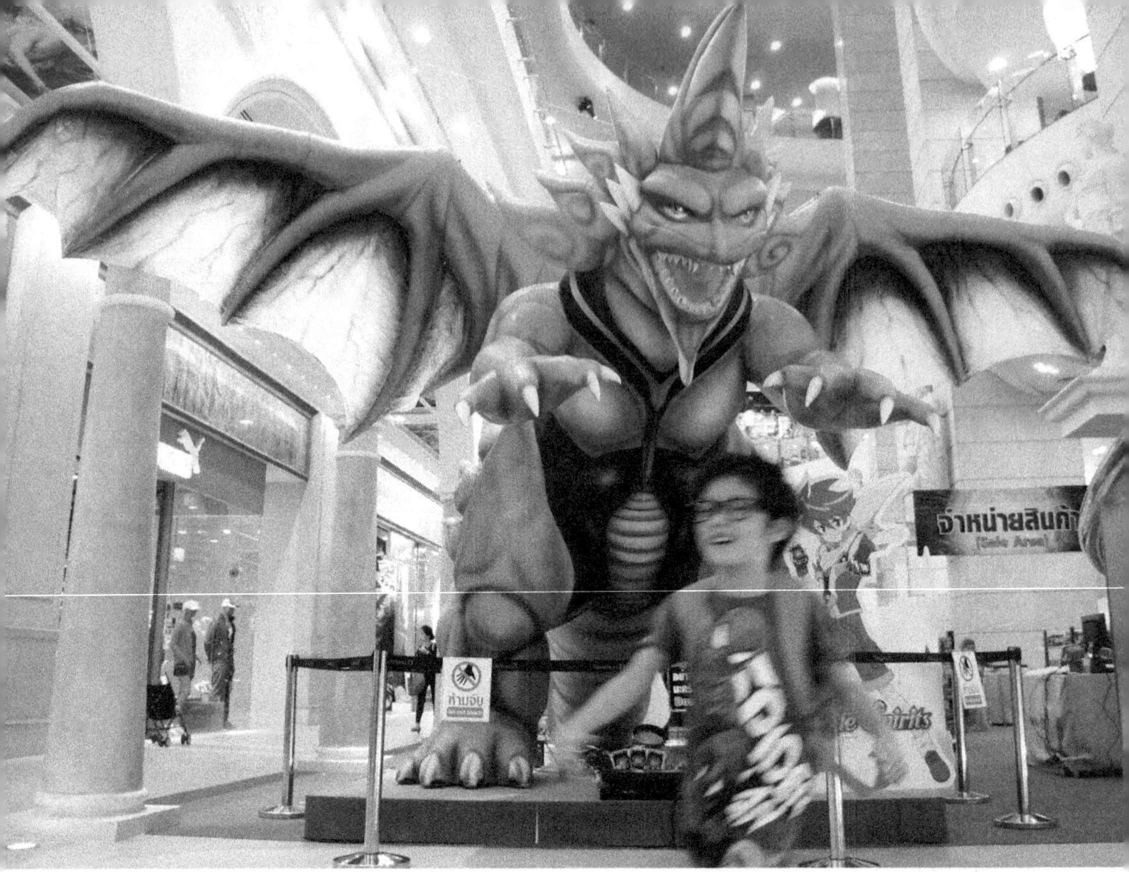
ห้ามจับ

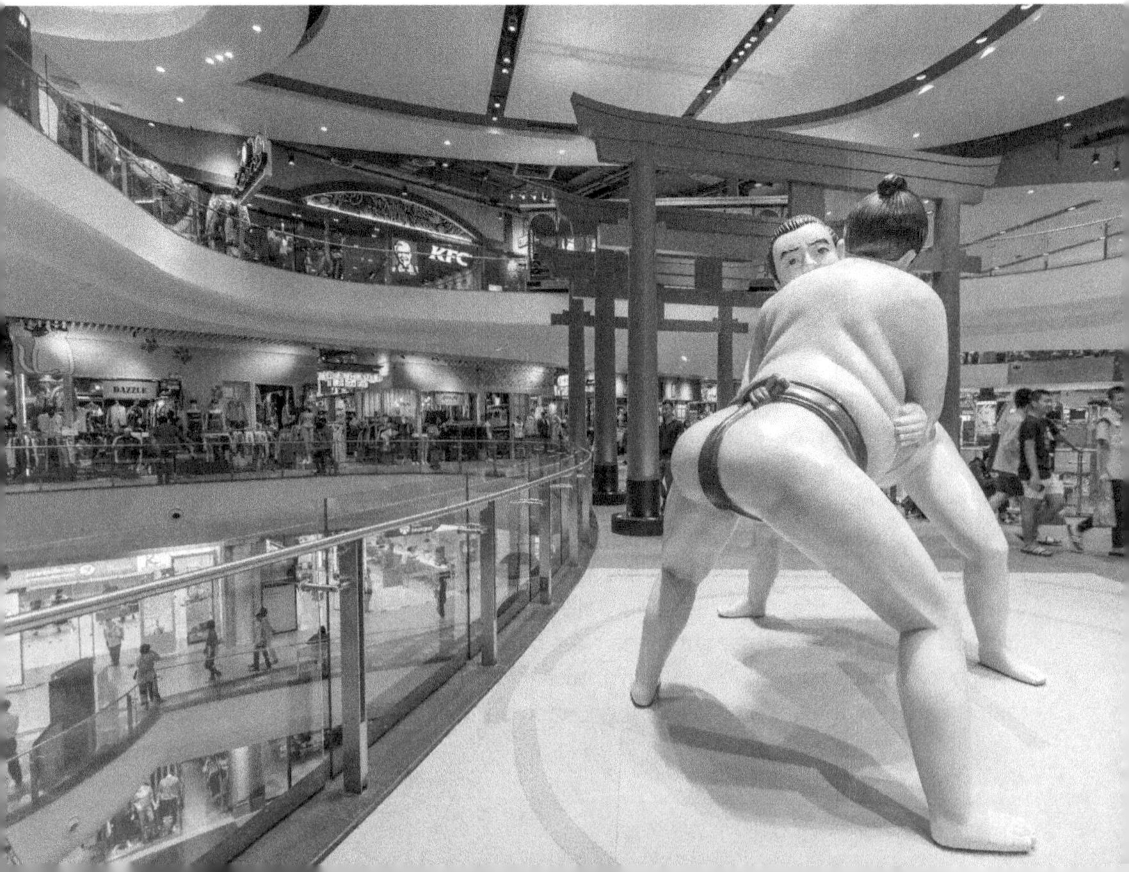
KFC
DAZZLE

and the Wharf, with bay windows and colourful slatted-wood facades. Jardinières in the shape of wooden barrels, a simple but life-sized copy of a cable car, stylised rails and an imitation of a cobbled pavement on the floor support the visual impact. Porch roofs and embossed tiles, brick facades, arched windows, signs and street lamps, whose light cases are molded with small pointed roofs and figurines of golden dragons, give a hint of the city's famous Chinatown. Sculptures of giant crabs and sea lions further associate the fifth floor with the Pacific and seafood restaurants in Fisherman's Wharf. The themed restrooms also clearly remind the visitors that these two levels function as food centres.[24]

Finally, in the main atrium of the fifth floor, a giant statue of an elongated Academy Award reaches from the fourth to the sixth storey, connecting the food courts with the top level and announcing another American theme – Hollywood. Although the sixth floor features some references to Hollywood, these are very restrained compared to the themed elements on the other floors.[25] A sculpture of a film team at work, a huge Hollywood sign and a globe inscribed with *Cinema City*, inspired by the Universal Studios logo, serve as a reminder of the concept chosen for this section of the mall. Inevitably, some thematic details are to be found in the restroom. They include dressing-room mirrors framed with light bulbs, production slates and star signs on the doors and floor, a life-sized image of an imaginary red-carpet event with photographers flashing their cameras towards visitors, film posters and even Walk-of-Fame-style signed imprints with messages on the walls.

From the ground level to the sixth floor, Terminal 21 thus suggests a quick around-the-world trip with areas designed to evoke impressions of eight cities and regions. Unlike the previous examples examined in this book, the contemporary interior reminiscent of the architecture of a flight terminal is omnipresent and clearly visible, steadfast against diverse interruptions.[26] To connect all the many themes under one roof and communicate the overall design concept among the different landmarks, gate signs are displayed in front of each escalator. Their unified colour, lettering and directions continuously remind visitors of the idea of hopping between airport terminals. Despite the discontinuity of the sometimes rather cartoonish-themed references scattered around the mall, the clash of styles caused by countless scenographic interventions does not overshadow the interior architecture of the building. In fact, some parts of the building, such as the massive atrium with its shiny curved surfaces, continue to stand out. The dynamic escalators that form a connection between the nine levels, with blue signs indicating each 'gate', also support the resemblance to an imaginary futuristic transport hub. The flight uniform-inspired costumes for mall employees at information desks and entrances underpin the overall impression, while the information booklet that looks like a passport adds to the fun.

IMAGE 14 *Terminal 21, Bangkok, Thailand. © Mooindy, Dreamstime.com.*

IMAGE 15 *Terminal 21, Bangkok, Thailand. © Geargodz, Dreamstime.com.*

4

Producing Experience

4.1 The magic of Disneyization

Montecasino, the Ibn Battuta Mall, the Villaggio and Terminal 21 represent four different results of *Disneyization*,[1] a term introduced by Alan Bryman to signify how the principles of Disney theme parks have been applied to a variety of social and economic sectors that spread from America across the world (2004: 1). Established in 1955 with the inauguration of Disneyland Resort in Anaheim, California, this holistic approach to designing a theme park based on Walt Disney's animated films has become synonymous with the visual simplification of a narrative – theme, story or history in a more general sense. Its financial success propelled the Disneyland Resort spin-offs, including Walt Disney World Resort in Orlando, Florida (1971), Tokyo Disney Resort (1983), Disneyland Resort Paris (1992), Hong Kong Disneyland Resort (2005) and Shanghai Disney Resort (2016). It was also soon taken over as a corporate strategy in other areas, incorporating individual themes into chain restaurants, heritage villages and shopping malls. In this context, Bryman talks about *transferred Disneyization* to indicate how four dimensions of Disneyization, namely, theming, performative labour, hybrid consumption and merchandising,[2] have been translated into other socioeconomic sectors (2004: 2).

Theming, as defined by Bryman, is the cultural practice of 'clothing institutions or objects in a narrative that is largely unrelated to the institution or object to which it is applied' (2004: 2). In the case studies presented here, the representation of external narratives,[3] which are not related to the sold goods and services nor have any direct connection to their regions, is evident. They tell big stories – the history of Italy (Montecasino, Villaggio), of the Arabian Peninsula and North Africa (the Ibn Battuta Mall), even of the world (Terminal 21). In doing so, themed malls, as a Postmodern phenomenon, contradict the very nature of Postmodernism, in which big stories are abandoned because of their association with ideology and political programmes (Sarup 1993: 146). Instead, Postmodernism favours local struggles, seeing them as a reflection of local creativity (1993: 146). In terms of scenographic strategy, themed shopping malls reinvent historical environments, aiming to involve visitors by means of a spatial experience and entertainment and making them an integral part of consumption (Bryman 2004: 41). These special setups are used to lure consumers out of their homes with the promise of something memorable. At the same time, they secure a traditional way of shopping that requires the buyer's presence at the place where the trade is being made. Bryman argues that theming distinguishes these malls not only from regular shopping malls but also from online, infomercial and outlet shopping (Bryman 2004: 41).

Performative labour, according to Bryman, has evolved out of the theatrical aspects of Disneyization and the growing tendency of the service industry to be constructed and viewed as a performance (2004: 103). It is facilitated by converting the workplace into a stage, transforming employees into performers and applying the vocabulary of theatre production to real-life circumstances (2004: 103). Perceiving commerce as theatre is based on the observation that people stay longer if the environment physically draws them in by offering 'variety, complexity, drama, and texture' and by inviting visitors 'to be actors on the urban stage' (2004: 58; Beyard et al. 2001: 98). The same is true of the emotional labour behind employees' performance, expressed through eye contact, smiling, gestures, body posture and friendly encounters with consumers, which is among the factors that sustain these businesses (Bryman 2004: 105–8). Sales, information and security personnel in Terminal 21 are not only dressed in accordance with the theme, but they also perform their duties. In the Villaggio, the gondoliers also play their part in the show despite the fact that, unlike their Las Vegas counterparts, they do not sing. The level of sincerity behind this behaviour[4] brings emotional labour close to acting. It is different from the routine friendliness generally encountered in commercial settings, giving the impression that employees also 'have fun' and blurring further the line between trade and theatre, work and play.

Hybrid consumption is defined as the interlocking of different industries that then become difficult to separate (Bryman 2004: 57). Led by economies of scope,[5] shopping malls did not just grow in size to accommodate the variety of offers when theming was introduced; they actually underwent a transformation into mixed-use spaces.[6] Most themed shopping malls are places of hybrid consumption per se. The four examples described here are no exception, as they combine shopping, restaurants, cinemas, theme parks, exhibitions and recreational areas. As such, hybrid consumption is not necessarily linked to scenography, because it can exist without it. However, by adding an overall narrative to the space, themed shopping malls also step into the role of tourist attraction. Quoting the manager of The Forum Shops at Caesar's Palace in Las Vegas, Bryman explains the movement towards themed environments as the pursuit of a 'pleasant' atmosphere, where visitors feel good and which facilitates the conditions for lingering. What scenography does for hybrid consumption in themed malls is visually to connect the diverse services into one unified entity, creating a 'wow' effect that prolongs consumers' stay and leads to them spending more money (Bryman 2004: 58). Even though research on consumer behaviour is far from an exact science, and its results are closely connected to consumer expectations, gender, age, their income and their socioeconomic background, some empirical data nevertheless document a significant relation between 'relative spending' and the 'attractiveness' of the shopping centre (Dennis 2005: 50). In addition to setting the tone for increased spending, theming also creates the circumstances in which the distinction between different forms of consumption drifts out of focus. Even if the origins of hybrid consumption lie in shopping arcades and department stores, Montecasino and the Villaggio leave little room for doubt: Las Vegas still serves as the global role model for contemporary incarnations by wrapping mixed-use resorts into a themed design (Bryman 2004: 61–2). In the realm of shopping-mall culture, where similar types of stores and services are offered, the combination of hybrid consumption with theming helps 'to differentiate sites that might otherwise appear unremarkable' and 'to create environments that are construed as being spectacular' (Bryman 2004: 76; Ritzer 2005: 259).

Transferred Disneyization, as it is applied in shopping malls, overlaps with the principles of expanded scenography laid out by Joslyn McKinney and Scott Palmer (2017: 8–13; Bryman 2004: 2). It introduces new spatial relations into the commercial public domain, including *relationality* – the way spectators confront imagined and staged realities in public spaces, *affectivity* – the manipulation of spaces, images and signs for the purpose of catching viewers' attention, and *materiality* – the communication of scenographic content through direct tactile encounters between spectators and their surroundings (McKinney et al. 2017: 8–13). Relationality is reflected in the way well-known environments appear in a new light, 'situating' consumers in unfamiliar scenographed spaces that activate the 'dramaturgical potential of the built environment' (McKinney et al. 2017: 8–10). This opens the possibilities for shoppers to gain fresh insights about themselves, others and the places they are in (McKinney et al. 2017: 8–10). Unlike scenography in theatre, whose affectivity usually works over time, gradually unravelling to reflect the play's dramaturgy, themed scenography aims to produce an immediate impact. It does so through carefully constructed spatial organisation and the sensory use of materials that create a direct bodily response. The close proximity of spectators to the scenography in themed environments has led to an exaggerated experience of materiality and, in some cases, themed concepts have even been structured around it. For example, beyond its capacity to seduce the audience visually, with high-tech fountains that establish associations with open urban spaces, water is used nowadays as a scenographic material in all its forms. As such, it forms the backdrop for skiing, skating, snowboarding, playing, walking through tunnels in aquariums and among ice sculptures, riding gondolas, and projecting video images, actually becoming an independent scenographic agent in its own right.

Themed commercial public spaces, including shopping malls, join the wide field of expanded scenography according to specific principles. They restructure the traditional design strategies inherent in Disneyization while continuing to blur the boundaries between life and theatre. Of course, theming cannot be solely attributed to Disneyland; there are many earlier examples of themed approaches to design other than in amusement parks, such as in restaurants, apartment blocks and film theatres (Bryman 2004: 23). Among the most prominent of these themes, Gottdiener identifies 'status, tropical paradise, wild west, classical civilisation, nostalgia, Arabian fantasy, urban motif, fortress architecture and surveillance, and modernism and progress' (1997: 144–51). Bryman adds more general terms to Gottdiener's classification, dividing themes into place, time, sports, music, cinema, fashion, commodities, architecture, the natural world, literature and morality or philosophy (2004: 18). Looking at our case studies from the perspective of expanded scenography, we can see that the spectrum of existing themed strategies has been broadened. Even though the leitmotif of the city of Venice in the Villaggio Mall is directly inspired by Grand Canal Shoppes, the use of this particular theme goes far back in history to Dreamland on Coney Island. One section of this amusement park called the Canals of Venice was destroyed in a fire in 1911. It had a canal with gondolas that ran along the street front, which incorporated ornamental facade elements of Doge's Palace into a colonnade, aspiring to a resemblance with Venetian architecture. In the Villaggio Mall, the theme used in Grand Canal Shoppes has been extended; three additional shopping streets have no canals, instead adding ancient Roman and late Baroque stylistic references to the main Renaissance theme. With its multiplex cinema, ice rink and Gondolania theme park, the mall has widened its offerings, moving the original concept of Grand Canal Shoppes further in the direction of entertainment and recreational facility. The tendency to expand an existing themed concept set by American examples can be also observed in the Shoppes at Venetian in Macau. This Las Vegas Sands project in China goes far beyond its origins. The mall in Macau covers an area of one million square feet (92,903.04 square metres), doubling the size of Grand Canal Shoppes with more than 350 stores and an extensive food court. Six shopping streets fork from the central Great Hall, ending in a ring road that contains three indoor canals with singing gondoliers waiting to take shoppers for a ride. Further expansion includes the advancement of scenographic techniques for the visualisation of Italian-themed architecture more generally. In Montecasino, an attempt to increase the level of 'authenticity' of the building facades has resulted in the use of aging techniques to make the scenography look more real. In addition, the lights are dimmed, street fronts irregular and alleys narrow, small piazzas have emerged, and the setting has been dressed with props such as washing lines, parked cars and birds.[7] The mall offers both diurnal and nocturnal atmospheres within a single shopping area, going beyond the unified high-key polish of Las Vegas.

Generally speaking, even if the themes of classical civilisation, Arabian fantasy and fortress architecture, as well as urban motifs and Hollywood are at the heart of the design concepts behind a few of our examples, their scope has clearly been widened. The numerous themes in the Ibn Battuta Mall are presented as part of an overarching theme of travel as a way of gathering knowledge. Moving through different courts, consumers encounter exhibits that tell stories about the discoveries of a specific historical period, broadening the entertainment approach to consumption by adding an educational aspect. In Terminal 21, the travel concept is taken even further. Exchanging a horizontal layout for a vertical use of space, this shopping mall serves as a melting pot for multiple themed directions within one overall setup of a transport hub. As a result, a new kind of metatheatrical dimension is added to theming. By uniting diverse 'destinations' under one roof, Terminal 21 highlights the transitional character of the visual narrative: these places can never truly be reached, regardless of how far one travels.

In the past, a promise to reach imagined or existing places was implied by life-sized means of transport, for example, the aeroplane exhibits in nineteenth-century department stores.[8] Walt Disney, however, introduced scale as an additional strategy to tap into 'otherness'. This traditional technique has been used for centuries in both architecture and scenography to test designs in three dimensions and to communicate artistic visions to others ahead of embarking on their realisation. It is logically inherent in planning themed environments. Naturally, Disney also used scaling for presentations, but he went a step further, combining it with other media. In a television broadcast of *Disneyland's 10th Anniversary Show* (1965), Disney announced new buildings and animatronics, which would become part of the Disneyland experience. In doing so, he demonstrated the process of design creation, from the conceptual drawings and storyboards to a finalised model (Hamilton 1965). The public was introduced to new features of the park with very detailed models that explained their future functions. Taking advantage of camera use and close-ups, the scale on screen was diminished and the audience was given an impression of how the planned infrastructure would be experienced on-site. For example, a riverbed was left out of Caribbean Town, leaving a walk-through path in the model. Positioned on a stand so as to be at the height of the viewer's sight line, the model made it possible for the camera to go inside and catch various perspectives from the audience's point of view. Spectators were thus embedded in an altered perception of the world. As he introduced the park's new sections, the Haunted Mansion, Pirates of the Caribbean and New Orleans Square, he explained the study of light on a model to enhance the theatrical atmosphere of the buildings and the park itself at night.

Beyond the implementation of these techniques for the purposes of design and presentation, Disney's enthusiasm for model, scale and forced perspective – techniques traditionally used in the film industry – resulted in the use of different scales for architecture and transportation in Disneyland. The aim was to reinforce the impression of 'entering another world'.[9] The same method was applied to a miniature Santa Fe railroad, cars and scenographed architecture, as in a themed area set up to recall an American town around 1900, to name just a few examples. To support the change in perception as spatial relations were so significantly altered, Disney took the utmost precautions to isolate the Disney world from its surroundings so that nothing might distract visitors and remind them of the reality outside the park's gates (Chung et al. 2001a: 277). Fading out the outside world has been ingrained in the shopping malls since their early days in the late 1950s, when their architecture supported 'introverted interior worlds, shut off to the outside' (Brune 2011: 21). As they are enclosed environments, scaling in themed shopping malls functions almost independently of their immediate surroundings. It is often employed to accentuate associations with certain topics and places or manipulate the perception of their size. Scaled means of transport are extensively used as scenography in Terminal 21, where visitors can find a replica of a San Francisco municipal railway wagon, a model of cars driving over the Golden Gate Bridge and a London double-decker bus. Upper floors of shop facades are scaled down in the Ibn Battuta Mall, the Villaggio Mall and Terminal 21 to fit under the ceilings of shopping alleys and make street fronts look taller. At the same time, other elements such as the columns in the Chinese court of the Ibn Battuta Mall, the Academy Award statue in the Hollywood-inspired area of Terminal 21 and the *maneki-neko* in its Tokyo section are all scaled up, either indicating grander spaces or underlining a connection to the theme.

If we look deeper, however, Disneyization goes beyond the narrative of themed concepts expressed with surface cosmetics, imaginative facades and playful combinations of scaled architectural styles. As a product meant for mass consumption, theming is an inherently intermedial phenomenon. The opening ceremony at Disneyland in the mid-1950s, which coincided with the emergence of the first shopping malls in North America, was followed by extensive media coverage: Disney's theming concept was spread far and wide to a variety of audiences. The ceremony was covered by ABC in a live broadcast using twenty-nine cameras, and the American public was presented with the new era of theme parks via television sets and post-production techniques. The introductions to different sections of the park were scripted and staged. The show included multiple hosts, musical numbers, interactions with the audience, flying doves as a symbol for peace in the 'atomic age' of Tomorrowland, inserts of animation sequences, cyclorama projections, demonstrations of atomic reactions and a simulation of a rocket trip to the moon, made possible by film. Through the skilful application of montage, magical transformations were inserted into theatrical acts performed on-site, for example, the ten-year anniversary cake was 'cut' into moving slices. In one of the first interviews he gave on the subject, Walt Disney explained his vision, which was to reach past the limitations of animated films and provide 'something live, something that will grow' (Chung et al. 2001a: 273). In practical terms, this was only realisable in combination with other media. Disney's idea of a themed space was thus one of change and adaptation, a way of morphing physical reality over time according to the needs of the public (2001a: 273). As Chuihua Judy Chung points out, Disney believed that imagination is the starting point from which reality is created and that the fantasy has to be realistic and believable in order to sell (2001a: 273). For the vast majority of visitors, Disneyland was first experienced on television, supported by post-production effects, and then afterwards through direct physical encounter. Chung explains that the translation process, in which the architecture was designed using the same approach as producing an animated film, was done by 'imagineers'. They used a combination of imagination and engineering to offer a cinematographic experience of the space, as if visitors were actually entering the Disneyland film (2001a: 276).

In fact, the experience of theme parks such as Disneyland and themed malls is regularly compared to cinematographic perception in terms of a film montage, while movement through them can be seen as progression through the scenes of a film (Aronson 1977: 73; Davis 1991: 13). This point of view is based on the observation that the narrative of themed spaces brings 'geographically and architecturally unrelated elements into a "logical whole"', as is done in film (Chung et al. 2001a: 276, 280). Bryman goes into more specific detail. Theming, he argues 'provides a veneer of meaning and symbolism to the objects to which it is applied' (2004: 15). Furthermore, he emphasises that it 'transcends [meanings] or at the very least is in addition to what they actually are' (Bryman 2004: 15). As on both stage and screen, images, symbols and props carry supplementary meanings in themed settings, which exceed their functional purposes. They tell stories, stir the imagination, announce action. In regard to Disney World Resort, Robert Venturi calls this approach 'symbolic of American utopia' (Chung et al. 2001a: 284). Consumers' lost sense of place comes as a result of their intermedial perception of themed shopping malls, which intertwine direct exposure through physical presence and indirect experience via still and moving images on computers, tablets and phones. Embedded in this context, symbols also figure as connecting elements in the overall spatial manipulation established by theming. Another reason for the lost sense of place and time, as well as the related spatial experience, is the cultural loss caused by decentralisation and consumers' drift from city centres towards suburban shopping malls, which started in the post-war period (Oc et al. 1997: 15–16). According to Peter Coleman, the re-establishment of this sense of place and the re-creation of local identity remain the key challenges to shopping-mall designers (2006: 445). As Warnaby et al. note, the shopping mall's success and its 'development as a force for marketplace creation' go hand in hand with the simultaneous development of 'marketplace turbulence and destruction' (2018: 278).

Efforts to cope with this phenomenon, as well as the urge to establish a unique selling point as affluence grew in tandem with competition, correspond with the emergence of 'experience shopping' and the advent of brand stores in the early 1980s. The goal was to strengthen 'a brand image as their [store's] sense of place' (Hosoya et al. 2001: 166; Pine II et al. 1999: 5). These shops were also a reaction to a reduction in the average time spent in malls, which sank significantly between 1980 and 1990 (Hassel 1996, cited in Chung et al. 2001b: 74–5). The shift towards experience and simulation, Coleman explains, focuses on '"feeling" and "collecting" the merchandise' and sophisticated approaches to the creation of drama, as businesses became 'stages for experience' (2006: 445–6; Pine II et al. 1999: 4). Differentiating between brand attitude, brand attachment and brand personality, Kim et al. describe the shopping-mall experience as 'a practical sense, feeling, cognition, and behavioural response to specific brand-related stimuli' (2015: 63). It is 'a response of customers toward the marketing activities offered by a shopping complex, which includes sensory, emotional, cognitive, and behavioral experience' (Kim et al. 2015: 68). An empirical analysis conducted by Kim et al. across five South Korean shopping malls shows that shopping-mall brands resonate positively on the consumer's satisfaction and loyalty (2015: 68–74). Experience as a brand is typically associated with the staged interiors of stores as 'environments with added value' (Hosoya et al., cited in Chung et al. 2001b: 166). This includes playing with toys or testing the recreational equipment in simulated outdoor conditions (Hahn 2002: 117). Theming then wraps the shopping experience in a specific narrative, which artificially strengthens the character of the shopping mall and gives the marketplace 'personality', hoping that its resonance will pay off with consumer loyalty. Theming, therefore, substantially contributes to the creation of the 'personality' of the brand, which is defined as the 'psychological reputation that reflects the individual personality in common and normal sense' (Kim et al. 2015: 68). It is a recognisable and profitable selling strategy that reassures consumers in their choices, stimulating their buying behaviour.

While the lack of social and political implications is masked, other shortcomings are more easily noticeable. A closer look at the shop facades in our case studies reveals an alienated interpretation of historical architectural styles that separates the buildings from their 'originals', an approach referred to by Venturi as 'decorated sheds'. Unlike architecture, which operates within the frame of generally accepted contemporary aesthetics, Anna Viebrock explains, scenography communicates history through the heightened stylisation of reality, using its comparative freedom to create more intense atmospheres (Brejzek 2017: 64–5). The connection between aesthetics and the capitalist economy in the late twentieth and early twenty-first centuries, reflected in architecture and acknowledged in the theoretical discourse on the subject (Böhme G. 1995; Haug 1986), applies to scenographed alleys in themed shopping malls only to a certain degree. Even though the desire to create an aesthetic and atmospheric pleasure for consumers is evident, theming here follows a specific path within a framework dictated by the economy: it goes beyond the limits of 'good taste' and 'dominant aesthetic ideas' imposed upon architects (Brejzek 2017: 76). Exaggerated design, strong colours, the reinterpretation of classical proportions, elaborate ornamentation and a combination of different styles are conquering the vast spaces of Montecasino, the Ibn Battuta Mall, the Villaggio and Terminal 21, creating environments that reflect kitsch, mimicry and artifice, and challenging generally accepted architectural aesthetics. They aspire neither to create beauty nor to hold a 'mirror to social reality',[10] but instead to forge an imaginative new objectivity that distances itself from mainstream architecture and the outside world. In exchange, they offer another version of reality that seeks to entertain by making us laugh, wonder and play. Therefore, in regard to the aesthetic approach, architects embarking on the adventure of designing scenography, Thea Brejzek suggests, 'need to leave the safe and aesthetically pleasing territory of symbolic representation on the stage behind and embrace the politicized domestic as a mirror of society, a conceptual move that would allow for the urban-builders of today to finally become world-makers in the theatre' (Brejzek 2017: 77).

Changes in the understanding of spatiality as a new way to introduce a sense of place in themed shopping malls, as Rob Schields recognises, have a wider impact on 'social spatialisation' at both the regional and global level (1989: 147–64). Shopping's ability to redirect spatial conditions dovetails with the very nature of scenography as a cultural practice. According to John McMorrough, 'It is the activity of shopping that allows it to constitute the effects of the city' (2001: 195). The lost sense of place, originally caused by an enclosure of the activity of shopping, now propelled themed design with a focus on city architecture, whose representation was always among the major features of scenography (Brejzek 2017: 75). An emphasis on the symbolism of architectural style, as opposed to its construction and function, exposed a conflict between the perception of fake street fronts in shopping malls and their use. The re-creation of the city as scenography resulted in facades detached from the construction, and set domestic and residential architecture as the stage for commerce (Venturi et al. 1979: 104). In the same way as in theme parks, the representation of history in themed malls is criticised 'for the omission of inequality and tensions' (Bryman 2004: 8). As Marcela Oteíza points out, 'the city adds its social and political history to the performances' and brings layers of meaning to site-specific environments (2017: 79). Along with the tendency for *disneyfication*, which is 'applied to the cultural realm in the form of stories and the depiction of history' (Bryman 2004: 8), using historical styles for inspiration is a deliberate scenographic strategy. Despite the effort, however, in the crack that opens between shopping-mall alleys performing as city streets and the unpredictability of an actual city as a performance site, the long history of the marketplace within an urban environment falls away without an echo.

4.2 Technological wizardry

Discussing imaginative production using mechanical apparatuses in the nineteenth century, Jonathan Crary identifies the Kaiserpanorama in the Unter den Linden boulevard in Berlin as 'one of the numerous sites on which we can credibly locate an "industrialization" of visual consumption … the physical and temporal alignment of body and machine correspond to the rhythms of factory production and to the way in which novelty and interruptions were introduced into assembly-line labor in order to prevent attention from veering into trance and daydream' (Crary 2001: 138). Regarding the design approach to commercial scenographic displays and installations, industrialisation inevitably infiltrated the creative process, changing it significantly. From the early days of department stores and the introduction of themed scenographic arrangements that predominantly referred to the exotic and opulent, displays of technological progress were never far behind (Gottdiener 1997: 35). Early issues of the magazine *Popular Mechanics* offer a historical survey of the mechanical devices used for shop-window displays. Among other inventions, these included a device exhibited in New York in 1913, which contained three compartments arranged vertically, one above the other, that operated as an elevator or stage lift in the theatre.[11] While one compartment was being exhibited in the shop window, the other two could be used to change displays, as on the theatrical stage.[12] The February 1932 issue of *Popular Mechanics* describes a revolving colour screen, a constantly changing colour curtain run by electric clock. According to the magazine, the curtain consisted of 'two revolving cylinders of red, blue and yellow translucent material, each housing an electric lamp, and an electric clock to rotate the cylinders'.[13] The quality of light in the shop window would change continually, and the exhibited items would be drenched in three different colours. In July 1941, the magazine published an article presenting the solenoid pendulum.[14] This device caused an element displayed in a shop window to swing, for example, a hand cut-out would wave left and right pointing in the direction of a product name.[15] Functional and aesthetic mechanical inventions of this kind, adapted for shop windows or store interiors, certainly caught the attention of passers-by, shaking them out of the daydream. Yet 'the mechanization of vision', as Crary observes, 'had no intrinsic link to objectivity or veracity but rather to new capacities for simulation, illusion, conjuration' (2001: 277–8).

The use of mechanical devices to create spectacular and illusionistic-themed scenography was, at first, a seasonal affair, begun by department stores between 1870 and 1890 during Christmas holidays. Usually, they were involved in staging Santa Claus in fairy-tale settings. In his historical review of holiday displays, William L. Bird quotes historian Ralph M. Hower, mentioning Macy's first animated shop window with moving figures driven by steam power in 1883 (Bird 2007: 24). An illustration in *Frank Leslie's Illustrated Newspaper* the following year shows Macy's Christmas display 'in which human-scale figures appear to be taking a trip on a panoramic track led by Santa in a triumphal car' (Bird 2007: 24). The opulence of Christmas shop windows grew during the 1920s and 1930s with increasingly extravagant light decorations, Christmas villages, caves and mechanical installations (Whitaker 2013: 74). Even the fragmented documentation of these shop-window displays divulges the effort and ambition department stores put into this marketing strategy in order to attract more consumers during the holiday season. Endeavours to outshine the competition included removing interior walls to connect shop windows for a continuous installation, as done by Tony Sarg for a Macy's display in New York in the early 1920s. The result reached theatre-stage dimensions, at least in length, and opened possibilities for even more elaborate Christmas displays. Sarg, a marionette theatre-maker by trade, crafted a spectacular panorama stretching 21 metres along five shop windows on Thirty-Fourth Street, with twenty-six mechanical compositions inspired by fairy tales (Bird 2007: 30). Further examples that reveal the history of mechanical Christmas displays and their dominance in the first half of the twentieth century include Santa's Circus (1920) by W. F. Larkin at Wanamaker's, a walk-through attraction with mechanical circus acts, Macy's animated window dressing Around the World at Christmas Time (1933) by Landy R. Hales (Bird 2007: 17–19), a trapdoor installation for delivering complimentary presents to children through a well-titled Snow White's Wishing Well (1938) at J. N. Adams & Co. (Bird 2007: 59), A Window on Williamsburg (1966) at Woodward & Lothrop with one hundred animated figures by Christian Hofmann in eight settings (Bird 2007: 128), and many others. From the 1920s to the 1960s, Bird recounts, mechanical displays that combined papier-mâché figures and electrical motors became 'an expressive medium for institutional selling and storytelling' (2007: 47).

The spectacular Christmas trimming practised by the department stores proceeded in the shopping malls, only on a much larger scale. By 1925, all of the shops in the pioneering themed mall, the Country Club Plaza, were decorated with the same kind of Christmas lighting, and Christmas trees were prominently positioned throughout the premises (Hahn 2002: 31). Additional elements, such as oversized lit candles used as street lanterns, also formed part of the display. After the Second World War, the spacious halls, atriums, courtyards and shopping streets of the early shopping malls allowed scenographic installations to become even more enormous in both size and richness. From the 1950s, huge Christmas trees entered the shopping malls' interiors as well as their exteriors, reaching heights as gravity-defying like the 65-metre pine in front of the Northgate Mall (Diltz 2018).[16] Giant scenographic installations were featured in airy courtyards and parking lots. Westfield Garden State Plaza, for example, featured a 15.5-metre Santa Claus emerging from a 7.6-metre chimney, installed every holiday season between the early 1960s and early 1980s along with an arch decorated with bells and animated Santas hammering out Christmas carols (Ervolino 2017). Christmas displays in the shopping malls did not continue the mechanical shows put on by the department stores: they restricted decking the halls with big trees and ornaments to a 'fence-lined route into a display setting for Santa'. As Bird notes, the malls might have been unwilling to distract consumers from the merchandise (Bird 2007: 139). Christmas lights, however, for which technology was improving constantly, became one of the dominant decorative elements in scenographic arrangements both inside and outside the shopping malls. They were patented by Edward H. Johnson in 1882 and improved for mass production by Albert Sadacca, whose Noma Electric Company, founded in 1925, became the world's largest manufacturer of Christmas lights (Davis 2012). These lights played a significant role in the fact that, from the early 1920s, electrical ornamentation was widely established as an indispensable part of scenographic Christmas installations.

Despite the ubiquity of electrical tricks, the charm and seduction of mechanical scenography nevertheless retain its attractiveness today. Most notably, Macy's in New York still pursues the tradition of mechanical displays that it began in the late nineteenth century. In the first decades of the twentieth century, its six shop windows on Broadway enchanted consumers year after year with animated themed settings. These ranged from the steam-punk extravaganza Make a Wish (2011) and the outer-space adventure of Santa's Journey to the Stars (2014) to the Herald Square model in The Perfect Gift Brings People Together (2017). Using the full arsenal of theatre-stage engineering on a small scale, Macy's shop-window displays involved the use of dwarf 'stage lifts', mechanical solutions for spinning, moving and flying effects, animated films and animatronics. Roya Sullivan, the company's national window director, explains that preparations for such elaborate scenography start a year in advance and require up to 200 people (Adamczyk 2014). In London, Harrods followed the example set by Macy's, launching animated displays such as The Harrods Christmas Express (2013). The motion of the steam train inspiring the theme was simulated by mechanics as well as by landscape animations on HD monitors set up as compartment windows, depicting 'the analogy between window shopping and the gaze upon exotic landscapes passing by the carriage window' (Goss 1993: 37). According to the *Daily Mail*, the effort involved fifty people and took three weeks to install (London 2013). Even more impressive was Harrods's 2014 themed setting dubbed The Land of Make Believe, with 'dancing' mannequins as ballerinas and a composition of a 'flying' Santa Claus on a sleigh stretching across two windows. In Paris, the Galeries Lafayette also holds on to the long tradition of extravagant Christmas displays. In 2017, the department store launched its funfair-inspired displays entitled Spectacular, Spectacular. The themed concept was extended beyond the shop windows, which were dressed with miniature animated rides, merry-go-rounds, a Ferris wheel, marionettes simulating circus acts and flying birds. Inside the department store, there was a giant rotating Christmas tree and a mobile composition of oversized sweets bouncing up and down in the main hall under the dome. Moreover, a virtual reality experience of a rollercoaster ride, delivered via a VR headset with moving seats, wind and sound effects, was installed on the second floor. To top it all off, Beth Ditto performed on opening night. Every weekend, carol singers, a magician and a tattoo studio on the third floor served as a special treat for consumers.

In Melbourne, Myer's animated displays from the last decade include a tribute to the children's book *Gingerbear Friends* by Jan Brett, designed by John Kerr and his team at Stage One. This 2013 set was an elaborate showcase of mechanics, animatronics and turntables, which took seven months and forty artisans to build. It was enhanced with an additional feature, a smartphone app that could be downloaded via QR code, which showed the creative process behind the display from its conception to its installation. Myer's 2017 Christmas window spectacle, aglow with light and mechanics, followed a narrative based on the children's book *The Completely & Utterly, Absolutely Perfect Christmas* by H. C. Floren, written especially for Myer's. The main character of the book, an Elf, is actually a Christmas decoration himself, who sets out on a journey to find better 'scenography' for a company. This scenographic journey leads him from one group of decorations to another, allowing a universal story to unfold about belonging and appreciating what one has. At the same time, readers are reminded of the long history and creative versatility of Christmas decorations.

Examples of technology-based scenographic displays in department stores are numerous, and not all of them can be considered here. The few we have looked at, however, are enough to illustrate the influence of the latest technological developments. In comparison with its historical precedents, Christmas-themed scenography in affluent department stores has extended its reach beyond the physical space of their shop windows. To cash in on the commercial value, the merchandising includes toys, a special edition of a children's book, a three-dimensional animated TV commercial, a virtual reality app and even 'making of' material. Despite all these changes, the attention and amazement provoked by the fanciful mechanical displays, in the past as much as now, are not the only things that draw in the numbers: Bird's historical overview shows that another fundamental appeal is the emotional response they awaken, memories and nostalgia, a child within (2007: 5). The enduring and persuasive power of applied technology in a commercial scenographic context sets the bar higher and expands its marketing strategy more every year.

At the moment, the use of technology for the purposes of scenographic installations in shopping malls involves experiments with HD screens, interactive displays and LED lights (Fritsch 2018). Duggal Visual Solutions' Lumipixels, an animated LED backlit board, for example, induces a sense of motion and fluidity by lighting the fabric graphics stretched in front of it.[17] In East and Southeast Asia, the Christmas extravaganza grows bigger year after year, especially in regions with a Western European colonial past. Harbour City Mall in Hong Kong, for example, cooperates with acclaimed designers to impress visitors with unique-themed displays every season, investing substantial funds in order to outshine the competition.[18] Among the many impressive Christmas arrangements, such as a Disney-themed setup with oversized Christmas baubles out of which Disney characters emerged, or the Snowie installation designed by Rami Niemi in 2016, a composition of snowmen that consisted of two oversized snowballs covered with thirty-two different designs, some technological marvels have also been presented. These have included the mechanical scenography of moving deer silhouettes in 2006, an elaborate light installation and choreographed drone show designed by George Chan in 2017, and three giant Santa spaceships with spinning propellers suspended from the ceiling.

When it comes to themed shopping malls, technology, at least in the scenographic context, plays a rather marginal role. Technological wonders like the *Myth of Atlantis* at The Forum Shops at Caesar's, complete with animatronics, stage lifts and pyrotechnic effects, or Dita von Teese's hologram show at Studio City are reserved for more spectacular environments such as Las Vegas or Macau. Apart from the Gondolania theme park at the Villaggio Mall, where technology certainly plays an important role, Montecasino, the Ibn Battuta Mall, Terminal 21 and even the Villaggio itself rely predominantly on traditional Christmas decoration. At Montecasino, an annual Christmas village transforms the mall's outdoor piazza into a European-style Christmas market. In the Tuscan setting, wooden booths decorated with lights and garlands support the simulation of an imaginary Italian town square during the Christmas holidays. In December 2019, equal effort was put into adorning Montecasino's interior. The decorations included massive light installations suspended from the ceiling and stretched between opposing facades in shopping alleys, as well as illuminated trees, ornaments, a gigantic teddy bear and Santa's sleigh made of lights, and a stage for Santa set against the backdrop of a stylised hut, positioned underneath a roofed baldachin construction decorated with lights and pine tree branches. The alleys were dressed such that they could easily be mistaken for the outdoor Christmas finery on display in European streets and squares. In 2015, the Ibn Battuta Mall was decked out with huge Christmas trees surrounded by oversized presents in the Tunisian court, Santa's hut and sleigh in the Persian court, and a scaled-down version of Santa's cottage in a winter setting with Christmas trees, loads of presents and a showman in the Chinese court. A prominent place for special scenographic arrangements was a platform beside the junk-ship replica on top of the fountain in the Chinese court. In 2016, it consisted of a printed backdrop on the walls that simulated the interior of Santa's cottage, with his chair, a fireplace and windows showing a winter landscape. In front, props such as piles of presents, big teddy bears and Christmas trees were arranged. Huge carpets were spread out for children to come onstage, use the set as a playground and take a photo with Santa. A small bridge enabled visitors to reach the stage by walking over the fountain edge, which surrounded the setting. The same approach was repeated in the Chinese court the following year, though with more elaborate scenography on the fountain platform. The winter scenery included a couple of houses, whose roofs were covered with tonnes of fake snow. Visitors could wander around among them. Santa's sleigh was used for complementary photo sessions with children. In all this Christmas scenography in the Ibn Battuta Mall, the use of technology was restricted to a heap of oversized Christmas presents wrapped in LED lighting, positioned on a turntable, which spun around in one of the courts during the 2017 holiday season. Likewise, Bangkok's Terminal 21 holds on to the tradition of positioning an enormous Christmas tree with wintery scenography around it by the main entrance, outside the mall. In the past few years, the mall's interior has been decorated with a composition of oversized presents and colourful balls suspended from the ceiling in the atrium (2014), a series of snowmen in historical costumes representing the countries included in the mall's themed design – such as one snowman dressed as a citizen of ancient Rome, one as a French painter and another as a member of the Queen of England's guard, among others (2015) – and copses of white trees with deer on the sky-bridge in front of the mall and partially within it (2017). The most dominant decorative element, however, is the lights. The ornamentation in Terminal 21 during the holiday season is heavily based on an LED lighting system that, in some years, stretched vertically over multiple levels of the mall, above the railings and permanent-themed scenery. In the Villaggio Mall, scarce documentation of any Christmas decoration in recent years gives only a hint of low-key efforts based mostly on LED lights wrapped around the indoor lanterns and hung above the shopping streets.

It is interesting to note that the Ibn Battuta Mall, the Villaggio Mall and Terminal 21 all continue traditions established in the Western world despite the fact that Christmas is not a national holiday in the United Arab Emirates, Qatar or Thailand. Its connotation in those places differs widely from the countries in which the cultural significance of Christmas evolved. Therefore, the scale of investment in Christmas decorations and the substantial profits associated with the holiday are not really comparable. Apart from the lighting, there is hardly any implementation of new technologies as scenography at Christmastime. Contemporary scenographic solutions seem to be reserved for individual shop windows, information boards, special occasions and promotions; they are not featured in the main halls, alleys or outdoors. In comparison with regular shopping malls, such as Hong Kong's Harbour City, which outshines its Western counterparts in both scale and presentation, Christmas ornamentation in the themed shopping malls we have looked at is thus restricted to a traditional kind of dressing. While the decorations offer shiny and sparkling effects, the scenography itself stays motionless. Having already built a strong visual identity, themed environments struggle to incorporate an additional narrative into the existing one; if it is not integrated into the regular set, as in Montecasino, Christmas iconography simply clashes with the historically scenographed surroundings. The tendency to depend on the established theme and on architectural mimicry exposes the limits of these commercial spaces' flexibility and adaptability, which Christmas literally brings to light. Drawing on Deleuze and Guattari, Crary suggests that 'anything with a permanent stable location in space is incapable of being inserted into a system of exchange and circulation and anything that is part of a code (a traditional or established pattern of behavior or representation) will resist being deployed in networks of abstract relations' (2001: 143–4).

Elsewhere, an upcoming mall, Destination 2028, has been announced by its developer, Westfield. The unveiled plans drop hints about changes heralding the next generation of shopping malls. Location-based technology for mobile phones, such as Beacons, which offer nearby information and promotions, is not the only new improvement to the shopping experience (Pilgrim 2017). According to the *Forbes* article 'The Future of the Shopping Mall Is Not about Shopping' by Jon Bird, new additions include 'AI-infused walkways, eye-scanners that personalise a consumer's visit, and smart changing rooms' (Bird J. 2018). Plans for a $2-billion 'tech-driven mega mall' called Dubai Square show an ambitiously planned complex with over 700,000 square metres of retail space, double the size of The Dubai Mall (Julien 2018). Technical advancement, according to developer Emaar Properties, will include features such as a 'smart fitting room with interactive mirrors and curated private fashion collections', and purchases will be enabled with 'custom-design mobile apps, barcode-scanning applications and radio-frequency identification' via mobile and desktop (Julien 2018). The entertainment area of the first floor will feature performances, concerts and theatre shows supported by three-dimensional projection mapping, theatrical sound and lighting equipment (Julien 2018). Technology-led developments of this kind inevitably move towards the adaptation of the shopping-mall landscape to cater to the changing needs of new generations of consumers. It seems, however, that theatricality will remain closely involved. The Cirque du Soleil's announcement that they will open a Creactive entertainment centre in Toronto Mall in 2019, which will give visitors the opportunity to stretch their muscles and test their artistic circus skills, points the way. According to Jon Bird: 'Stores will be stages, delivering "classroom retail" – showcasing the makers and processes behind products and brands. Event areas will host showpiece interactive activities and events' (2018).

Overall, adaptability has established itself as an important parameter when it comes to keeping up with an ever-changing market. The question is only whether the themed shopping malls will be able to follow this trend and expand their capacities for simulation and illusion, or whether they will be frozen in time like their own scenography. Since the first mechanical devices entered the scenographic world for commercial purposes, technology has heralded the transformation of displays, enhancing static arrangements of desired and desirable objects with movement, theatricality and light. It is interesting to note how themed shopping malls, despite their theatrical and performative orientation, diverge from this path, gripping onto an old-fashioned way of scenographing themed environments, and the nostalgia and sentiment that go along with it. On the other hand, the role of window displays and decorative installations continues to change rapidly in accordance with the new technology. As Eileen Fritsch notes, 'Stores today function as showrooms, gathering places or distribution centers' (2018). They do not aim solely to sell consumer goods, but rather physically to embody the brand's image, 'serving as innovators, consultants and execution partners' (Fritsch 2018). Display technology follows this new orientation. The Postmodern agenda, however, does not consider technology a determining instance in cultural production, but rather tools that 'offer some privileged representational shorthand for grasping a network of power and control' (Jameson 1991: 37–8). Even so, discussions of technology in the context of commercial scenography highlight one issue that, elsewhere, often remains unacknowledged. As technology in scenography extends its impact beyond product promotion, reaching into the broader realm of popular culture, and as our understanding of its consequences grows deeper, the ethics of designers' actions emerges as a topic demanding attention.

4.3 Aquatic fairy tales

From their original, purely functional purpose, namely, to provide drinking and bathing water, the decorative role of fountains and wells in the town squares of European cities evolved over time to become their dominant feature (Tabački 2017b: 171). As fixtures in open urban spaces, they became synonymous with the city, its urban structure and, consequently, with the marketplace, traditionally located in the town square. At the same time, together with the architecture that surrounded them, fountains provided the scenography for processions, festivities and the theatricality of the marketplace, which was seen 'as a symbol of the stage upon which Everyman played his earthly role' (Carlson 1989: 17). As Marvin Carlson acknowledges, from the late Middle Ages and early Renaissance, 'theatre existed as an important part of urban life without any specific architectural element being devoted to its exclusive use' (1989: 14). Among them, artificial fountains are documented as part of the scenography for royal entrances as a way to overlay and increase the value of existing city structures, as in the case of Charles VI's arrival in Paris in 1380 (1989: 22). In addition, David Wiles mentions the Eastern Procession play held in Lucerne in 1583, which was staged in front of the fountain in the city square, reminding us of the presence of water as scenography in a site-specific context and its very long history (2003: 106).

With shopping-mall culture emerging in North America after the Second World War, this water iconography was transported first into courtyards and later into mall interiors. The initial idea to establish a new kind of community centre in the American suburbs, inspired by the urban matrix of European town squares, encouraged developers and architects to incorporate decorative fountains and ponds into the shopping malls from the very beginning. They were installed in the courtyards of Shopper's World in Framingham

(1948–51), Northland in Detroit (1954) and Marshall Field's Old Orchard Shopping Center in Skokie (1956), to name only a few. Their transition into the indoor spaces of enclosed shopping malls can be credited to Victor Gruen, who included a pond with a fountain in the design of Southdale Mall's central hall (1956). The idea was welcomed by other developers, and fountains became a standard component of shopping-mall interiors throughout the 1960s – from the Moorestown Mall (1963) and the Westfield Topanga Mall (1964) to Cinderella City (1968), the Eastwood Mall (1969) and many others. In some cases, they became a mall's distinguishing characteristic, such as the fountain in the Plymouth Meeting Mall (1966), even appearing as iconic postcard images. In the 1970s, fountain landscapes became increasingly elaborate, and the shooter reached impressive heights at the Berkshire Mall (1970), the Belden Village Mall (1970), the Eastridge Shopping Center (1971), the Staten Island Mall (1973) and the Deptford Mall (1975). Positioned in the spacious halls of these shopping malls, the fountains were supposed to simulate an open urban environment and help recreate its atmosphere. At the same time, the presence of water was associated with nature, which, according to Jon Goss, influenced the naturalisation of the shopping experience and mitigated 'the alienation inherent in commodity production and consumption' (1993: 36). 'Fountains', he argues, 'signify civilized urban space, while on a larger scale, the importance of the waterfront to retail environments is due to their association with sport and recreation, historic trade, and the potential for a new life of adventure (being cast away, press-ganged or ticketed on a departing ship)' (1993: 36).

In the four shopping malls used here as case studies, fountains are incorporated into the chosen themes in different ways. In Montecasino, a large number of fountains are used to complement the compound's exterior. They range from Baroque-inspired opulence in front of The Palazzo Montecasino hotel, decorated with sculptures spraying water towards the central cascade, at the entrance to the Montecasino shopping mall, as a fixture on the roundabout, and in the centre of the oval Baroque staircases to the more contemporary musical fountain on the piazza, which offers visitors a ten-minute show combining light effects and spectacular water displays 'dancing' to the rhythm of the music. Another fountain can be found in one of the mall's interior piazzas, designed with medieval architectural references to harmonise with its themed surroundings. In the Ibn Battuta Mall, a large rectangular fountain is positioned in the central hall of the Chinese court. Apart from its decorative and symbolic functions, it is used to set the scene for the Chinese junk beached in one of its corners. In the Villaggio, a luxurious fountain stands in Via Domo shopping street. As light from the glass dome above flashes on the water, it accentuates the two high-end stores, Louis Vuitton and Gucci, that flank the basin. The latter's shape, in the middle of nods to sixteenth- and seventeenth-century Italian architecture, is inspired by an Arabesque design, so different cultural references clash in a single entity. In Terminal 21, a fountain supports the Roman theme on the ground floor by incorporating a statue of Nike of Samothrace.

Alongside the inclusion of fountains in themed environments, the development of fountain technology in the following decades increased the power of shooters to reach dazzling heights. This influenced their outdoor location, usually in the shopping mall plazas and along the promenades. Combined with light effects, music and projections, fountains became a leitmotif and an attraction in their own right. At the end of the 1990s, the opening of the Bellagio resort in Las Vegas and its modern-day shopping arcade Via Bellagio marked a new era in the history of fountain displays. Conceived by Wet Design, the Bellagio fountain on the Strip comprises 1,203 nozzles and shooters (Kopytoff 1999). In harmony with music and 4,500 lights, choreographed water streams present aquatic gymnastics of a special kind, shooting water up to 140 metres in the air.[19] This is made possible by a special robotic nozzle, the Oarsman, created by Wet Design to enable a variety of gracefully waving water jets and smooth transitions between the jets' heights and movements in time with the music (Mraz 2003). Fed by electricity and input data, the Oarsman positions its nozzle on an X-Y axis and adjusts the stream height while taking water directly from its source (lake or water basin) without using pipes (Mraz 2003).

It did not take long for this concept to be incorporated into shopping mall complexes in other parts of the world. In Downtown Dubai, surrounded by The Dubai Mall, the Burj Khalifa skyscraper and Souk Al Bahar, a 275-metre-long string of jets and shooters stretches along the artificial lake. Dancing to the beat of popular tunes, the fountain creates a variety of displays, and its Extreme Shooters reach heights of up to 150 metres. An even more ambitious fountain system was created in front of The Shoppes at Marina Bay Sands, a shopping mall in Singapore. Its fifteen-minute public show entitled *Spectra* was developed by the Australian branch of the company Imagination. It opened in July 2017. Fountain technology installed in the bay facilitates different spraying options such as pyramids, gyroscopic arcs, straight jets, lava and mist, which are used as water screens for lasers, lights and animated projections (Tabački 2017a: 124). Four of the show's acts are visually abstract artistic reflections on Singapore's roots, cultural history and future prospects (2017a: 124). The show, which took two years to develop, uses more than 110 types of LED lights and lasers, as well as specially developed underwater 500W LED fixtures that provide a rich colour spectrum (Wee 2017). The technology includes timecode synchronisation software, which triggers the lasers, lighting, projections and fountains to the sound of music composed for the show.[20] The previous Marina Bay public entertainment piece, Wonder Full (2011), designed by Laservision, ran for six years and revolved around the circle of life. Using a cinematographic approach, Wonder Full projected film footage, digital animation and lasers onto three liquid 'walls' of water droplets sprayed by a fountain system (2017a: 124). This system of water displays combined with music, lights and pyrotechnic effects took three years to develop. The presentation system was controlled by Laservision's Digital Data Pump Series III via twenty media servers.[21] A projection surface of fine droplets of water required '18 individually controlled fountains reaching up to 20 metres in height, in conjunction with independent tilt mechanisms [to create] a wide range of stunning liquid patterns'.[22]

While sheltered from rain and snow, the use of water for decorative, entertainment, educational and recreational purposes took over more and more retail space over the years, becoming, in some cases, the dominant feature of shopping malls' infrastructure. As previously mentioned, in the West Edmonton Mall (1981), an artificial pond was used for submarine tours, animal shows and other attractions in the past, and still serves today as a stage for elaborate scenography with a replica of a life-sized ship. The West Edmonton Mall's vast waterpark is one of its most sought-out facilities. The scale and size of aquariums, meanwhile, reached enormous proportions. The Dubai Mall, developed by Emaar Properties and designed by DP Architects Pte, houses a 10-million-litre aquarium tank and underwater zoo. It features a tunnel that passes through it, displaying over 140 different species and offering visitors an immersive experience. Its front glass wall measures 51 metres in length and 11 metres in height, providing an overwhelming scenography of underwater life on the mall's ground floor.

Before the invention of air-conditioning, department stores had to face a noticeable decrease in visitors and lower revenue in hot summer months, so special offers, events, sales and exhibitions had to be established to bridge those periods (Whitaker 2013: 78). Nowadays, air-conditioning is not the only shopping-mall infrastructure that lets visitors cool off in the heat. In the past few decades, water in its solid state, initially represented by ice rinks, has been extended to cover artificial ski slopes and snow towns. Recreational ice rinks appeared in some shopping malls as early as the 1950s, as in the Garden State Plaza in Paramus, New Jersey (1957) (Cohen 1996: 1057). They are still an important attraction today, especially in places where the climate is hot and dry throughout the year. Ice rinks can be found at the Siam Discovery Centre (1973), an upscale shopping mall in Bangkok; at the Sunway Pyramid (1997) in Bandar Sunway, Malaysia; at the SM Mall of Asia (2006) in Pasay City, the Philippines; at The Dubai Mall (2008); and many others. Forming part of the Gondolania theme park, the ice rink at the Villaggio Mall is surrounded by an arched colonnade and mock Renaissance facades under the blue sky ceiling, embedding Southern Italian flair into a winter landscape. The ambition to provide exotic and extreme attractions has long led developers to pursue a constant search for novelties that would secure their market share. This also influenced the appearance of ski slopes in malls. Madrid's Xanadu Shopping Mall (2003) introduced an indoor ski slope as part of a shopping experience provided by 250 retail outlets, offering a drastic temperature change from Spain's Mediterranean climate. The slope's hall is scattered with faux pine trees and artificial outcrops of rocks along the walls, and bars and restaurants sit above the snow park. Ski Dubai at the Mall of the Emirates (2005) is another indoor snow park scenographed with a ski slope, ski lifts, a rocky landscape, trees, towers, an ice cave and even a penguin colony. A sophisticated cooling system for the 400-metre-long slope is combined with technology to produce real snow. Developed by Malcolm Clulow, it sows ice particles into a fine mist of sprayed water and so creates snow crystals. A slightly different kind of winter environment is offered at the Gateway Ekamai Shopping Mall (2012) in Bangkok: Snow Town is a children's playground with a tiny slope and lots of snow to play with. Its scenography depicts a rather eclectic version of an imaginary European town square mixed with Hello Kitty igloo-lounges and a Japanese restaurant.

With regard to the themed malls, water was first established as a leitmotif in Grand Canal Shoppes (1999) at the Venetian resort in Las Vegas. As the mall's theme is inspired by the city of Venice, the presence of water is already visible on the Strip, with an artificial lagoon and two bridges that invite passers-by to enter the premises. Gondoliers stand ready at designated piers to take visitors for a ride, whether outside the resort or within it. The same experience was exported to the Arabian Peninsula, in the Villaggio Mall in Doha (2006) and to Asia, with the opening of the Venetian Macao (2007) in China and The Grand Venice Mall (2015) in Greater Noida, India. Designed by Aedas and HKS Architects, the scale of the Venetian Macao surpasses its Las Vegas predecessor by far, earning its status as one of the largest casino and gaming resorts in the world.[23] Almost half a million square metres of retail space, a giant replica of Grand Canal Shoppes, offers visitors gondola rides along three indoor canals and around an outdoor lagoon. As part of the scenography of a themed landscape, these indoor canals have thus introduced another kind of movement through retail environments and added to their theatricality through the singing performances of the costumed gondoliers. They also encourage an exchange of roles, turning spectators into performers as soon as they step into the gondola, themselves then becoming part of the performance. In comparison to the use of water for solely decorative purposes, Grand Canal Shoppes and its global counterparts have used it to add kinaesthetic and tactile sensations to the visual and aural in the overall theatrical experience offered by themed shopping malls.

Early attempts to incorporate the sense of touch into theatrical performance go back to the Futurist movement of the beginning of the twentieth century (Aronson 2018: 41). As Arnold Aronson explains, the ambition was to use touch in order to penetrate the 'audience space or a shared performance/ spectator area' and actively involve the audience in the performance (2018: 41). In these terms, the theatricality of themed shopping malls continues to blur the divide between performers and spectators. The malls reinforce the use of senses beyond hearing and vision, expanding their impact to touch, smell, taste and kinaesthesia, which have been stamped private and archaic in a predominantly digital culture (Pallasmaa 2005: 16). The presence of water in themed environments, represented by fountains, canals, ice rinks and ski slopes, supports tactility in our experience of scenography. The site-specific setting in themed malls, including the architecture itself, confronts us with spatial relations and, as Juhani Pallasmaa observes, 'expresses and relates man's being in the world' (2005: 16). The interactive possibilities offered by aquatic, icy and snowy landscapes within scenographic architecture connect us with our immediate surroundings, reconstructing the real sensory input and so addressing the growing alienation and detachment imposed by digital technology. Even on short rides along indoor canals, during which visitors sit still, the rocking gondolas influence the motion of their bodies in a different way than when they are walking. It also changes the point of view from which they perceive the scenography. An extreme activation of the kinaesthetic sense is achieved through skiing, gliding and skating.

However, regarding the tactile experience of water, the following needs to be taken into consideration. Because of a sustained belief that skin does not provide specific receptors for detecting wetness, it must be assumed that our senses 'learn' this from experience (Filingeri et al. 2014: 1457–69; Tabački 2017b: 176–7). According to Filingeri et al., sensory tests show that the perception of wetness during static contact increases significantly with cold wet stimuli in comparison with warm or lukewarm wet stimuli, making temperature more relevant to the experience of wetness than the wetness itself (2014: 1457–69). Dynamic contact, however, which is usually the type provided in themed environments, increases the sensation of wetness regardless of the temperature of the stimuli (2014:1457–69). Although our understanding of how our nervous system connects central and peripheral tactile and thermal stimuli is still poor, the dynamic interaction with water is understood to be a relevant aspect of our experience of the physical world around us. Following the announcement of projects such as the futuristic water-themed shopping mall proposed for China's Dongfeng Town, we are left with no doubt that the presence of water in shopping malls, whether they are themed or not, will continue. The element's capacity to activate our senses and penetrate a shared performance or spectator area[24] makes water a unique scenographic component that actively involves consumers in a performance. Therefore, a better understanding of how the perception of water as scenography can influence our experience could lead to its more meaningful implementation.

5

Consuming Experience

5.1 Flâneurs or active consumers?

In *The Arcade Project*, Walter Benjamin uses the term *flâneur* to describe somebody engaged in the practice of walking around observing the marketplace (1999: 427). *Flânerie* was established in Parisian shopping arcades, he writes, as a consequence of the narrow sidewalks and carriage traffic (1999: 32).[1] The flâneur's knowledge, Benjamin argues, 'is akin to the occult science of industrial fluctuations. He is a spy for the capitalists, on assignment in the realm of consumers' (1999: 427). By the late nineteenth century, the value of observation as 'sustained looking' at products, which happened in motion as shoppers wandered through the marketplace from one merchant to another, 'became inseparable from the effects of dynamic, kinetic, and rhythmic modalities of experience and form' (Crary 2001: 282). According to Jonathan Crary, empirical studies show that even though the peripheral area of the retina provides only partial or distorted visual information, it simultaneously delivers heightened sensitivity to movement (2001: 290). Because we perceive the world by gathering information while we move around and explore our surroundings, perception and action cannot be considered independently of each other (Ingold 1992: 41, 45), whether in life or in the marketplace.

Visiting a themed mall, just as entering a theme park, begins with leaving the car in a parking lot or getting off public transport and walking onto the premises (Gottdiener 1997: 112). As such, themed places are experienced by pedestrians. Even though our locomotion also relies on mechanical means – escalators, elevators and, in theme parks, a variety of rides – we nevertheless engage with these spaces predominantly as flâneurs. Once inside, consumers' movement is controlled by both architecture and scenography, which direct circulation (Aronson 2018: 31; Schechner 1994: 7). Contrary to the layout of the mall as it was originally established, with department stores anchoring each end of the main shopping streets and thus setting shoppers' primary route and direction, our four case studies present a different pattern of walkways. The main anchors in the Montecasino complex are the casino area and Madame Zingara, a dinner cirque entertainment venue. The net of curved shopping alleys, which includes a food court, leads towards these two points. While the main entrance allows visitors to step directly into the casino, all Montecasino's doors lead shoppers through the mall before they reach Madame Zingara, which is not in any direct line of sight. The Ibn Battuta Mall, meanwhile, has only one longer shopping street, leading through the Indian court, apart from side alleys that run in straight spokes between the entrances and the main axis. At one end, this street concludes with the ancient junk, a scenographic element of the Chinese court. At the other end, shoppers can see the distant beginnings of a shopping alley in the Persian court. Although visitors need to pass through it to get there, they see nothing of the impressively ornate Indian court. This court, including its dominant scenographic installation of Al-Jazari's water clock, is out of their sight line; visitors can see its splendour only shortly before they enter it. With some exceptions in the Persian, Egyptian and Tunisian courts, all the other alleys are angled, offering only segmented eye-catchers at the end of each walkway. Pop-up stalls and huge banners positioned in the middle of the shopping streets are additional obstacles, making it difficult to have a good view of the theme that continues ahead. Because the walkway in front of it is covered, an armillary sphere located on the mall's main axis ahead of the Egyptian court is only visible from a short distance. In the Villaggio Mall, Canal Street and Sportif Street lead towards the ice rink and Gondolania theme park, while Via Domo hosts a restaurant at the end of its shops. Carrefour Street and Veneto Street head to the cinema. Via Domo is the only street with an unbroken sight line, so shoppers can see the restaurant. The other anchors are just visible when visitors have walked the length of the shopping streets. Terminal 21 is organised vertically, with escalators as the dominant means of transport between its floors. There are no department stores in the mall. What triggers the vertical movement is a promise that the next floor will offer a different set of shops in accordance with its theme. The leisure and entertainment area on the sixth floor and the two levels of the food court on the fourth and the fifth floors could be considered anchors that draw shoppers upstairs, though this is only relevant to visitors who want to use these services.

In all these examples, the department stores that used to act as magnets directing movement are replaced with the promise of a different experience waiting in the themed courts or gaming, dining and entertainment venues ahead, hidden around corners and out of sight lines. In some places, the scenography of the mall gives clear visual cues to attract attention, pulling consumers in one direction or another. Elsewhere, it relies on the effect of surprise, the sudden revelation of another theme. In such settings, visitors are guided by spatial interventions that trigger their curiosity and draw them into another part of the mall, either as a fixed point in a sight line or as a transit zone that sets the mood on the way to a desired destination. By predetermining suggestive routes that inspire individual wayfinding, this kind of scenography supports visitors' impulse to 'personalise' space; it allows them to create their own movement patterns instead of submitting to the directions provided by the shopping mall map (Kutnicki 2018: 405). Together, architecture and scenography lead consumers along predetermined paths, making them feel as if they were choosing their own routes and so influencing their behaviour.

Linking arcades to the entertainment industry, Benjamin discusses 'the experience of the flâneur, who abandons himself to the phantasmagorias of the marketplace' (1999: 14). Even if they are not performance spaces in their own right, themed shopping malls still illustrate the transformation of everyday places into the performative and theatrical. This is at least partly accomplished by the spatial layout, which sets the parameters for consumers' possible movement patterns. In site-specific theatre, guiding the audience through either enclosed or open urban environments has a direct influence on their transformation into performers. Similarly, shopping alleys produce the same result when it comes to moving the spectator/consumer, 'whose presence defines the environment, and without whom the event cannot exist' (Aronson 2018: 190). In his analysis of spaces built for entertainment and amusement, Arnold Aronson emphasises that 'the crowd may become not only part of the decor which helps to transform the space, but also actual performers' (2018: 32). 'When the movement patterns and disposition of the crowd against specialised architectural backgrounds are controlled to some degree', he adds, 'the experience of viewing the crowd on the part of individual spectators becomes a performance of sorts' (2018: 32). This phenomenon is also discussed by Richard Schechner. He highlights the 'subtle and ever-shifting' relationship between bodily movement and space in connection with theatricality beyond the classic stage (1994: 2). The 'spatial, plastic stage architecture' of shopping malls, which steers the displacement of consumers' bodies, is compared to the looped patterns of Frederick Kiesler's *Endless Theatre* (Aronson 2018: 53, 70–1; Schechner 1994: xxxi). Aronson reminds us of Kiesler's arguments regarding the shortcomings of the proscenium stage, identifying motion as the only element essential to spectators' experience of theatrical space (2018: 53). Kiesler acknowledges that 'the plastic element of this stage is not scenery, but man' (2018: 53). It is therefore apparent that, regardless of its 'staging', Aronson points out, scenography in themed environments is alone not sufficient to transform place into theatre; even though it facilitates the perception of the mundane as theatrical, scenography functions more as a frame (2018: 32). In order to complete the process, the 'electromagnetic' movement of consumers along the shopping alleys is necessary, merging performance and spectatorship in an architecturally unified whole. The walkways in the examples provided here are embedded in angular layouts, which, according to Kiesler, suggest confinement. However, the feeling of endlessness experienced by shoppers walking along those alleys echoes Kiesler's assertion that continuity of movement is the precondition for spectators' actual experience of theatrical space (2018: 71–2). In it, Lefebvre argues, 'a spatial action overcomes conflicts, at least momentarily, even though it does not resolve them; it opens a way from everyday concerns to collective joy' (1991: 222).

A fascination with motion as a way to experience 'total theatre' was widely discussed among the avant-garde of the early twentieth century. Kiesler was not the only one to point out that movement was essential to the environmental concepts of theatre that emerged out of the need to break away from the frontal view of the proscenium stage and the passivity of seated spectators. In his historical overview of environmental scenography, Aronson mentions Andrzej Pronaszko and Szmon Syrkus's design for The Theatre of the Future for the Polish Universal Exposition in Poznan (1928), Nikolai Okhlopkov's scenographed environments for mass spectacles in Russia (1932–4) and Jacques Polieri's Theatre of Total Movement (1957, 1962) (2018: 78, 97–107). All of these designers clearly demonstrated a desire for spectators to move, either by walking or by mechanical means. Their attempts to achieve this found common ground by connecting the stage and the auditorium in order to 'create a greater sense of reality than was being achieved on the proscenium stage – in life, events occur all around us, not merely in front of us' (Aronson 2018: 111). The walkways through themed shopping malls mirror those avant-garde theatrical experiments regarding spectators' movement even though the setting and the cultural context have changed. Walking along shopping alleys, using escalators and lifts or taking a gondola ride on indoor canals, consumers dive into the life happening all around them. Schechner's concept of negotiation with the space (Schechner 1968: 50, cited in Aronson 2018: 151), which happens in site-specific environments altered by scenography, is evident in themed shopping malls. Consumers 'negotiate' their movements with scenographic spaces according to settings consciously arranged by the designers. It is a give-and-take relationship that constitutes itself in the process of testing ways to explore the unfamiliar.

In the process of spatial negotiation, 'experience' is inseparable from mobility, which is rooted in the human need to broaden our horizons and reach beyond experiences we can create in our direct surroundings (König 2008: 157). The promise of gaining a different kind of shopping experience boosts the number of visitors to themed malls,[2] establishing them as a legitimate destination for mass tourism (Ritzer 2005: 120). Because of the nature of such meticulously constructed spaces, consumers' immersion depends on a range of features that guide their actions. As a consequence, their movement through the shopping mall is seen by some as passive and submissive to social control, an unconscious activity of navigation led by the mall's physical layout and the consumer's interpretation of global symbols (Jewell 2001: 357, 359). 'By reducing the effort in the process of navigation', Nicholas Jewell argues, 'the mall once again allows us to withdraw, and gives simultaneous autonomy and uniformity to our patterns of movement' (2001: 357). Jewell sees this as a 'directional "trust"' that influences shoppers' motion (2001: 357).

Discussing the concept of flânerie, Zygmunt Bauman claims that shopping malls have caused the downfall of modern flâneurs because they leave no room for imagination and so restrict shoppers' freedom (1997: 264). Similarly, Jon Goss says that what we witness in shopping malls today is not so much flânerie itself, but 'a nostalgia for its form which only marks its effective absence' (1993: 35). On the other hand, Rob Shields refuses the reduction of shoppers to passive consumers (1989: 13). He argues that many visitors to themed shopping malls are indeed flâneurs enjoying the fantasy world as an escape from the routine of their everyday lives. As such, his depiction recalls the daydreaming effect established in the nineteenth-century shopping arcades described by Benjamin. Likewise, Jacob C. Miller's exploration of embodiment as an affective experience, based on his ethnographic fieldwork at the Abasto Shopping Mall in Buenos Aires, notes the mall's 'ability to work as a therapeutic space' and 'the dissolution of subjectivity as the mind fades into the noise generated by the mall's affective techniques, encouraging visitors to lose themselves' (2014: 57). This correlates with Mark Gottdiener's analysis of Disneyland. Theming is successful, according to Gottdiener, 'not because it materializes the myths of American society or fantasies, but largely because it liberates people from the constrains of everyday life' (Gottdiener 1997: 114). The connection between flânerie and the capacity to let loose is seen by Michel de Certeau as an attempt 'to escape an imposed spatial system' (1985: 122–45; Wiles 2003: 87). The act of walking through a city is equated with claiming freedom and identity (De Certeau 1985: 122–45; Wiles 2003: 87). These observations see shoppers as active agents who not only pursue mall planners' goals but adjust those goals to their own needs. Such positions on flânerie, as an act of taking the initiative, align with Colin Campbell's characterisation of modern consumption 'as a voluntaristic, self-directed and creative process in which cultural ideals are necessarily implicated' (2005: 464). Mark Gottdiener also emphasises consumers' proactive approach to commodities and shopping (1997: 7). He sees it as a process of self-actualisation 'by seeking ways of satisfying their desires and pursuing personal fulfillment through the market that express deeply-held image of the self' (1997: 7).

Flânerie today is not, of course, what it was in the nineteenth century. Modern flâneurs are target-oriented consumers collecting puzzle pieces together in order to complete an image of themselves that was formed long before any concrete action was taken. Regardless, however, of what consumers seek to fulfil their needs – things to buy, attractions to see, unfamiliar places to explore – they all hope for the adventure that the act of consumption promises it will provide. So how does scenography relate to a discussion on active and passive flânerie? Target-oriented consumerism presupposes an active awareness of the surroundings. Human perception, rooted in our primal survival instincts, is used to its best advantage not only during our own movement but also when we perceive movement around us (Abel 2018: 39). Correspondingly, in the act of perceiving scenography as the constructed architectural environment, we also perceive others, whose movements we register and whose reactions prompt us, in turn, to become conscious of ourselves (2018: 23). Embedded in the scenographed reality of themed shopping malls as we move and watch others move, we thus perceive the reality of our existence differently than in everyday places. The more intensely we connect with a new environment, the more intensely we feel our own existence (2018: 25). We pay more attention when we are somewhere unfamiliar because the new and unusual settings around us cause our senses to remain alert (2018: 30). In contrast to ordinary shopping malls, where the architecture stays in the background, themed shopping malls place scenography front and centre, showing off its uniqueness and aggressively demanding attention. As a result, these malls expand our personal involvement. They force us to look around by provoking surprise, irritation and astonishment, heightening our multisensory awareness of and attention to the world around us, making us active explorers of an unknown territory. We are encouraged to move through the space according to our own initiative, either to wander around in curiosity or to run away. One way or another, the scenography moves us, amplifying our bodily sensations, and lets us reflect upon ourselves through our own actions and the actions of the other consumers around us. The perception of scenography in themed shopping malls cannot, therefore, be considered the daydreaming lethargy Benjamin attributes to arcades and passages. Rather, in this new and different commercial context, our bodies are awakened by the intensity with which themed malls frame the reality of our existence.

During the nineteenth century, the relationship between subjectivity and perception was reconfigured. Jonathan Crary acknowledges that in all the variety of ways in which the topic was tackled as part of our biological heritage, attention was seen as inseparable from movement (2001: 42). Therefore, discussing shoppers' perception of their surroundings in themed malls from the perspective of motion could help us understand how an active exploration of this particular scenographic setting influences feelings of participation through a direct connection with the environment. While our multisensory experience of a mall echoes our bodily inhabitation of the world at large, the exposure of our senses to such controlled surroundings is usually determined by the given layout of pathways. These emphasise certain aspects of the environment and dictate how they are shown to us. As Tim Ingold explains, showing something to somebody causes some aspect of that environment to be unveiled 'so that it can be apprehended directly' (2000: 21). Through this relationship, the perceiver is directly involved in the world, discovering its immanent meanings (Ingold 2000: 21). Even though our perceptive apparatus receives more impulses in themed areas than in regular shopping malls, 'showing' visitors the environment by leading them along pre-planned routes and so directing their attention still rely heavily on vision – a sense generally associated with un-involvement and distance. This implies the existence of a gap between close-range bodily involvement and the detachment required by vision.

Looking at this issue from a psychological point of view, the first thing to consider would be visual flow. This effect, which appears when we are in motion, causes the impression that the environment is moving towards us (Durgin 2009: 43). Interestingly, visual flow appears slower when we are moving than when we are standing still and our surroundings move around us (2009: 43). This means that we receive distorted information from our senses about our own motion. In themed malls, consumers travel along shopping alleys by walking at different speeds, as well as by taking the stairs or the escalators. The pace and kind of movement are determined either by the input of external stimuli or by the machines used for locomotion. In any case, the visual flow moves with consumers and stays constant in relation to their speed. It has been known for many years that visual flow is perceived to be slower during self-motion, but this has only recently been quantitatively investigated (2009: 44). These investigations show that the speed of the street fronts passing by as usually experienced by pedestrians walking through a city seems to be slower than it would if the roles were reversed, and the streets were moving at the same speed while onlookers were standing still. In our everyday lives, this is not much of a problem (2009: 44). In fact, the slowdown of perceived speed enables greater precision in our visual judgement (2009: 46) and more visual input from our surroundings. In the context of the environmental scenography of shopping malls and the movement of consumers, the relationship between real and perceived speed will always stay the same. In a controlled environment, slowing down the visual flow while people moved, for example, by using projections, would allow us to perceive our movement more precisely and absorb more information from the environment. On the other hand, speeding up the visual flow would further distort our perception of our own speed and reduce the information absorbed from the environment.

The dependence of our visual perception on our walking speed is demonstrated in the treadmill experiment. According to Frank Durgin, when participants were blindfolded after spending just twenty seconds running on a treadmill, where there is no visual flow, they typically walked farther than they believed. This is despite the fact that, generally speaking, people have a very good idea of how far they have walked when their sight is restricted (Durgin 2009: 43). One possible explanation, Durgin suggests, is that the participants tended to walk too far because they did not register any progress while they were on the treadmill (2009: 43). Tests with projections in controlled environments show that visual flow that is near walking pace is perceived slower and is easier to differentiate when walking than when standing still, even when the speeds in the retinal image are the same (2009: 44). Overall, the experiments show that projecting very slow visual flow while people are walking gives those people the impression that there is no movement at all even in cases where the movement would be clearly visible if they were standing still (2009: 46). As a result, considering our poor ability to distinguish between slow visual speed values, visual flow can be seen as an advantage for scenographic perception in site-specific conditions, as it enables us to glean more information from our surroundings.

James J. Gibson, who is credited as one of the most influential theoreticians on the subject of perception in motion, describes visual perception as the process of actively plucking information from the environment, while visual space is defined by data such as the texture gradients on surfaces. Gibson depicts the active observer as one who is continuously moving eyes, head and body. Although the observer's self-motion causes an endless flux of images across the retina, Gibson notes that there are parameters among those changing images that stay constant and deliver crucial information. In themed malls, this might be the unvarying size of floor and wall tiles, columns or railings along the way. As well as providing necessary input, the unchanging 'invariants' can be used in an instant, without needing to be processed, transformed or manipulated in any way (Gibson 1950: 154, 216; Goldstein 1981: 193). In this context, Gibson understands environmental perception through movement as a direct process that does not require any mental intervention (Goldstein 1981: 193). Here, perception means 'considering the stimuli in the environment, rather than considering what happens to these stimuli after they enter a person's eye' (1981: 193). In line with this observation, walking through the shopping alleys of themed malls enables participating consumers to move among invariable patterns, extract them and process the impact of the environment directly. Consequently, visual perception during self-motion must inherently be considered a precondition for the embodiment of those consumers in scenographic surroundings, which allow them to be in the moment and so belong to the world.

In a different approach, the phenomenological point of view presented by Edmund Husserl asserts that perception revolves around the sensations of the body in a given environment (1983: 51; 1989: 152–3). 'The lived body', with its capacity to move 'immediately and spontaneously', is seen as the centre of experience (1989: 159). In other words, bodily sensation through movement results in perception, which makes it the main method by which we encounter the external world (1989: 159–60). According to Husserl, the body, with its direct, lived experience and capacity for self-motion, intertwines 'with the rest of psychic life in its totality' (1989: 168–9). Consequently, our experience of the environment in all directions begins from the body as a centre and 'zero point of all these orientations' (1989: 165–6). Our perception of surrounding objects and things is thus always relative to the position of our body, which changes constantly as we move (1989). The distinctiveness of Husserl's take on bodily sensation is that it goes two ways: we can touch objects to discover their properties (e.g. texture or temperature), or we can sense our 'embodied self' by performing exactly the same procedure. This reflects the core of Husserl's phenomenology, which is based on eidetic reduction, the search for the essence and uniqueness of each particular experience. It demands we remove all prior knowledge about sensory encounters with our surroundings in order to focus our awareness solely on our immediate sensory input and so to isolate the phenomenon in question.

For Maurice Merleau-Ponty, the position of the body in space is not determined in relation to other coordinates or objects, but by 'the anchoring of the active body in an object, the situation of the body in face of its task' (1962: 115). His argument says, movement is an essential aspect for understanding how the body inhabits space because it actively uses it (1962: 117). Action is thus seen as a way to coexist with the place that is occupied; the experience of movement is what provides access to the world and so gives us the opportunity to discover ourselves (1962: 162). According to Merleau-Ponty, the relationships that we establish with the objects around us through sight and movement guide us towards the 'intersensory unity of a "world"' (1962: 159). He recognises vision as action, as an experience of light that opens us to the world (Ingold 2000: 258; Merleau-Ponty 1962: 438). He notes, however, that this cannot be accomplished by vision without movement (Ingold 2000: 263; Merleau-Ponty 1964: 162). Merleau-Ponty's conception of visual space is that it surrounds and passes through the perceiver, immersing oneself in the visible world: perceiving with the body, as we do, we are acknowledging not only the space around us but also the space within ourselves (McKinney et al. 2009: 169; Merleau-Ponty 1962: 206).

Moving from phenomenology to social anthropology, Tim Ingold draws on Gibson and Merleau-Ponty in order to discredit the generally accepted position that equates vision with distance. Instead, he looks to establish the participatory role played by the sense of sight. Contrary to anthropological analyses that see vision as cold and detached in comparison to hearing, which is warm and bonding, Ingold backs up Gibson's position on vision as a direct sense and Merleau-Ponty's argument that vision is the way for us to open ourselves to the world. For both Gibson and Merleau-Ponty, as for Husserl, the existence of the senses is established through the moving body and its involvement with the environment (Ingold 2000: 268). Accordingly, the interaction between physical movement and vision seems to be the key to founding a two-way relationship in shopping malls. As such, it is a crucial factor in transforming the marketplace into theatre by immersing consumers in a site-specific environment.

Movement links the theatrical and immersive in a mutually dependent way, leaving consumers no choice but to become part of the performance that happens in places of gathering. In themed shopping malls, which are built to direct movement intentionally through an exaggerated visual layout, active flânerie offers the opportunity to understand 'new kinds of bodily movements and relationships within the social realm' (Jewell 2001: 359). It also opens a door to address the concept of belonging through the use of scenography in the sphere of consumerism. Apart from enabling us to explain the connection between vision, movement and immersion in a site-specific context, the study of perception during self-motion could also potentially lead towards a more meaningful use of scenography and new dynamics of movement not only in commercial spaces but also in the theatre. In controlled environments, some phenomena such as visual flow have the potential to accentuate the dramaturgy of place and increase the audience's immersion in the spectacle. As Roger Copeland notes, attempts to restore an immediate sensory experience for the audience that shapes their perception through digital media may be naive (Copeland 1990: 42, cited in Giesekam 2007: 6). However, Ingold reminds us, as we become more skilled at perceiving the environment, 'the world will appear ... in greater richness' (2000: 55). In the scenographic context, this may be the way to 'rediscover what it means to *belong*' (2000: 246).

5.2 Surface semiotics

Consumption as a process of 'signification and communication' is, according to Baudrillard, 'a system of exchange, and the equivalent of a language' (1998: 60). 'The circulation, purchase, sale, appropriation of differentiated goods and signs/objects today', he adds, 'constitute our language, our code, the code by which the entire society communicates and converses' (1998: 80). Madan Sarup points out that Baudrillard's understanding of consumption is not determined by a use-value relationship but by the consumption of signs (1993: 162). In this context, the market as a built environment went through a shift in perception as well, becoming a sign in its own right. Drawing on observations made by Françoise Choay, Mark Gottdiener explains that 'the transformation from a signifying to an anti-signifying environment' began with the rise of capitalism, as buildings lost their 'religious and cosmological referents and became "sign-functions" of their societal role' (1997: 27; Choay 1986: 170). Seeing the history of capital and the history of a signification structure as intertwined and mutually dependent, Gottdiener argues that the role of systems of meaning has been 'essential to capitalist development since its earliest beginnings' (1997: 48). Scenography as a marketing strategy that comes into focus with theming 'reduces the product to its image and the consumer experience to its symbolic content' (Gottdiener 1997: 74). This corresponds with the use of scenography as a cultural practice of changing an environment's primary function through images and symbolic representations, no matter whether the given space is a theatrical stage, an amusement park or a shopping mall. As Gottdiener points out, this is precisely what themed commercial spaces aspire to: the creation of symbolic content led by consumer desire, which shifts attention away from the place's real function, namely, the realisation of capital and the promotion of sales (1997: 75).

In its attempt to offer solutions to the urban problems facing nineteenth-century industrial cities, early Modernist thinking looked to the future by radically distancing itself from the past. The use of ornamentation and symbolic references to past styles was equated with crime, which influenced a loss of the symbolic in architecture. It was only with the advent of Postmodernism that signification found its way back to city architecture. The use of architectural symbols as a means for visual communication has been thoroughly examined by Robert Venturi, Denise Scott Brown and Steven Izenour in their classic work *Learning from Las Vegas* (1972). Using the commercial backdrop of Las Vegas as a case study, they tackle the issue of symbols banned from architecture by Modernist tendencies (Venturi et al. 1979: 139). In Las Vegas, the relationship between people and space has long been facilitated through signs (1979: 139), making the city the ideal place to study their use in architecture. In the late 1960s, Las Vegas was subordinated to road traffic and viewed primarily from the perspective of car drivers; the symbols dominated because the architecture was not sufficient to communicate content (1979: 24). Twenty years later, this city was the birthplace of themed shopping malls, which provided another type of architecture ruled by signs, only this time meant to communicate with pedestrians. Describing the changes that took place in Las Vegas from the 1970s to the year 2000, Venturi et al. refer to the city's development 'from iconography to scenography ... from strip to mall ... from vulgar to dramatique' (Chung et al. 2001a: 617). Imbued with clashing symbols and iconographic architectural references, this is essential for each themed mall's articulation and advertisement 'as a particular place in competition with other locations' (Gottdiener 1997: 82). The production of meaning, the use of ornamentation and signs in the mall, Ursprung argues, challenges us to re-evaluate their relationship to form and to the semiotics of space carried out by scenographic interventions especially in times when, 'ornament is once more moving centre stage' (2014: 27).

If we start with the assumption that all meaning is culturally constructed, as Tim Ingold suggests, this implies that the shopping mall stripped of theming is a place 'empty of significance' (1992: 39).[3] In most cases, as Gottdiener notes in his analysis of the Mall of America, 'apart from the skilful deployment of images, [the mall] has no relation to any real places or cultures around the globe' (1997: 88). As theming is a simulation of historically embedded codes, symbols and environments, it is 'fundamentally disconnected from the use-value of the commodities with which [it is] associated' (Gottdiener 1997: 76). The exploitation of scenography in this context merely adds to the tension instead of solving the problem. Swinging between 'duck-house' and 'decorated shed', architectural typologies established by Venturi et al., the scenography of the shopping mall overlaps with its architecture without really being connected to it. Even though the themed design takes centre stage, symbols are still used to communicate the space's function, not because the mall's appearance is insufficient but because it is misleading. Being attention seekers, themed malls follow the tradition of the 'decorated shed' restaurants, which Venturi et al. used as a reference. To attract prospective customers as they were driving by, the outsides of these restaurants were covered in disproportionate decoration. In the malls that serve as our case studies here, it is possible to note the following: even if they expand their themed narrative to various degrees to encompass their exteriors, they are either embedded in a matrix of city streets (the Ibn Battuta Mall, Terminal 21) or situated within larger compounds and recreational complexes (Montecasino, the Villaggio Mall). The contemporary consumer visits them purposefully rather than being seduced by their appearance while happening to pass by. Independently of their chosen theme, these malls are established symbols (of consumerism) just like any other tourist attraction. But it is not their exterior that acts as a magnet encouraging passers-by to stop and use their services; it is their interiors that differentiate them from others and keep consumers inside by providing a unique experience. After all, this is where the spectacle takes place.

With differentiation as a primary goal, themed shopping malls offer an overload of signifying spaces that contradict not only the construction beneath (Venturi et al. 1979: 164), but also what is on offer as well. Even though some

Italian brands are represented in the Villaggio, the majority of the mall's stores and services have nothing in common with Italy nor with the Venetian theme. Likewise, there is no apparent connection between the stores and the cities or regions that provide inspiration for the themes in Terminal 21 and the Ibn Battuta Mall. The same applies to Montecasino: apart from a few Italian restaurants, the link to Italy is not established through either shopping or services. Regional ties have been dramatically weakened in all of them, and the places used to inspire themes have become dominated by an international mix of retailers and services. As a result, the content is now more or less the same in both 'authentic' and 'themed' places yet still reflects the eminent lack of connection between the design of a space and what is sold there. In some cases, symbolism and function clash strangely. The verses of a short poem (*tanka*) written in Japanese on the restroom wall in the Tokyo-themed section of Terminal 21 contain a promise to return from the mountain Inaba if the loved one continues to wait like a pine tree.[4] Even if toilets are typically places where all kinds of graffiti messages are scribbled on the walls, this traditional Japanese declaration of love still seems oddly out of place. It is additionally illustrated with an artificial pine tree, fixed perpendicularly to the wall beside the Asian poem, and positioned between urinals and cubicles. Overall, it creates a rather comic spectacle. While avoiding a connection to the place and loosening ties to the immediate surroundings, the scenographic use of such signs and ornaments is also implemented to add layers of meaning to a space that has none. In Montecasino, display vitrines with posters from the Teatro alla Scala for the operas *Tosca* and *Così Fan Tutte* mix modern announcements for films, concerts and shows with ones from the past.[5] Interestingly enough, reality is mixed with fantasy in the process of accumulating meaning, thus constituting a parallel semiotic level.

The introduction of signs to indicate imaginary destinations, as in Terminal 21, points towards the cities that visitors can expect to encounter on the next floor. They have been introduced solely to support the narrative rather than to direct consumers towards a specific place in the mall. Purely functional boards pointing out exits or stores, designed according to the theme, are merged with the theatrical use of signs to tell a story, thereby establishing a meta-mapping of physical space. Here, the use of symbols not only exceeds the form but also uses scenography to provide an extension of the place, setting a new standard in spatial communication and negotiation. With their commercial success, themed malls demonstrate the effectiveness of visual sign language and the triumph of symbolism over form in everyday places. In times when authenticity is highly improbable, if not entirely impossible, the malls make simulation a 'real thing'. Jon Goss sees this type of spatial and temporal displacement, facilitated by the 'sign-saturated place and its constant motion', as characteristic of the Postmodern world (1993: 33). He claims it is part of the shopping centre's transition from 'a Modern rational Utopia to a Postmodern Heterotopia' (1993: 33). Associating the mall with a transport hub, as is done with the use of signs in Terminal 21, is also grounded in the fact that the two types of structure are increasingly similar in both design and conception (Gottdiener 1997: 96; Pimlott 2007: 271–316). Gottdiener argues that it is not surprising that the twin functions of the air terminal and the mall – 'air transfer and retailing – merge through conscious design' (1997: 94). Signs, the bearers of visual references to airport gates, are positioned in front of each escalator. They indicate the theme of the floor above or below, according to where that particular escalator leads: consumers moving between the mall's different levels are continuously confronted with them. While announcing the change of theme, these signs simultaneously emphasise the transitional aspect of the mall, which architecture alone cannot accomplish. Both airports and shopping malls, Gottdiener says, 'are overendowed with sign systems'; they are 'extreme cases of semanticized environments' (1997: 100), places that depend on a clearly recognisable system of symbols to guide consumers and travellers as they move through the labyrinthine buildings.

Looking at the effect of signs in shopping malls from the perspective of consumer movement, it can be seen that they lead visitors on erratic paths in order to expose them to as many shops as possible (Koolhaas 2001a: 414). When they are applied to directing you to where you want to go, Rem Koolhaas points out, shopping mall signs guide you along 'unwanted detours, turn you back when you're lost' (2001a: 414). As a consequence, signs not only act as indispensable devices for directing movement but also lead consumers into corners of the mall that could otherwise be overlooked. They make sure that shoppers pass as many stores as possible, supporting their visibility and securing their profits. In an interview with Venturi conducted by Rem Koolhaas and Hans Ulrich Obrist, the dominance of iconography as an essential architectural element is emphasised. According to Venturi, it has taken over the primacy of space in contemporary architecture (Chung et al. 2001b: 593). Signs, he claims, are more relevant than buildings themselves (2001b: 616): using words and letters, they transmit the purpose of a place and stand as a counterpart to other architectural elements. Their typology, scale and graphic-design style carry an additional, secondary message, giving more detailed information about a particular function by pointing out the entrance (Venturi et al. 1979: 113–14). In themed malls, where spatial design remains only loosely connected to the shops' content and offers, signs navigate us to what we are looking for. Thanks to their explicit, symbolic, decorative and practical role, signs thus simplify and settle the contradictions laid out by the dominant imagery of a theme. As Gottdiener recognises, scenographic strategies can transform the complexity of meaning into a 'cartoonish facade produced to disguise an ordinary retailing establishment' (1998: 85). Yet 'when the real world changes into simple images', Debord writes, 'simple images become real beings and effective motivations of a hypnotic behavior' (1970: §18). The semiotic arsenal in themed shopping malls, which drives our movement, demonstrates the fact that we can become part of the mall's spectacle only through mediation by signs and images (1970: §18).

Drawing on the terms 'performativity or performative', as defined by Fischer-Lichte et al., Antje Böhme notes that signs in shopping malls, as locators for spectacle, can only be analysed in the context of the performative processes through which they constitute meaning (2012: 43; Fischer-Lichte et al. 2005: 234–42). In themed shopping malls, she argues, meaning is produced by simplified signs and ornamental fragments of (mostly historical) architectural styles, which keep the main theme aesthetically unified (Böhme A. 2012: 133). Its informational content, which we glean by actively observing environments heavily equipped with signifiers, triggers our actions and sets the place's performativity in motion. As meanings are produced, bodies move and the performance is created. However, Fischer-Lichte et al. point out, meanings in shopping malls are not transmitted to the perceiving visitors through interpretation; they are generated through the process of perception (2005: 20; Böhme 2012: 43).[6] Furthermore, consumption, the driving force behind the mall's performative processes, is not only the end result but actually part of this transmission of meanings. In fact, it is the production of meanings that enables the consumption of scenography in the first place. In this context, Tim Ingold equates perception and consumption, as 'persons and environment are mutually constitutive components of the same world' and 'meanings embodied in environmental objects are "drawn into" the experience of subjects' (1992: 51). He calls these meanings 'affordances' or 'use-values'. According to Ingold, the 'dialectics of the interface between persons and environment should be understood in terms of a dichotomy not between culture and nature but between effectivities and affordances – between the action capabilities of subjects and the possibilities for action offered by objects' (1992: 51-2).

In *Learning from Las Vegas*, Venturi et al. highlight architects' refusal to deal with the symbolism of their immediate surroundings, such as the form language of suburban residential architecture in the late 1960s and early 1970s. This is seen as a rejection of commercialism and of the middle-class aspiration to climb the social ladder it represents. Venturi et al. also emphasise the fact that architectural form and language alone cannot achieve the impact that symbols have on spatial relations (1979: 180). Fifty years later, the lessons offered by Las Vegas are reflected in themed shopping malls around the world because, as McMorrough notes, 'rather than shopping (as an activity) taking place in the city (as a place), the city (as an idea) is taking place within shopping (as a place)' (2001: 194). The success of Montecasino, the Ibn Battuta Mall, the Villaggio and Terminal 21 demonstrates 'the need for meaning' (Gottdiener

1997: 115). These malls reflect a hope that the consumption of 'otherness' through signs in the material environment of a public space will satisfy a desire for community and inclusivity.

The increasing numbers flocking to themed destinations thus demonstrate not only the human need for gathering and for collective escapism as a way to ease the harsh realities of life but also people's ongoing search for their own identity (Gottdiener 1997: 125; Jewell 2001: 332). In the realm of globalised popular culture, malls are a place for us to congregate for consumption surrounded by scenography. The images and signs are supposed to bridge the gap between our physical presence, anchored in the immediate locality, and the desires of our aspiring selves, which are projected in the signified globality. Yet even if signs are embedded in themed landscapes, their agency functions only on the surface, offering orientation in the physical space around us or in the imaginary space around our stylistic identities. As Jewell suggests, they afford some degree of comfort by providing a special kind of cultural tourism (2001: 331) but, while they enhance the ideal of a global community, they are merely indulging consumers with fragmented images. They fail to impact the body on a deeper level: that which would address the shift towards the rising autonomy and independence from both local and global influences that occur in modern consumption (2001: 331). The way signs 'move us' seems to be restricted to the physicality of our bodies, leaving performativity as the production of meaning without any substantial significance.

5.3 The body in the forged reality

Suggestions for how to broaden the sensory impact on theatre audiences, now an inseparable part of flagship stores' and shopping malls' corporate identities, started with avant-garde concepts for theatre buildings at the beginning of the twentieth century. Expanding the futurist agenda, the unrealised ideas of Oskar Strnad, Walter Gropius, László Moholy-Nagy, Farkas Molnár and Filippo Marinetti, among others, wanted to embody the audience in the performance and to reconfigure the relationship between the stage and the spectators' area in different ways. Aronson describes how the effect of machines dispensing appropriate smells in order to intensify the experience of a 'total environment', tested exclusively at the Théâtre d'Art in Paris as early as the end of the nineteenth century, was incorporated into the progressive theatrical concepts of Molnár's *U-Theatre*, Marinetti's *Total Theatre* and Otto Piene's *The Theatre That Moves* (2018: 64, 78). Nowadays, firms like Allsense, Air Aroma, Branded Smell and The Aroma Company specialise in marketing technology for a corporate signature scent, aiming to create an emotional connection with patrons and a 'memorable experience'.[7] Shopping malls are no exception to this trend. Some of Allsense's clients include Singapore's ION Orchard, 313@Somerset, Palais Renaissance and Forum Shopping Mall.[8]

Other tools and tricks have also been put into effect to deepen the audience's immersion in the themed shopping experience. In these settings, painted sky ceilings are reminiscent of James Blanding Sloan's concept of a theatre enveloped in a dome construction serving as a screen for the projection of sky scenes (Aronson 2018: 65). Aronson reminds us that weather simulations, such as the realistic staging of a rainstorm, showcased at Miracle Mile Shops in Las Vegas (Beyard et al. 2001: 163), were also envisioned by Sloan in his plans for the 'Infidome' theatre (1939) as well as by Antonin Artaud in his manifesto the *Theatre of Cruelty* (1958) (2018: 65–6). Furthermore, to intensify the sensory input on the audience, many theatre-makers and designers proposed staging action in several places at the same time – an approach occasionally taken in all four of our case studies. The theatrical avant-garde of the twentieth century advocated the abolition of the stage and audience area, to be replaced by a unique environment in which both spectators and performers shared the same space,[9] a feature that dominates today's themed commercial spaces.

While scenography in the theatre cannot generally be approached by the audience and is meant predominantly to create an audio-visual impact from a distance or via media, themed shopping malls expose the artificiality of scenography in close proximity to the viewer. In doing so, they have contributed to the creation of the unified performance space promoted in the twentieth century, though the setting is perhaps not exactly what those previously mentioned avant-garde theatre-makers and designers had in mind. The real city is thrilling because of the unknown and mysterious hiding around corners. With no dark wings or alleys in which to hide obvious deceit and build the fantasy, brightly lit shopping streets foster our excitement based solely on what we see and how it makes us feel. 'Bright light', argues Pallasmaa, 'paralyzes the imagination' (2005: 46). However, such direct exposure to light also sets the preconditions for a unique perception of themed space. Scenography in shopping malls, constructed around scaled proportions,[10] unified heights, missing traces of time[11] and the imitation of materiality, distorts visitors' visual and tactile experience as well as their hearing, which is a crucial feature in the articulation of space and its understanding (Pallasmaa 2005: 49). The different quality of sound compared to an open urban environment causes disorientation, changing our perception of space as a whole. In his criticism of the dominant visual bias in contemporary architecture, and the corresponding loss of plasticity and tactility, Juhani Pallasmaa broaches the issue of detachment between the construction and the reality of matter, which 'turns architecture into stage sets for the eye, into a scenography devoid of the authenticity of matter and construction' (2005: 31). Not only the difference between the 'light' materiality of scenography and the solid materiality of architecture is perceptible using the haptic sense but their echoes are also different. Even if, in some malls, consumers can hear recorded birdsong, other acoustic references such as the sound of cars, church bells and general noise characteristic of a city environment are all missing. Visitors hear people talking, but the sound of their voices is different. The smell of the city, especially specific ones such as of Venice on the Adriatic Sea, is exchanged for the smell of food and perfumed air. The active involvement of all these senses frames our reality within the imaginary world of the themed mall, enhancing the sense of 'otherness' through cultural references, background noise and the smell and taste of 'ethnic' cuisine in the food court (Goss 1993: 34). Moving through the themed space, visitors exchange the experience of an urban setting for staged environmental scenography. Instead of confronting the shopping alleys in the same way as city architecture – approaching, entering, touching, smelling, feeling its materiality – shoppers in the mall revert to 'the formal appreciation of a facade' (Pallasmaa 2005: 63); their sensory exchange differs due to the incoherent link between construction and materiality, reality and fiction, inside and outside.

As Pallasmaa notes, we experience architecture through the tectonic language of buildings: 'we behold, touch, listen and measure the world with our entire bodily existence, and the experiential world becomes organised and articulated around the centre of the body' (Pallasmaa 2005: 64).[12] Using this principle as its base, scenography in themed shopping malls is instrumental in the establishment of parallel worlds. It sets up a new sensory relationship with the space around us, where nothing is what it seems, displacing us in an area beyond our previous understanding of materiality. The visual appearance of the scenography does not correspond with how the material feels under our fingers. The set in themed malls invites consumers to forge a new kind of bond with the marketplace, through which they can become 'co-creators' of the performance by acknowledging the possibility of a different kind of experience (McKinney 2012: 221). The transfer of purely scenographic stimuli, both sensory and cognitive, which effect the change Schechner sees as the essence of theatre, makes a significant contribution to the theatricality of themed shopping malls. Denying familiar sensory impulses creates a 'brief interruption of reality' (Baudrillard 1998: 34): 'The image, the sign, the message – all these things we "consume" – represent our tranquillity consecrated by distance from the world, a distance more comforted by the allusion to the real (even where the allusion is violent) than compromised by it' (1998: 34).

This phenomenon, according to Madan Sarup, represents the transition from Modernism to Postmodernism, and the introduction of 'models of simulacra': constructed worlds 'which have no referent or ground in any "reality" except their own' (1993: 163). Drawing on Baudrillard, Sarup calls further attention to the dominance of images and simulacra in consumer society and the loss of the relationship 'to an outside, to an "external" reality' (1993: 164). This sense of detachment and its consequences run deep, according to Mark Pimlott's analyses of the shopping mall. 'Existence within the realm of representations, particularly when enhanced by the aura of spectacle', he argues, 'creates distance from reality, from the self, and from the possibility of encounters with the other' (Pimlott 2007: 295). Living in increasingly simulated environments ruled by signifiers, we have lost the insights afforded by direct experience and knowledge (1993: 164). Taking into account that 'there is no longer a realm of the "real" versus that of "imitation" or "mimicry" but rather a level in which there are only simulations' (1993: 164), it would be not adequate to describe scenography in themed malls as copying an 'original' or 'reality'; the only thing it can be is self-referential.

Inherited from 1980s and 1990s architectural academia, an understanding of visuality as being anchored in language, meaning and conceptualisation (Mitrović 2013: 23, 75) is reflected in the architectural approach to scenography taken by early entertainment centres and themed sections in shopping malls. Here, interaction was replaced with the narrative and stories derived from the main theme. Even though this tendency is still inseparable from themed environments today, the linguistic and conceptual approach to scenography for commercial purposes began, at the end of the 1990s, to be enriched with new possibilities for interaction, opening the door for an experience of space outside of language. In addition to semiotics, the consumption of place started to transpire through other senses as well, gradually incorporating hearing, smell, touch and bodily movement. While simplifying reality to make the experience more attractive, shopping malls' scenography was thus progressively directed to activate all our senses and build upon our embodied memory in order to immerse us in their imaginary worlds. This memory, which enables us to perceive space or appreciate the texture of a surface, is gained through an exploration of the existing physical world. According to Henri Lefebvre (1991), our perception of space is based on the physical relationships that happen through human interaction and communication in a particular place. However experimental, environmental or imaginative that place may be, he argues, we perceive our surroundings and develop assumptions based on what we experience and the context within which it occurs. Lefebvre maintains that any attempt 'to understand the contemporary world that ... ignore[s] spatial considerations' is doomed to remain 'partial and incomplete' (Unwin 2000: 13); our knowledge of the world is grounded in the sensory spatial relationship that exists between it and our bodies.

Even nowadays, in times when online commerce challenges traditional shopping habits (Bader 2016: 21), it is hard to deny the impact of scenographic strategies in shopping malls. While abandoned or repurposed facilities remind us that the concept is not successful by default, themed shopping malls still attract astronomical numbers of visitors every year.[13] The 2017 financial report published by the Las Vegas Sands Corporation, whose properties include the themed resorts The Venetian Macao, The Parisian Macao and The Venetian Las Vegas, shows that the malls are the corporation's second-highest earners, responsible for 10.2 per cent of total revenue, only 4.5 per cent behind the casinos.[14] Even if this success is driven by buying, Schechner notes, it is not limited to it. Bryman points out how the entertainment offered by the malls' scenography stimulates the excitement of the senses and works as 'a mechanism for distinguishing a service from that of its competitors even though the actual services may otherwise be more or less identical' (2004: 17). The scenography in themed shopping malls takes and condenses real and believable elements, such as ornaments, columns and arches, from the places that inspired the theme, which it then rearranges in an imaginative way. In doing so, the malls create a reality that communicates with our senses differently precisely because it is not actually real (Böhme A. 2012: 84). 'Illusionistic designs carry the visitor off to an idealized world', Bader points out, '– a kind of hyperreality – that is free of filth, chaos, and garbage' (Bader 2016: 18; Hampel 2010). According to Baudrillard, this hyperreality dissolves the tension between reality and illusion by going too far (Sarup 1993: 166). In becoming 'more real than real ... it has become the only existence' (1993: 166).

Nevertheless, by merging the real with the imaginary, hyperreality is full of contradictions, as it relies simultaneously 'on sensory perception as much as it does on control and suggests urbanity despite the fact that it isolates itself both spatially as well as socially from its immediate environment' (Bader 2016: 11). In this context, it opens the question of social and political responsibility inherent in the creation of a parallel universe free from the complexity of reality. It leads us to ask whether the scenography of themed malls continues the process of making 'the world [a] hedonistic but meaningless visual journey', distracting and detaching consumers through simulacra of reality. Or does it confront this situation by demanding the involvement of all our senses, reinforcing a 'body-centred and integrated experience of the world' (Pallasmaa 2005: 22)? If the task of architecture is to 'concretise and structure our being in the world' as it 'reflects, materialises and eternalises ideas and images of ideal life' in order for us to recognise who we are (2005: 71), is it not then the task of scenography to question exactly this, our need for the stability and permanence expressed by architecture? Instead, should it then expose us to the mimicry, the artifice and the ephemeral, reminding us of the unstoppable flow of life and its countless ways of experiencing the world? Confronting us with visual deception, manipulating our hearing, deliberately addressing our senses of smell, touch and bodily movement, the scenography of themed shopping malls targets our body and its senses in a way that is only rarely possible in the theatre, thus forging a new reality that challenges our very thinking and being.

6

The Deceitful Charm of Scenography

6.1 The echoes of history

From prehistoric ceremonial sites indicated with signs and drawings on cave walls, where the earliest forms of theatre took place,[1] to elaborately designed alleys in themed shopping malls, environmental scenography has always been a process of appropriating a place for the purpose of a happening. The careful and considered choice of location for rituals and festivities, still apparent in contemporary scenographic practice in the theatre, sets the starting point from which scenography first began to contribute to the transformation of place into cultural space (Schechner 1990: 119). As the setting for social gathering, performance and the scattering of attendants after closing hours, shopping malls continue the long tradition of collective experiences embedded in trade and entertainment, carrying on the essential characteristics of theatre (1990: 121).

There are some obvious similarities in concept and function between the shopping mall and some of its historical precedents, such as the Oriental bazaar, which make it tempting to draw direct parallels between them. However, Walter M. Weiss reminds us to keep a few crucial differences in mind (1994: 60). He points out the importance of the spiritual component, the religion that determines the rhythm of the bazaar (1994: 60). This also concerns the position of the mosque in relation to the bazaar's architectural layout, as it is never far away (Hmood 2017: 264). In Western Europe, the withdrawal of the marketplace from the city squares into market halls, whose 'function was to shelter the transaction of business while permitting the authorities to control it', marks the moment of separation between spirituality and market business (Lefebvre 1991: 265). 'The cathedral church was certainly not far away', Lefebvre elaborates, 'but its tower no longer bore the symbols of knowledge and power' (1991). From this point of view, academic references to shopping malls as today's 'cathedrals of consumption' could be misleading.[2] Pilgrimages to shopping centres and the mass obsession with consumer goods lack any connection to spirituality and religion. If a parallel were to be drawn here, it might be linked to gatherings and the theatricality of religious festivals, which were traditionally held in marketplaces with a church or cathedral as scenography (Mumford 1996: 55); the connection would not necessarily be between two places for happenings. Richard Goldthwaite explains that a change in spending habits and the emergence of consumer society began in Renaissance Italy, a period marked by its redefinition of secularity and separation of what was sacred. 'Man buys intentionally as the result of a deliberate decision informed by the values of his culture,' Goldthwaite argues. 'The totality of his consumption, therefore, has a certain coherence' (2002: 154). 'To the extent that the goods man surrounds himself with help establish, and maintain, his relations with other men', he elaborates, 'consumption involves him in a sort of ritual activity; and even if certain kinds of consumption seem only to satisfy personal pleasure rather than make a social statement, it is nevertheless likely that those pleasures themselves are socially conditioned' (2002: 154). During the Middle Ages and the Renaissance, the emergence of an early form of consumerism strengthened the marketplace's theatrical ties while, at the same time, gradually veering away from the spiritual component: as it became 'the center for trade, recreation, and social intercourse, it was in fact the stage on which the new urban bourgeois class played out their lives' (Carlson 1989: 17).

The Industrial Revolution brought further divide, this time between the production of goods (unseen) and their marketing (seen). This coincided with the establishment of the proscenium theatre in the eighteenth and nineteenth centuries (Schechner 1990: 124). Design effort was put into only what was meant for exposure (the facade, the proscenium, scenography) and not what remained hidden (the stage entrance, the fly gallery, backstage, the construction). This gap was emphasised by the heavy ornamentation of historic-revival movements, which caused architectural critics to express their discontent as early as the mid-nineteenth century. Ruskin's plea for decency and honesty in architecture clearly reflects this tendency, arguing against the decorative and deceptive features that were associated with stage designs of the time. In his essay *The Seven Lamps of Architecture*, Ruskin highlights three kinds of 'Architectural Deceits': '1st. The suggestion of a mode of structure or support, other than the true one; as in pendants of late Gothic roofs. 2nd. The painting of surfaces to represent some other material than that of which they actually consist (as in the marbling of wood), or the deceptive representation of sculpted ornament upon them. 3rd. The use of cast or machine-made ornaments of any kind' (1898: 62).

All three techniques are, of course, used for scenographic representations of architecture onstage, equating scenography in the theatre with a cultural practice of deceit and falseness. Ruskin was tackling the same notions of truth, revelation and sublime as Edward Gordon Craig did half a century later in his attempt to modernise scenography and step away from the deceptive portrayal of architecture onstage. In his essay, Ruskin argues that 'while a man's sense and conscience, aided by Revelation, are always enough, if earnestly directed, to enable him to discover what is right, neither his sense, nor conscience, nor feeling, is ever enough, because they are not intended, to determine for him what is possible' (1898: 2). Craig, on the other hand, agitating against representation, promoted 'suggestion' as a means 'to create the atmosphere of mystery that was considered most conducive to the perception and revelation of Truth and Beauty' (Eynat-Confino 1987: 25). To Craig, 'suggestion' as a way of using symbols to visualise 'the inexpressible in things' seemed more appropriate for mystical and spiritual discovery (1987: 25). Instead of insisting on authenticity of materiality, as Ruskin did in the field of architecture, Craig focused on feeling, atmosphere and movement, trying to achieve a 'mystical union with the universal rhythms of nature in such a way as to directly express the soul' (1987: 113).

The introduction of electric light in the nineteenth century, and its implementation in arcades and passages, lit the streets as brightly as a stage, causing city architecture to be perceived as a theatrical set. 'The arcade is a city,' Benjamin writes, 'a world in miniature, in which customers will find everything they need' (1999: 873). Correspondingly, in theatre, light was used to focus the audience's attention on the stage and scenography, while the auditorium was darkened (Schechner 1990: 140). The recurring tension between what was exposed and what was hidden was now associated with the repression of desires in the subconscious, causing representations in architecture to 'belong to the dream consciousness of the collective', a state from which it was necessary to awaken (Benjamin 1999: 858). Referring to Sigfried Giedion's thesis regarding nineteenth-century architecture and the relationship between construction and the subconscious, Benjamin posed a hypothetical question: 'Wouldn't it be better to say "the role of bodily processes" – around which "artistic" architectures gather, like dreams around the framework of physiological processes?' (1999: 858). The exposure to the dreamlike paved the way for the scenographic to unfold in places of trade, despite the rationalisation that took place in the nineteenth century. Establishing different speciality sections and grouping consumer goods, the emerging department stores exerted considerable effort to make themselves 'warm, well-appointed, and elegant settings that helped inflame the consumer's fantasies – in a word, enchanting' (Ritzer 2005: 90). Like the fashionable corsets that shaped the feminine silhouette by squeezing the body and seriously harming it, the scenographic illusion in arcades and department stores reinforced the divide between production processes, which included the extensive exploitation of labour and resources, and the presentation of the final product, which exploited theatricality, covering harsh realities with otherworldly settings.

By changing the milieu in which it was applied, this approach opposed the foundations of scenography as it is understood today. In theatre, scenography is seen as the artistic practice of visually shaping the inner essence of a story, bringing the inside to the outside, and thus enabling communication with what was previously hidden. However, as Jonathan Crary shows in his analysis of Georges Seurat's painting *Parade de cirque* (1888) and unfinished drawing *A Shop and Two Figures* (1882), what came to light was actually 'the emptiness of a modern relation of display and consumption' (2001: 195). According to Crary, representations of an economic environment as a circus sideshow in Parade de cirque and of a nineteenth-century shopping street in A Shop and Two Figures are 'the ubiquity of the subjective experience of "shopping" and its construction as spectacle' (2001: 196). Pointing out the price displayed on the entrance behind the central figure of a musician at the Circus Corvi outside the Cinematographe, which simultaneously functions as scenography, Crary sees a symbolic 'new limit of rationalization and disenchantment in art practice' (2001: 196, 279).

The tension and contradictions between the shown and the hidden, spectacle and consumption, were supported by the advertising strategies that developed in the constantly increasing competition of a growing consumer market. This opened the door for themed scenography to release its persuasive power. According to Mark Gottdiener, the American department stores of the nineteenth century played a crucial role in the introduction of thematic environments, not only with their settings but also with their catalogues (1997: 58). By 'converting industrial goods into an image', he explains, catalogues spread thematic appeal to millions of homes by mail. They transformed desirable commodities into 'images and representations that tapped into cognitive associations that were pure symbols', and so prepared the way for themed environments to emerge (1997: 59). Visual overexposure to images accelerated after the Second World War. In the 1950s and 1960s, advertising strategies expanded rapidly beyond prints in catalogues, newspapers and magazines to include radio and television, creating a multibillion-dollar industry and securing the foundation for themed environments (1997: 66). Accordingly, themed areas in stores, shopping malls and recreational facilities can be seen as the materialisation of symbols established through marketing, highly effective in the realisation of capital and, as such, an 'extension of television, magazine, and newspaper advertising' (1997: 70).

In the twentieth century, Gottdiener says, 'it has become more important for the survival of capitalism to succeed in the realization and circulation of capital through commodity production within an environment that remains highly competitive' (1997: 46). Drawing on Baudrillard's critical analysis of Marx, Gottdiener also points out that 'the continual expansion of capital is no longer so much the problem of production, or capital valorisation in commodities at the factory, but of consumption, or capital realization at the market' (1997: 46). Likewise, human geographers tend to agree that consumption is not the end result of economic production; it is a two-way process as the consumption, in turn, effects further investment in production (Jones 2012: 78) and influences economic growth. As the whole industry thus depends on the creation of images and environments that make us buy one product over another (2012: 78), the exploitation of scenography to enhance shops' appearance, as well as their wider settings, has firmly established its position in the production of goods in capitalist society. As Jon Goss acknowledges, by manufacturing an 'idealized representation of past or distant public spaces', shopping malls transform the constructed environment into an object with market value (1993: 19). Looking at themed environments, the exploitation of scenography to circulate commodities and realise profits highlights the link between scenographic techniques and the practice of making images in Postmodern society. This reflects the cultural production of privately owned market spaces through a heightened sense of reality (1993: 19, 21). As a result, scenography in the commercial context is tied to everyday life, becoming part of the process of visually shaping the world economy and global society through consumption (Jones 2012: 78).

As their objectives have, since the late 1980s and early 1990s, included the rapid development of tourism, the United Arab Emirates, Qatar, Thailand and South Africa have been through an unprecedented transition during the economic shifts that have taken place. One prominent example, the city of Dubai, has seen drastic urbanisation and restructuring of the traditional marketplace (Goldthwaite 2002: 56; Pacione 2005: 260). What started in 1956 with the construction of a single concrete building has become a vibrant metropolis with sixty-five at the moment operating shopping malls,[3] three of which are themed. Scenography, the long-standing cultural practice of reshaping a given environment into a cultural space, has been widely adopted by Dubai's shopping malls, supporting the rate of change in both market and society. Scenographic interventions during the city's annual Shopping Festival, which takes place from December to January, are sponsored by twenty-five of its malls. So far, these interventions have included hot-air balloons and oversized butterflies in the Bur Juman Mall, a gigantic balloon-spaceman floating through the Dubai Marina Mall, and numerous theatrical performances, dances, concerts, laser shows and other events.

Unfortunately, although Qatar, Thailand and South Africa, in addition to the United Arab Emirates, each developed their own individual approach to theming, building on the concept's origins in the United States, it seems prior reflection on the challenges created by quick development was never involved. Instead, as our case studies demonstrate, theming is used to cover their tracks. Echoing the nineteenth-century corset mentioned earlier, the scenography of themed shopping malls hides the conditions behind the circulation of capital while intensifying exposure on highly competitive markets. This time, however, it is not meant to shield the subconscious but rather to ease the consumer's conscience. Meanwhile, the discrepancies characteristic of an overly hasty urbanisation process reflect what Fredric Jameson describes as the abolishment of the distinction between inside and outside (1991: 98). This binary relation, inherent in the embodiment of city streets in the inner spaces of commercial passages, which started with shopping arcades and continued in the aisles of department stores and alleys in shopping malls, now defines 'the concept of the postmodern "city"' (1991: 98).

Exchanging the 'authentic' for a stand-in, introduced with the enclosure of the open marketplace and city streets, falls into a long tradition of using substitutes to imitate real materials in commercial settings. At the 1851 Great Exhibition in the Crystal Palace in London, mass production for the working classes took centre stage as industrialists presented cheaper versions of products and demonstrated affordable alternatives to originals (Friemert 1984: 46). Substitutes were also present in the Crystal Palace in another form, namely in themed courts – Egyptian, Greek, Assyrian, Roman, Byzantine, medieval English and Renaissance Italian.[4] Designed by Owen Jones, the courts supported the narrative of the exhibition by recreating 'imaginative geographies' that reflected the history of human civilisation. Quoting Timothy Mitchell, Crary highlights nineteenth-century exhibitions as places that turned ordinary visitors into 'tourists or anthropologists, addressing an object-world as the endless representation of some further meaning or reality' (Crary 2001: 236).[5] The question of whether the 'representation of the world could in some way be life-enhancing' went hand in hand with the nineteenth-century discourse that focused on the primacy of visual stimuli as a trigger producing physical and psychological changes in the viewer (2001: 163). Crary also references Stéphane Mallarmé, who describes items at the London Exhibition in the Albert Hall (1871) as a 'tantalizing surface of experience', an 'overload of possible diversions, pleasures, and spectacles' (2001: 122). Nineteenth-century exhibitions, therefore, played a crucial role in introducing scenographic representations of 'otherness' into commercial places, filtering objects and spaces out of their original contexts and putting them in a different cultural environment on the stage of 'the pseudo-festival of the European expositions'. This prepared 'the dead ground out of which might arise [a] hoped-for ritual civic theater of the future and, as an implied consequence of such a cultural reform, an impossibly attentive observer-participant' (Mallarmé, cited in Crary 2001: 124).

Spatial simulations propelled by Postmodernism thus seem to be a logical outcome of the long process of cultural reform carried out by heightening observers' attention using scenographic interventions. In the commercial context of exhibitions and marketplaces, the theatrical approach to cultural exchange and the displacement of historical references paved the way for the contemporary decadence visible in themed shopping malls. As it did so, scenography was exposed as the practice responsible for creating the preconditions necessary for the cultural repositioning of public space. The conjunction of consumption and leisure initiated by shopping malls in the 1950s for one particular segment of the population constructed 'community experiences around the cultural taste of white middle-class suburbanites' (Cohen 1996: 1063–4). Since then, this phenomenon has spread its influence far beyond the borders of suburbia, reaching out to the masses but targeting individual desires. According to Wolfgang König, consumer society involves neither the total manipulation of consumers by the economic system nor their total freedom of choice (2008: 215). He emphasises that consumerism is stimulated by needs and wants as well as by the sociocultural impulses delivered by the society we inhabit (2008: 215). Desire, Baudrillard clarifies, fuelled by the feeling that something is lacking, signifies itself in needs, which are significantly different from enjoyment and satisfaction (1998: 75, 77). As he explains, in the same way as labour power denies the relationship between the worker and the product of his labour, and the exchange value of commodities has nothing to do with personal exchange, needs 'are produced as system elements, not as a relationship of an individual to an object' (1998: 75). Baudrillard describes needs as 'the most advanced form of the rational systematization of the productive forces at the individual level, where "consumption" takes over logically and necessarily from production' (1998: 75).

As the historical overview shows, scenographic interventions in Montecasino, the Ibn Battuta Mall, the Villaggio and Terminal 21 continue the tendency of indulging consumers with worlds in which established sociocultural needs and desires are visualised. Their dependence on consumption and exchange transforms spaces designated for the realisation of capital into commodities in and of themselves, embodying consumers in themed narratives with which they cannot truly connect. If there is no personal involvement in the process of exchange, the environment becomes only a projection, a flat surface that cannot be penetrated. No matter how hard we try to enter, it always shuts us out. So, from the historical perspective, crediting scenographic strategies in themed shopping malls with being the instruments responsible for consumerism would not be appropriate. As König asserts, they are, at best, 'consumption intensifiers' (*Konsumverstärker*), not creators (2008: 215). Nevertheless, the agency of aesthetics in consumer society should not be underestimated (Böhme G. 1995: 48). It gives designers the opportunity to direct attention, Crary argues, influence spatial dynamics and steer consumers' needs, ultimately putting designers in the position of power (2001: 74). The gap that exists between the real experience and an image of reality, as Debord describes (1970: §7), is widened in themed shopping malls as simulacra are expanded and signs continue their domination over signifiers. This creates a space for language to enter the process of spatial design and configuration. The result is a confluence of consumption, scenography and language, giving scenography a loud and echoing voice that reiterates individuals' needs as a 'speech effect' (Baudrillard 1998: 80). Even if our bodies cannot penetrate its surface, the resonance it produces goes deep into our consciousness.

6.2 The aesthetic universe

Comparing Modern and Postmodern art, Fredric Jameson recognises 'a new kind of flatness or depthlessness, a new kind of superficiality in the most literal sense' as a major feature of Postmodernism (1991: 9). A predominant focus on the aesthetic appeal of scenography in themed shopping malls reflects this notion rather literally by flattening the diversity and edginess of open urban spaces. When scenographic elements such as street fronts, typically used in theatrical settings to reference architecture, were transferred into malls, shopping streets became mere images of themselves. Attempts to translate architectural aesthetics into a scenographic appropriation of place propelled pastiche into the shopping environment.[6] By creating a simulacrum, 'the identical copy for which no original has ever existed', scenography has become only a vague reflection of the places it used as inspiration, presenting more of a medial image of a source, an 'intensifier', than a real sense of an actual place (Jameson 1991: 18, 46).

But considering that what we chiefly consume in these days of the rapid development of digital technologies is the image rather than the architecture itself (Jameson 1991: 99), scenography in themed malls seems to offer us exactly what we expect. As direct, bodily encounters with our surroundings gradually recede in favour of experiences via digital images, the 'flatness' of this theatrical physicality equates it with 'a sign or logo for architecture itself' (1991: 101). Contrary to both the urban matrices of inner cities, which spread continuously over time, and artificially constructed themed environments such as Disney World, there are no dominant visual, acoustic or olfactory references that lead visitors through themed malls, helping them to orient themselves. Consumers are led from one spot to another not by a visible highlight, usually spotted from afar in open urban environments, but by means of predetermined, universally pleasing routes and signs. Attractions are promptly revealed, suddenly and unexpectedly exposed. This kind of disclosure contradicts contemporary modifications of the place both onstage and in environmental theatre, where scene-changing happens gradually in front of the audience as the drama evolves. An old-fashioned approach to scenography, as it is practised in themed shopping malls, places the focus on its aesthetic qualities, flattening three-dimensional space instead of shaping or 'breaking' it physically or stylistically, and failing to make it adaptable for all the different kinds of 'plays' that might occur in the marketplace. Yet, this bias opposes Marc Augé's criticism of the shopping mall as a 'non-place'.[7] 'Money and commodities', Lefebvre reminds us, 'were destined to bring with them not only a "culture" but also a space' (1991: 265). Indeed, due to scenography's specific aesthetic agency, themed environments are actually given strong characteristics of place, though not the ones we usually mean: the result is place as a commodity.

It is interesting to note that, despite the aesthetic monotony introduced with corporate branding strategies, themed shopping malls still aspire to a certain level of diversity within the worldwide homogenisation of consumption. This is accomplished through the entertainment provided by themed narratives. As the Villaggio Mall demonstrates, even if homogenisation is hard to escape, attempts are still made to differentiate the mall aesthetically and conceptually from its global counterparts. George Ritzer calls this phenomenon 'homogeneous diversity' (2005: 182). Cultural differences have a profound influence on the modification process, yet beneath all the efforts to stand out with regard to uniqueness of design, individual brands, and distinctive products and services, shopping malls offer extremely similar content almost everywhere. Sanitisation, the process of filtering reality and eliminating everything considered offensive (Ritzer 2005: 183), has infiltrated aesthetics as well, making it harder for designers to break away from uniformity. The shift towards establishing interaction with the setting, instead of with other shoppers (2005: 185), directs efforts to create aesthetically pleasing interiors that 'communicate' with consumers. Staying on the safe side with a relatively narrow spectrum of themes, shopping malls continue to follow a mainstream approach to design because they want to appeal to the masses (Gottdiener 1997: 156).

The less consumption has to do with obtaining goods rather than amusement (Ritzer 2005: 192), the more aesthetics will require scenographic strategies to put on a show in order to keep commercial settings fun, adventurous and, above all, profitable. After all, today's consumers expect commercial environments to entertain them (Gottdiener 1997: 75). Ritzer describes the phenomenon in more detail: 'Eatertainment, shoppertainment, and retailtainment are also all about the creation of sets where consumers can eat their food or buy their commodities in fantastic theatrical settings' (2005: 192). With its interpretation of historical architectural styles, the scenography of themed shopping malls does not aim for accuracy but entertainment (Gottdiener 1997: 121). The urge to pursue authenticity and reality, which drove Max Reinhardt to Venice in 1934 to stage *The Merchant of Venice* in the Campo San Trovaso square (Aronson 2018: 44–5), has been exchanged for using visual aesthetics and the physical simulation of 'Venice' to bring its narratives to malls in Doha, Las Vegas, Macau and Greater Noida. On special occasions around Christmas and New Year, a twelve-minute scene from *The Merchant of Venice* is played twice a day in the themed setting of The Grand Venice Mall in Greater Noida. Scenographic narratives are visually structured to tell the story of one (Montecasino, the Villaggio) or multiple themes (the Ibn Battuta Mall, Terminal 21), involving consumers in an exploration and, consequently, in a specific kind of silent dialogue with the space. Narrative is seen as a precondition for the consumption of experience because social connections are forged through the stories that are being told (Böhme A. 2012: 82).[8] In accordance with their new commercial purpose, the reinterpretation of historical references in Montecasino, the Ibn Battuta Mall, the Villaggio and Terminal 21 happens in a new way. It puts the focus on heightening consumers' sensations and leads towards an experience driven by hedonism and intensity (Tsai 2010: 323).

The connection between emotional embodiment and sensing the space has been thoroughly explored by cultural geographers (Davidson et al. 2004: 523). As Axel Buether notes, the emotional impact of spatial perception reflects the atmosphere of the perceived space (2018: 72). From the psychological point of view, the mere-exposure effect suggests that individuals' aesthetic preference increases towards objects and environments that are perceived continuously, especially when exposure is unconscious. Consequently, aesthetic sensations are closely related to a deep familiarity with the things and places we then experience as beautiful (Richter 2018: 160–2). Empathy grows with immersion, making staged environments more appealing to our senses than our everyday surroundings (Buether 2018: 72). In turn, Tsai argues, immersion is established through emotional impact, which causes a temporary sense of blissfulness (2010: 323).

A cross-regional survey conducted in four shopping centres in Japan, Australia, Great Britain and the United States,[9] and published by Shu-pei Tsai in *The Service Industries Journal*, presents a holistic entertainment experience as the concurrence of four feelings, namely, exhilaration, exploration, relaxation and socialisation, demonstrating their significant effect on patronage frequency and purchase amount (Tsai 2010: 332). The empirical approach that Tsai lays out highlights the relevance of combining different aspects of experience for competitiveness on the market rather than conceptualising shopping malls around a single kind of encounter (2010: 332). Looking at Tsai's survey results from a scenographic perspective, it is interesting to note that exploration combined with emotionality was positively associated with shopping behaviour in terms of both patronage frequency and purchase amount, while exhilaration had the same association only with patronage frequency (2010: 333–4). Furthermore, scenography-related attributes such as atmosphere, product arrangement, mall image[10] and special events were found to be equally important contributors to the holistic entertainment experience, though atmosphere did not show a direct impact on either patronage frequency or purchase amount (2010: 333–4). Product arrangement,[11] on the other hand, related positively to both aspects (2010: 335). Following the results of his research, Tsai suggests that the 'drivers for the holistic entertainment experience are recognized as also taking root in quality and aesthetic excellence, ease and comfort, and the mall's symbolism and functionality' (2010: 333). The combined cognitive and sociocultural factors embedded in emotionality, Tsai explains, create that holistic entertainment experience. Its effectiveness then substantially influences the success of the shopping mall in question.

The aesthetic approach to the scenography of commercial spaces such as themed malls cannot be viewed independently from capital, of course, as it serves only one purpose – to secure profits. Designers are encouraged to morph, dwarf, rescale, simplify and caricature reality. In a truly Postmodern manner, diverse elements and components 'float at a certain distance from each other in a miraculous stasis or suspension, which, like the constellations, is certain to come apart in the next minute' (Jameson 1991: 100). As Jameson identifies, this is vividly represented in the Postmodern approach to historicism, as demonstrated by some malls 'whose various elements – architrave, column, arch, order, lintel, dormer, and dome – begin with the slow force of cosmological processes to flee each other in space ... endowed for a last brief moment with the glowing autonomy of the psychic signifier ... before being blown out into the dust of empty spaces' (1991: 100). The act of breaking free of Modernist repression in regard to play and resistance to consumption has unleashed a dreamy weightlessness of daring, kitsch and even aesthetically off-putting designs, which can be played with and consumed (1991: 101). At the same time, these designs function as a disguise of the subconscious, the hidden raw architecture of the building, a construction that holds the floating elements together for as long as the play of consumption lasts. The mediating function of this playground, which establishes scenographed space as a commodity, shows the relevance of narrative and aesthetics for the successful placement of malls as products in increasingly competitive markets. It also, notably, raises fundamental questions regarding the sociopolitical consequences of this aesthetic formulation (1991: 104). An awareness of the power of aesthetics inevitably brings the issue of responsibility into play.

6.3 Social interaction with a price tag

When shopping malls first began to emerge in the 1950s, they incorporated social facilities in the form of community clubs, movie theatres, bowling alleys, and children's gymnasiums and playgrounds, as in the Garden State Plaza (1957). Designating spaces to be used for gathering and socialising was based on an ambition to make shopping malls 'the heart of suburban life' (Cohen 1996: 1058). From these early examples, social features in themed malls went beyond the physicality of the place. Nowadays, those features in malls such as Montecasino, the Ibn Battuta Mall, the Villaggio and Terminal 21 are not only represented by scenographic techniques and their narratives, which aim to bring people together by providing a unique experience. Nor are they exclusively associated with the social activity of consumption. Indeed, visits to themed shopping malls and visits to the theatre are related beyond the desire for cultural input and the purchase of goods and services. The connecting aspect is the need for a social experience through participation in the spectacle, which unfolds in both places as 'a social relation among people mediated by images' (Debord 1970: §4; Pine II et al. 1999: 47).

Building on Lefebvre's 'space of representation', Rob Shields uses the West Edmonton Mall as an example of 'a space in which the social imaginary is opened to new visions' (1989: 6–8). According to Shields, such a space calls for a rejection of a rational conception of the world by prompting a 'different logic of space and a different capital logic' (1989: 6–8). This involves the transformation, through the use of symbols and metaphors, of spatial reality and locations into a metaconcept, thus influencing a shift in 'material culture and social structuration' (1989: 6–8). Adjustments in spatial understanding, Shields argues, 'constitute changes in individual's *spatiality* and social spatialisations' (1989: 8). He claims that being a member of a consumer community surpasses other social identities, even that of being a citizen (1989: 11). In a similar vein, Debord argues that 'the economy over social life had brought into the definition of all human realization an obvious degradation of being into having' (1970: §17).

In his book *Shopping Town: Designing the City in Suburban America*, Gruen looks back critically at the evolution of shopping centres. He claims that the principles he defined concerning a responsible approach to malls' urban, social and environmental aspects have been neglected by their developers (Gruen et al. 2014: 226). His objective, which started with the Southdale Center, was to establish a contemporary urban typology and create a modern-day agora, a centre for social gatherings in the scattered residential areas of American suburbia. Gruen's plea to future projects was to incorporate the shopping-mall concept in densely populated inner-cities and use the model to revitalise their centres (Gruen et al. 2014: 225–6). At the beginning of the twenty-first century, his vision has become a reality in city centres around the world. Contrary to Gruen's expectations, however, the strategy has not been as concerned with revitalisation as with 'total control' (Venturi et al. 1979: 176). This is reflected in a rather limited approach to improving social conditions in places of trade. Venturi recognises the problem in the decision-making processes of building advisory boards and committees, which have a direct influence on the availability of social space in city centres. Yet the ambition to escape the city's control in themed shopping environments, which continue on the path laid out by Walt Disney, seems to have fallen wide of the mark. In fact, the initial idea behind Disney's meticulously planned theme parks was itself based on control,[12] rooted in Modernist architectural concepts that grew from the leftovers of chaotic nineteenth-century living conditions and evinced a clear aim to restructure and remodel the city. The goal 'to recreate a sensibility of public space' that began with layering a city's infrastructure and hiding visually unattractive functional services underground profoundly influenced Disneyland's conception (Chung et al. 2001a: 288–9). It exchanged the wish to re-establish the social in the city for control over who or what is meant to be seen and who or what is not. In the architectural sphere, this notion was challenged already at the beginning of the 1970s with the first buildings that exposed their underlying construction and installations. While these became an integral part of the aesthetic and introduced new architectural styles, themed malls and theme parks alike stubbornly held on to their Modernist inheritance, struggling not only to find new forms of visual expression but also to unfold their social potential beyond the stories they told.

While some empirical studies acknowledge the social mixture in regular shopping malls, showing that high-end malls also attract low-income visitors and so influence the general democratisation of consumption,[13] themed malls offer the opportunity to advance consumers' social layering even further (Ritzer 2005: 199). By creating an environment that can be consumed visually without having to pay an entrance fee, the scenography of the themed mall allows even those visitors who cannot afford to participate in the consumption of goods at least to take part in experiencing the place's atmosphere. The very idea of theming a mall, Tracy C. Davis notes, especially if executed in an extremely literal way, 'levels all classes of society to a common experience' (1991: 1–15). However, because full immersion depends on the interaction that accompanies the purchase of goods and services, the consumption of any ephemeral aspects is only part of the experience. Although strolling along scenographed alleys and window-shopping do hold a certain appeal, these activities are also a reminder to those who cannot fully participate of the limits imposed by social conditioning. On the other hand, scenographic strategies in themed malls support the exploitation of affluent consumers as they encourage these visitors to prolong their stay and lead them 'to buy more than they need; to spend more than they should' (Ritzer 2005: 52). As it thus directly influences an increase in demand for products and services, scenography plays a central role in securing the successful operation of capitalism and the market economy. The assertion that consumers have a choice not to participate, at least to a degree and within the constraints imposed by their social conditioning, is tricky. As Ritzer points out, theming makes alternative forms of consumption less attractive and increases the challenge of breaking free (2005). In other words, the scenographic settings in shopping malls do not make it easy for visitors to choose something else.

The simultaneous coexistence of choice and constraint is due, in part, to the fact that themed commercial environments even out the imbalance between Max Weber's notion of Western 'disenchantment', a result of the rationalisation and bureaucracy inherent in capitalism and consumption (Ritzer 2005: 57), and scenographic seduction in places where capital is realised, which manipulates the consumer by means of artificial 'enchantment'. This argument draws on Baudrillard's description of seduction as 'the possibility of reenchanting our lives' through play and illusion (2005: 68). The enchantment happens in relation not only to quality (2005: 88) but also to change, since the essence of magic, as of scenography, is fluidity – the transformation of one spatial construct into another. Scenographing carefully structured, classified and organised places is a process of alteration: layers of meaning are added to a sanitised and sterile environment that, despite its diversity of products and services, would otherwise have very little to offer. Employing a layout that encourages mobility through a wide variety of attractive options, the scenography of themed malls supports the illusion of freedom (of choice) and individuality by pushing consumers forward in constant flow. Rem Koolhaas refers to the way we move through the shopping mall as 'at the same time aimless and purposeful' and, as such, 'one of the last tangible ways in which we experience freedom' (2001a: 412). But tangible encounters in scenographed malls are precisely calculated. The touch of water in fountains and canals, the smell of perfume and food, the sound of birds singing, and even the materiality of the facades on upper floors and ceilings, which are out of our reach, connect us with the space through a series of emotional associations. They are grounded in our memories of how it feels to be in the middle of a city, and are consciously positioned in the mall to make us stop, gaze, wonder and, ultimately, spend. In a consumer society, Baudrillard sees the pressure to produce more individualism as bearing a direct connection to the repression inherent in the system (1998: 84). What is experienced as freedom, he argues, is the result of consumption, 'a powerful element of social control' facilitated 'by the atomization of consuming individuals', which requires 'ever greater *bureaucratic constraint* on the processes of consumption' (1998: 84). In the themed environment, therefore, 'choice' is not really a choice at all.

As Nicholas Jewell has noted, architecture that neglects the social context 'in which it operates – particularly in the case of a building as nakedly capitalistic as the shopping mall – is one that risks obsolescence' (2015: 18). The social responsibility of shopping-mall developers, architects and designers continues to revolve around the need for greater transparency and the inclusion of local communities in the decision-making process (Coleman 2006: 257). The hope is that this might open up the rigid objectives set by a single-minded focus on profits and the market. With a growing awareness of environmental implications, public concerns regarding the sustainability of both materials and energy could prove useful in the mediation between community needs and the neo-liberal agenda (Coleman 2006: 257). In such a constellation, socialising, as a way of *being* with others, becomes inseparable from *having* things to buy. Clearly, the strategy of theming in shopping malls is directly aimed at exploiting a basic human need for the purpose of turning a profit.

6.4 Public space as a political stage

The freedom associated with strolling along a shopping alley (Koolhaas 2001a: 412), considered in regard to the social aspects of themed malls, is also closely connected to the politics of safety. As Bart Somers, the controversial mayor of Mechelen, who has turned what was once the dirtiest city in Belgium, with the country's highest crime rates, into a paradigm of harmonious community among 138 nationalities, once said in an interview, 'There is no freedom without safety.'[14] He sees his determined approach to fighting crime in the city as a necessary precondition for implementing liberal and social politics. In turn, these politics then contribute to citizens' feelings of freedom. In the controlled environment of the themed mall, as of theme parks, apparent freedom is cultivated by careful consideration of the mall's visual impact, its pathways and shoppers' movement along them (Bryman 2004: 143; Ritzer

2005: 82). The shift in focus during the current phase of capitalism towards maintaining control of consumers has caused alleys to be organised and designed to expose shops and 'to get [consumers] to spend as much as possible' (Ritzer 2005: 54). Ritzer suggests that this control is also established on an emotional level 'by offering bright, cheery, and upbeat environments' (2005: 81), which promote feelings of safety. Contradicting the liveliness of the real city, marketplaces and street festivities in the midst of aged facades, dirty corners and petty crimes, the scenographic mimesis of clean and brightly lit streets in themed shopping malls reassures consumers that they are in a safe place. Here, they can move around freely and concentrate on shopping undistracted by any happenings outside the mall. The myth of happiness and safety reinforced by neo-traditional principles of 'new urbanism' (Bryman 2004: 48–9), which resonate in scenographic interpretations of the city in themed shopping malls, also carries a political connotation in its ambition to keep the complexities of life under control.

Aiming for 'global appeal', Nicholas Jewell observes, shopping malls have traded safety and consistency for the unpredictable nature of urban situations marked by surprise and contrast (2001: 328). Safety, as Jewell points out, is 'based on the perception of being with your own kind' (2001: 328). Exploiting scenography for this purpose, therefore, leads towards complicity in the process of filtering reality and creating the conditions for exclusion. Continuous attempts to eliminate the 'undesirable' from shopping malls have been repeatedly backed by court decisions (Cohen 1996: 1078). As a consequence, this has led to the persistent notion of an idealised world in which crime and poverty are sidelined in order to enable shoppers' undisturbed consumption (König 2008: 75). The ambition to keep enclosed commercial places inviting and desirable, however, was not invented in shopping malls. Benjamin mentions that the entrances to nineteenth-century shopping arcades were 'strictly forbidden to anyone who [was] dirty or to carriers of heavy loads; smoking and spitting [were] likewise prohibited here'.[15] Still, activities such as prostitution and gambling were as much part of the arcades (Benjamin 1999: 489ff) as they are of malls, especially in places where the malls themselves are located within larger recreational or gambling complexes. The statue of a prostitute in the Europa Boulevard of the West Edmonton Mall pays homage to the 'undesirable' activities that were and, indeed, still are a traditional part of city life. In line with the development of digital technologies, safety measures are constantly expanding to include new tools such as mass push notifications for mobile phones.[16] As Megan Leonhardt reports, Homeland Security and American shopping malls are both testing the same software for facial recognition and licence plate scanning (2016). The political implications of selection and exclusion based on watch lists or visitors' criminal records are still debatable when it comes to a discussion of freedom and safety. Some scholars see it as a direct confrontation with the shopping mall's established rules, the encouragement of undesirable activities and the legal challenge of political rights in court (Goss 1993: 42). The hope is to 'expose the ersatz and profoundly undemocratic nature of public space and the controlled carnival manufactured in the contemporary retail environment' (Goss 1993: 42).

With regard to scenography in themed shopping malls, another kind of control seems equally relevant. Alongside criticism of Disney's treatment of literary sources,[17] many academics have also raised the issue of imagination control in the conglomerate's theme parks (Bryman 2004: 135; Campbell 2005: 179ff; Gottdiener 1997: 158; Ritzer 2005: 60). 'The more he [the consumer] accepts recognizing himself in the dominant images of need', Guy Debord says, 'the less he understands his own existence and his own desires. The externality of the spectacle in relation to the active man appears in the fact that his own gestures are no longer his but those of another who represents them to him' (1970: §30). Encouraging simplification and exclusion in design, Alan Bryman argues, trivialises the originals in the same way as does adapting literary sources, taking away their complexity and the different levels of meaning they embody. The precisely designed and executed scenography in shopping malls, as in the theme parks, restricts visitors' imagination and thus forces them into passivity; it shuts down any possibility for creative interaction with the space and makes them mere 'onlookers – revelling in the imagination of others (Walt and his Imagineers) – rather than being active participants in the use of the imagination' (Bryman 2004: 135; Gottdiener 1997: 158). George Ritzer reminds us of Colin Campbell's observation that the capacity for individual fantasy is essential to understanding modern consumerism, as the nature of fantasy is never to be entirely fulfilled but rather to continue to generate an endless, unsatisfied need for new consumer goods and services (Campbell 2005: 179ff; Ritzer 2005: 60). To construct imagined worlds, Tim Ingold asserts, one needs to disengage from the world (1992: 52), quite a challenge in places built on consumers' total immersion. In conditions where the 'outside' world is completely sealed off and visitors' focus is trained exclusively on a unified themed design (Bryman 2004: 137–8), the dominant visual input leaves hardly any space for creative freedom in shopping malls and theme parks alike. According to annual visit rates, there is no doubt that such surroundings induce a certain level of enchantment, but it is one with a controlled and predictable outcome, stripped of anything unexpected and truly adventurous (Ritzer 2005: 88). Considering that it seems to be crucial to consumption, prompting feelings of safety that boost spending (Bryman 2004: 155), it should not be surprising that control exceeds the physicality of space and goes deeper into our consciousness, actually distracting us from the process of drifting and creative daydreaming by demanding attention.

Using terminology introduced by Karen Barad, Kathleen Irwin emphasises how exclusion in scenography is 'generative, constitutive, destabilizing and leads to productive inquiries into how differences and exclusions are made' (2017: 120; Barad 2012: 77). 'The sense of the cut (or absence)', Irwin writes, 'is not foreign to how meaning is made on stage' (2017: 120). Yet exclusions in scenographic interpretations of the city in themed malls are the product of decisions led neither by attempts to create meaning, as onstage, nor by functional zoning objectives, as in cities, but by the pursuit of conditions ideal for the realisation of capital. Unfortunately, the aims of mall developers do not align with consumers' needs or expectations of public space. In her study of American cities in the early 1960s, Jane Jacobs stresses the human need for visual clarity in city districts (1993: 194). She specifies two possibilities for making inner order visible on the outside, namely, accentuation and indication (1993: 194), both of which are essential characteristics of scenography. Her use of the term 'indication' relates to Irwin's notion of exclusion in scenography, and she explains it as referring to a segment standing for the whole or the possibility of filtering reality as an artistic practice (1993: 194). While acknowledging its roads as the most important visual aspect of a city, Jacobs criticises the contradictory effect of apparently interminable street sections in urban America (1993: 194). The streets' materiality, she explains, and their variety of buildings, shop fronts and signs combine to form a blend of diversity and intensity that demands optical interruptions and discontinuity. This is lost, however, in the anonymity of distance on long blocks, which makes the streets seem endless (1993: 194). Reinterpretations of cities in the megastructures of themed shopping malls follow a similar pattern, using simplified facades to recall the original architectural paradigm. As a result, they repeat the contradiction Jacobs identifies, demonstrating a scenographic tendency that Irwin calls 'endlessly citing other things' (2017: 121). Both physical and metaphorical, this 'endlessness' draws a parallel with the theatrical concepts developed by the 1920s European avant-garde. By referencing the city through indication, themed malls neglect the human need to look away from shop window displays in order to connect with the city itself.

In the conflict between the centrality of commerce, community and private ownership of public space (Cohen 1996: 1068), scenographed areas in themed malls are caught up in the dispute regarding the free expression of political thought, assemblies and demonstrations. These rights are traditionally upheld in public spaces but, as they are seen as a threat to business, many attempts continue to be made to exclude politics from shopping malls. Jon Goss mentions several court cases against malls that 'actively discriminate against potential minority tenants, employees, and mall users' (1993: 26). Even though differences between the malls must be acknowledged, political expression has, generally speaking, been filtered through the perspective of business profits (Cohen 1996: 1068). Until 1996, only six American states' 'supreme courts protected citizens' rights of free speech in privately owned shopping centers' (Cohen: 1070). Most of the court cases based their arguments on the claim that the mall is a public space and 'equivalent to a town center' (Cohen 1996: 1070; Goss 1993: 27).

Looking at this issue in a global context, political connotations differ according to regional sociopolitical conditions. In regard to the themed environment of The Palazzo Montecasino, Achille Mbembe argues that 'these new spaces are setting up new boundaries and distances increasingly based on class' (2004: 402). In places where commodities are displayed and private interest rules, 'neither critical debate nor critical reasoning takes place' (2004: 402). Mbembe refers to theming as an 'architecture of hysteria', which 'asks the spectator to forget that it is itself a sign of forgetting' (2004: 402). In South Africa, he asserts, creating suggestions of history by recapturing architectural features of distant places actively suppresses regional memories. This makes theming responsible for a return to the 'archaic', for slowing down or halting rapid changes in society, contemplation of past times or something that has been lost (2004: 403).

Contrary to the situation in Johannesburg, personal freedom in Dubai, Mike Davis notes, 'derives strictly from the business plan, not from a constitution, much less "inalienable rights"' (2006: 62). Continuing the liberal economic approach set during the 1980s, the United Arab Emirates has established 'free-trade zones where 100 per cent foreign ownership is allowed, with no individual or corporate taxes or import/export duties whatsoever' (Davis 2006: 62; Pacione 2005: 257). But apart from beneficial trading conditions, Davis emphasises, freedom in Dubai extends to permission to 'carouse and debauch – not to organize unions or publish critical opinions' (2006: 64). Between the seemingly unlimited possibilities for affluent residents and expats on one side and the modern-day slavery of migrant labourers on the other (2006: 65–6), the feeling of 'freedom' experienced through consumption in Dubai's shopping malls conquers a middle ground that goes as deep as consumers' pockets. Despite its reputation as the Bangkok of the Middle East (Davis 2006: 64), Dubai has not yet caught up with Thailand in the use of malls as a platform for political disobedience. While themed malls around the world have mostly managed to hold on to their apolitical position, about thirty people took the opportunity to protest in Terminal 21 on 1 June 2014. The action was part of a mass demonstration against the Thai coup d'état, which took place on 22 May 2014, and included protesters gathered around the shopping mall (Mooney et al. 2014).

A disconnect between themed businesses and politics is not a new phenomenon. Of course, there is a fundamental contradiction between political awareness and aspirations to create fantasy worlds set apart from the realities of life. The apolitical tradition of themed places goes back to the beginnings of modern-day theme parks, as introduced by Walt Disney after the Second World War. In *Disneyland's 10th Anniversary Show* (1965), Walt Disney takes a rollercoaster ride with the Shah of Iran Mohammad Reza Pahlavi and his wife Farah Diba. Their visit to Berlin two years later caused massive protests, out of which West Germany's radical left-wing Red Army Faction (RAF) was born. Disney's promotional film features additional politically problematic content, showing entertainment acts like the dance performances of Native Americans, a boat driver 'shooting' animatronic hippos during the rainforest ride and the introduction of a separate lane for female drivers. The fact is that such political elements were quickly removed in favour of the 'comfort and pleasure' inherent in the theme park concept. This was transferred into themed shopping malls, and ease was promoted as 'the new justice' (Koolhaas 2001a: 415). Initiatives to remove a statue of an indigenous man with a lollipop headdress and to silence the scream accompanying a pair of suspended mechanical female legs in the West Edmonton Mall are examples of ill-considered themed scenography that were corrected due to public demand (Kent 2018; Williamson 1992: 227).

A rising awareness of the political dimension of scenography was reflected in the introduction of politics as a major theme of the Prague Quadrennial in 2015. In fact, scenography is increasingly being acknowledged as possessing the potential to 'operate critically and responsibly by ... exploring the possibilities that exist for intervening in the world's becoming' (Irwin 2017: 115). As a result, finding ways to align the political basis of scenography with the role of political art in Postmodern times, especially in a commercial context, could lead to greater exposure and impact than it has in the theatre. As Fredric Jameson urges, political art should aim for new representations of 'the world space of multinational capital ... in which we may again begin to grasp our positioning as individual and collective subjects and regain a capacity to act and struggle which is at present neutralized by our spatial as well as our social confusion' (1991: 54). While this notion is accepted and practised in the theatre, commercial themed environments are lagging behind. They still fail to acknowledge the importance of public spaces as stages for progressive political thought, whether they are privately owned or not. In this situation, the only chance scenography has of reclaiming a culturally relevant position within the capitalist market agenda, 'designed around individually customized experiences', is in the hands of its creators – to stubbornly 'insist on politico-economic embedded-ness of design practices' in order to make a difference (Rufford 2018: 13).

7

Spatial Flexibility: A Yearning

7.1 The fluidity of market changes

A report published by the Center for Gaming Research at the University of Nevada for the period 1984–2018 shows a change in gaming versus non-gaming revenues in Las Vegas from 1999 onwards (Schwartz 2019). In 1999, non-gaming income on the Strip, including earnings from accommodation, food, beverages and other services, took the lead, accounting for 51.91 per cent of total revenue and leaving gaming behind for the first time with 48.08 per cent (2019). Since that year, gaming profits have continued to decline, eventually sinking to 34.34 per cent in 2018, while other sources of income have increased steadily over the last two decades, reaching up to 65.66 per cent in the same year (2019). In the course of this development, themed shopping malls in resorts and multipurpose complexes have advanced as tourist magnets and have joined the city's top earners, headed by entertainment on the Strip.

The connection between 'enjoyment and spending', as demonstrated in Las Vegas, has forged an unbreakable alliance between theatre and commerce, propelling scenographic architecture forward as a spatial intervention whose purpose is solely to entertain (Chung in Chung et al. 2001a: 292).[1] But consumption, according to Baudrillard, is not a function of enjoyment. It is 'a function of production and, hence, like all material production, not an individual function, but an immediately and totally collective one' (1998: 78). Baudrillard defines enjoyment as 'consumption for oneself, as something autonomous and final', which essentially does not relate to consumption itself (1998: 78). Through the system of exchange, he explains, all consumers are equally involved (1998: 78). Placing the scenography of shopping malls in the context of production, rather than consumption, corresponds with the role scenography plays in the theatre, where it produces meaning. According to Fischer-Lichte, scenography, as it generates meaning through perception, becomes responsible for forging stronger ties between the theatre and other aspects of life. In doing so, contradictory as it may sound, it influences the modernisation of public spaces as theatre (2013: 219–39). Even if no entrance fees are charged, this 'modernisation' process has little to do with the utopian projects expounded by Richard Wagner, Louis Napoleon Parker and Max Reinhardt, who strove towards the appropriation of public space in order to make theatre accessible to everyone. Charles Moore's remark on Disneyland, that 'payment' is required to enter a 'public' life (Chung in Chung et al. 2001a: 280), is just as relevant to themed shopping malls. Since Disneyland and the Walt Disney World Resort first opened their doors, attracting dazzling numbers of visitors every year since,[2] the Disney empire has helped establish a modern-day themed culture, where paying to participate in this special form of public theatre is taken for granted. Although the income from its theme parks is just part of Disney's annual revenue,[3] theming is nevertheless highlighted as a serious business.

As places that lie between rationalisation and simulacra (Ritzer 2005: 180), themed shopping malls have, both conceptually and stylistically, crossed over from their Modernist heritage into Postmodern times, remaining in transition in the same way as the retail business itself (Lyotard, cited in Ritzer 2005: 178, note no. 2). Consequently, the scenographic approach to entertainment architecture perfectly fits the unclear distinction between real and unreal (Ritzer 2005: 180). Not only Robert Venturi asserts that iconographic architecture can be 'universal and contextual – in terms of both technology and the content of its signage', but he also sees the danger of taking a scenographic approach to architecture, because 'it becomes an exotic theatre rather than an actual place' (Chung et al. 2001b: 616–17). Venturi's notion of the 'city as theatre' refers to the production of meaning through the use of surface facades, turning public spaces into scenes 'with the theatre serving as the central point of reference' (Brejzek 2015: 26–7).

As theatre and architecture have merged, scenography has been caught in a crossfire of negative criticism. In his essay 'Rappel à l'ordre: The case for the Tectonic', Kenneth Frampton equates scenography with packaging and commodification, and argues against the reduction of architecture to scenography (1996: 516).[4] Meanwhile, an extensive body of theoretical work from the field of scenography has brought to light a multidisciplinary understanding of its impact on the 'negotiation of the triad of space, surface and spectator in both the production of space and the production of meaning' (Brejzek 2015: 28). The Ibn Battuta Mall and the Villaggio Mall have a unique connection to Las Vegas, as they are examples of scenographic architecture built on land taken from the desert with no specific meaning or relation to the rest of the city. Yet this is not the case in all the examples examined in this book. Achille Mbembe points out the conflict at The Palazzo Montecasino caused by private developers inserting 'borrowed imagery' into the city matrix in a response to the failure of politics to deal with problems of the actual place – the city centre. '"Exotic" local and faraway styles', he notes, 'are theatrically restaged in simulated environments, where they contribute to the paradoxical reconciliation of place and ephemerality' (2004: 401). The discord precipitated by the ornamentation of the city, Mbembe contends, is grounded in a reaction to Modernist architecture and the observation that banning ornamentation from facades produced buildings that functioned as ornaments themselves (Venturi et al. 1979: 192).

The resulting counter-movement brought about a new position on the use of scenography for the purpose of internalising public space through themed narratives. In the process, Mbembe argues, changes are pushed into the structure and character of the city: 'By saturating its public, social, and cultural spheres with the commodity and by asserting its identity as a city of consumption mindful of the status of the ornament, the arts of commercial entertainment, and imaginary travel, Johannesburg has become a metropolis' (2004: 402). Similarly, borrowed images and ornamentation at the Ibn Battuta Mall and the Villaggio support the desire of developers in Dubai and Doha for their cities to be recognised as globally relevant tourist and shopping destinations, far beyond the places' local identity. Slogans tempting visitors to the United Arab Emirates – 'Discover all that's possible' – and Qatar – 'Where dreams come to life' – clearly contain promises of adventure and new experiences delivered through the consumption of fantasy, which here delivers real outcomes. As it redirects the perception of the city's identity, 'unreal' scenographic imagery is exchanged for real, hard currency.

The quote that concludes the famous discussion on ornament in or as architecture in *Learning from Las Vegas*, namely, Pugin's statement that 'It is all right to decorate construction but never construct decoration' (Venturi et al. 1977: 163), echoes the historical outcry of architects against scenography as a built environment. Although they have had their fair share in the modernisation of public space as theatre, themed shopping malls have overstepped the boundaries of accepted taste. In their daring and exaggerated use of all the stylistic devices at their disposal, including ornamentation, the malls have indeed expanded the production of meaning. At the same time, however, they have reduced the discipline's potential to simple mimicry. The misuse of scenography for commercial purposes in this way, especially in the last fifty years, has discredited it as a cultural practice in the production of space; it has eliminated scenography's essence, which, in the theatrical context, is to comment, react and perform, not make spaces 'pretty'. It has reintroduced 'decoration' into theoretical discourse, a term banished by Modernist pioneers Edward Gordon Craig and Adolphe Appia more than a century ago. Today, environmental scenography is understood as agency, a driving force that carries the potential to change public space into a realm of in-between, a place not entirely real and yet not completely simulated, but live and vivid because of its performativity.

Located in the crack between the Modernist continuity of narrative and Postmodern fragmented images and historical recollections, scenography in themed shopping malls plays with visual references. The result is a spatial construct that does not tell us how things were but how they could have been. Describing the idealisation of villages and small towns as a themed narrative, Jon Goss chronicles the tendency to mix historical design with commercial content in themed entertainment complexes developed in the late 1960s and the 1970s. His examples include the Spanish American hacienda in the Pruneyard Shopping Center in Campbell, California, the thirteenth-century Italian village in the Borgata of Scottsdale in Arizona and quaint New England Pickering Wharf in Salem, Massachusetts (1993: 23). Montecasino follows the same impulse, and it is also recognisable in the Ibn Battuta Mall, the Villaggio and even Terminal 21. These narratives, Chung explains, draw on Walt Disney's concept of Disneyland and the Celebration community (1996),[5] selling 'a lifestyle, not architecture' (2001a: 296). To some degree, they attempt to recreate 'an old way of life' (2001a: 296).

The approach to architecture and urbanism visible in themed environments such as Disneyland or Celebration exposes Disney's small-town nostalgia as a symbol of 'lost youth and the intimate scale of a midwestern small towns' (Gottdiener 1997: 126). The liminal character of this nostalgia is represented by the neo-traditional propensities of new urbanism and reflected in the hope that transitioning towards a simplified lifestyle, implementing social control and blending out the complexities of life will bring back a lost sense of community. The strategy, of course, has clear limitations, not least, Goss notes, concerning wistfulness for the traditional marketplace (1993: 28; Bryman 2004: 48). As they transform architectural references to times gone by into scenography, themed shopping malls bring fragments of the city into a filtered narrative free of any inherent danger to a real social order (Goss 1993: 28). 'The contrived retail carnival', Goss says, 'denies the potentiality for disorder and collective social transgression of the liminal zone at the same time that it celebrates its form' (1993: 28). Scenographic interpretations of urban nostalgia and the sentiments that accompany it act as collective tranquillisers; they can bring about hardly any kind of change.

Walt Disney's initial goal, to create a theme park that captured spatial reality in a cinematographic way, an animation that came to life, has since been taken over by the developers and designers of themed shopping malls. With the swift advances of digital technology, efforts to recreate 'downtown' as a cinematographic experience have turned form back into image, appropriating the scenography of public spaces as sets for photography and video: the flat surfaces of mock city facades are compressed further into the 'depthlessness' of digital images by cell phones, tablets and cameras. In 2012, before the Villaggio Mall was expanded with Via Domo and Sportif Street, a large backdrop of a shopping street along a Venetian canal covered the entire arched entrance to Sportif Street. A gondola was positioned in front of it, offering visitors the opportunity to step into it and take a photo, posing in the fantastic setting of Venice. A life-sized image, traditionally employed in theatre to indicate the place, is also used as a backdrop on studio sets for film and television productions. The frame of the camera lens cuts the connection to the image's immediate surroundings and tricks the viewer, who completes what is missing by imagining what has been left out of the shot. This expanded impact of theatricality through technology is similar to the digital extension of existing spaces using the post-production techniques common in film, video and television. In this way, scenography in themed malls fulfils a social role by satisfying the human need to experience a thrill. The impact is facilitated by exposure and engagement with different worlds or dream locations, and the promise of excitement without risk, which is already exploited by the film and video game industry. As Goss points out, the shopping mall 'sells paradoxical experiences to its customers, who can safely experience danger, confront the Other as a familiar, be tourists without going on vacation, go to the beach in the depths of winter, and be outside when in' (1993: 40).

Apart from this temporary, short-lived effect, the original intention and expectation for themed places to capture the spirit of animated films were bound to fail. The gap between the direct presence of the audience in an existing theatrical space and the spatial and temporal displacement of a filmic experience was always likely to remain unbridgeable. The very nature of a discontinuous cinematographic space is supported by editing techniques, aspect ratios, shot sizes and the endless possibilities offered in post-production for the creation of computer-generated images (CGI). As a result, it is extremely difficult to compare this with the immediacy of exploring real environments and being exposed to them through all our senses, even if we accept that there is no such thing as an unmediated experience (Copeland 1990: 42; Giesekam 2007: 6; Power 2008: 149). For now, even virtual-reality technology, which makes possible the simulation of movement, walking and exploring computer-generated surroundings, is clearly limited when it comes to our sensory input. It restrains our experience, showing us only fragments framed by the rendered matrix of a 3D model and the VR device. In fact, this technology establishes yet another level of 'depthlessness', enabling scenography to produce synchronous double 'flatness'. Therefore, comparisons of the experience of space (and scenography) offered by a mall to that offered by film, television or video games[6] are only relevant at a metaphorical level, as these two things are not truly comparable. Contemporary scenographic discourse covers an in-depth discussion of the difference between direct exposure to immediate surroundings and exposure facilitated by technology.[7]

The disappearance of (three-dimensional) shopping space also happens due to market saturation, demographic changes and developments in the retail economy, among other influences. Abandoned shopping malls, remembered in the archives of independent American websites, offer a source for the history of this architectural typology based on 'shared social experiences' and 'personal perspective' (Lepik 2016: 7). Scholars warn, however, that the destiny of some ill-fated shopping centres 'does not mean that [the mall's] influence is waning; its demise in native habitats only serves to enhance its legibility within the urban fabric' (McMorrough 2001: 202). The phenomenon is explained as a consequence of the rapid spread of a specific urban plan, which peaked, at least in the United States, as early as the 1970s. Still, its persistent use has fundamentally transformed the way we apprehend the traditional shopping street, offering clues about the contemporary perception of the city, because 'an understanding of the urban street becomes an understanding of the mall. As gentrification, commercialization and theming – all forces implied by the logic of shopping – become increasingly accepted as strategies to revive the city, the artificial effectively becomes the real' (McMorrough 2001: 202; Shields 1989: 13). Apart from its location and attractivity, Shields suggests, the 'carnivalesque appropriation as a site for *flânerie*' has become a determining factor in the mall's success or failure (1989: 13).

Apparently, the disappearance and abandonment of suburban malls are neither straightforwardly related to the themed shopping experience nor a process with an inevitable outcome. The New South China Mall (2005),[8] located in the city of Dongguan, spent its first decade struggling to defend its investment. This megastructure, with 5 million square feet (464,515 square metres) of leasable space, twice the size of the Mall of America, was the first themed shopping mall in China. Divided into seven zones, it depicts iconographic references to Venice, Rome, Paris and Amsterdam, as well as drawing associations with Egypt, California and Caribbean landscapes. It includes canals with gondolas, smaller versions of the Arc de Triomphe and St. Mark's Campanile, and an accompanying theme park. When it opened in 2005, the New South China Mall had only twelve tenants, and the vast commercial space stayed empty. It took ten years and two attempts to revitalise the place, which welcomed less than 10 per cent of the mall's visitor capacity during this period. As Johan Nylander reports, the last attempt at modernisation finally came to fruition in 2015, thanks to an updated marketing strategy that targeted middle-class citizens.[9] According to mall consultant Ted deSwart, the mall's shaky start was rooted in the choice of location in a city without an airport and no highway connection to the mall itself. The initial attempt to target an upper-class clientele in a prefecture-level city like Dongguan, which is inhabited mostly by the middle classes and immigrant workers, had to be reconsidered in the process of modernisation (Nylander 2015). Being the first mall of this size in China, the lack of local experience running such a megastructure cannot be disregarded.[10]

Looking at the bigger picture, by the middle of the financial crisis in 2010, up to 20 per cent of malls in the United States were struggling to stay in business (Bruegmann 2016: 94). The financial challenges facing these shopping centres were a reality in Europe as well. In 2018, the BBC reported that 'about £2.5bn worth of shopping centres and retail parks [were] up for sale in towns and cities across the UK' (Harby 2018). Canterbury City Council struck a deal to take over Whitefriars Shopping Centre and, in Shrewsbury, Shropshire Council bought three malls to support their regeneration (Harby 2018). Robert Bruegmann attributes the decline to an overbuilt retail market, time-consuming shopping in oversized spaces, an increase in specialised stand-alone stores with quicker access to products and better-targeted offers, and, of course, the rising popularity of online shopping (2016: 95). While experts in the field propose a shift towards the experience economy,[11] other strategies are already in place to cope with the situation. The reverse transformation of some abandoned malls into avenues with parking spaces in front of the shops (e.g. what was once the Park Forest Plaza near Chicago) is bringing shopping streets back to their original layout, the starting point from which Gruen developed the pedestrian concept of the mall (Herman 2001: 472). Daniel Herman argues that shopping centres never became 'true city centers' but, as some malls deteriorated and the concept was abandoned, conditions were established to reconfigure those areas back into the real city (2001: 472).

Financial crises and declines in revenue concern shopping malls and city centres alike. In order to stay profitable, Bruegmann notes, both sides need mixed-use environments that draw people and address the basic human needs to socialise and be entertained. These two aspects were always closely linked to the traditional marketplace (Bruegmann 2016: 96–7). Over a period of ten years, Ellen Dunham-Jones and June Williamson followed the refurbishment of abandoned or economically weak shopping malls. Their consequent report presents numerous cases of interventions in the United States, including reappropriating space for healthcare facilities (Vanderbilt Health at One Hundred Oaks Mall in Nashville), offices (Google at Mayfield Mall in Silicon Valley, Ford at Fairlane Town Center in Detroit) and educational institutions (Austin Community College at Highland Mall in Austin, Texas). These examples all demonstrate a more sustainable approach to existing infrastructure (Dunham-Jones et al. 2017: 84–91). Replacement, on the other hand, a strategy that 'requires the demolition of the retail building and its substitution with a completely new urban area', demands substantial investments without any guarantee that the new concept will be successful (Cavoto et al. 2015: 183). Cinderella Mall in Englewood, Colorado, built in 1968 and demolished in 1999, was replaced with Englewood Civic Centre, a combination of city hall and outdoor retail, which due to the lack of profitability is facing another revamp only twenty years later (Arnold E. 2019). As reported by Englewood Herald, redevelopment that will include building of a new 'area with a hotel, offices, apartments and smaller retail' is currently under consideration (2019).

Following recent demographic shifts in US suburbia, Gregory Marinic describes the transformation of two old shopping malls: the Sharpstown Mall, Houston, into an ethnic cultural and service hub for immigrant communities and the Euclid Square Mall, Cleveland, into 'church street'. In both examples, Marinic points out the malls' conscious spatial configuration, which facilitates alterations for alternative purposes in a 'higher performance future' (2016: 47–67). In response to an increase in the Latin American population and the abandonment of national mid-range retailers in the late 1990s and early 2000s, the Sharpstown Mall (1961) was gradually remodelled as a Latin American marketplace with 90 per cent occupancy by non-national retailers, 6,000 square feet (557.42 square metres) of space for community activities, a new performance stage in the food court and additional performance spaces for local musicians and cultural events (Marinic 2016: 54–7). Similarly, the rise of the African American community in the suburb of Euclid has brought about a change in the tenants of the Euclid Square Mall (1977), which now uses 60 per cent of its space to host faith-based non-profit organisations, including twenty African American churches, services, an online Gospel radio station and piano lessons, alongside minimal retail.[12] Using these malls, Marinic reminds us of the temporality of architectural practices, especially in the commercial retail industry, and the need for a sustainable approach that will allow participatory modification from original intentions and the reinforcement of cultural identities in accordance with the 'basic human desire to occupy and redefine space' (2016: 48, 52).

Within the framework of 'future alternative uses, the notion of flexibility, and an ability to respond to shifting socioeconomic conditions', scenography, due to its inherent temporality, offers the ideal tool for redefining the mall according to changing market conditions, and for the intentional design of adaptable spaces (Marinic 2016: 65). Ultimately, as Nicholas Jewell argues, 'a mall does not exist as a real place, rather as an abstract idea that constitutes a "brand", but one which is rendered inflexible over time and hence impotent by its physical materialization' (2001: 334). Going back to the origins of enclosed markets in ancient Greece, where this book began, Jewell's remark recalls the real meaning of the term 'agora', which does not necessarily refer to a specific place or building. Rather, it is a more fluid construct, referencing the 'market' or 'doing business' in a broader sense – the acts of meeting and exchange. In this context, scenography makes a wider range of participatory interventions possible, supporting the market's intrinsic fluidity, which architecture alone cannot do. It is designers' responsibility to combine the two and use the potential of scenographic architecture to approach a sense of the atmosphere of the marketplace without trying to reconstruct the place itself.

A shift towards spatial concepts whose performativity does not rely on themed narratives, but rather on its relation to our bodies, 'produce[s] a state of heightened attention to the here and now' and sharpens our perception of the spaces we occupy, which may prove a useful strategy (Ursprung 2014: 13). Such environments do not necessarily need a plot: the choreography of movement and guidance through the space is facilitated purely by the surroundings (2014: 18). There is still a lot to learn from contemporary theatre and the way scenography 'renders place eventful through interventional means' (Hann 2019: 127), and how it uses ephemeral and environmental tools to translate the literal and physical not into 'seeing' but into 'feeling'. Regarding the transfer of knowledge, Lyotard suggests that it should be about the organisation of actualised data into an efficient strategy and their rearrangement in a new way in order to invent a 'new game'. Bearing this in mind, the process calls for imaginative input from future creators (1984: 43–4, 51; Sarup 1993: 139). Using scenographic vocabulary, the important thing is that focus is placed on scenographic 'doing' instead of scenographic 'being'.

7.2 Flexibility matters

Approaching commercial scenography as a form of agency corresponds with the perception of shopping as 'the most unstable, most short-lived, and most vulnerable to the threat of decline and obsolescence' (Leong 2001: 130–1). Its dependence on external factors such as fashions and the economy forces it to make constant adjustments. Affluent, Postmodern consumers are predominantly concerned with the symbolic value of purchased goods and are influenced in their choices both by their surroundings and by ever-changing trends, which can shift buying behaviour quickly (Hahn 2002: 20). Closely tied to changes in consumer preferences, 'shopping ... is continually being reinvented, reformulated, and reshaped to keep up with the most subtle changes in society' (Leong 2001: 130–1). Barbara Hahn's analysis of consumer behaviour in the United States shows that, in the late phase of capitalism, the market does not dictate buying habits as it used to (2002: 14–21). Now, it is consumers who influence the market, forcing it to adapt to their current needs and elusive desires (2002: 20).

A constant state of flux is quite a challenge for architecture, a discipline that is anchored in stability and durability, with restricted possibilities for transformation. It is also important to acknowledge that the themed shopping malls discussed here were all designed by architects whose portfolios do not demonstrate any experience in designing for the stage. This dichotomy, Thea Brejzek argues, needs to change in order to 'embrace the politicized domestic as a mirror of society, a conceptual move that would allow for the urban city-builders of today to finally become world-makers in the theatre' (2017: 77). The nature of scenography, rooted in instability, short-lived and always changing, offers a possibility to reflect upon life and its developments through performativity. In contrast to the regular shopping mall (Herman 2001: 528, 531), the scenographic architecture of themed shopping malls seeks attention. Its goal is to stand out, draw in potential consumers and secure profits. But, as appearance is placed in the foreground, visual oversaturation masks a total absence of depth and true performativity. At best, it is a stand-in, a placeholder, filling in the blanks in the absence of true scenographic agency. It seems as if the architects who were once at the forefront of generating advanced ideas in support of performative spaces have indeed exposed themselves as amateurs in the realm of scenography (Brejzek 2017).

Progressive ideas of flexible theatrical structures and performative architecture, such as the Fun Palace by Cedric Price and Joan Littlewood (1961), Space Theatre and Study '63 by Sean Kenny (1960–3), The Walking City by Archigram (1964) and Le théâtre de l'Est parisien by Josef Svoboda (1972–4), among others, emerged in architectural and theatrical discourse during the 1960s and 1970s (Bittner 2016: 75; Tabački 2014: 67–92). It was at the same time that shopping malls started to spread across the United States. Apart from obvious differences between these two types of architecture, both flexible theatres and the early shopping malls were initially based on an ambition to create an overlap between culture and society. But that is where the similarity ended. Post-war experiments in the field of performative architecture found fertile soil in contemporary spectacles and their 'en-suite' theatres (the Cirque du Soleil, Dragone), shaking the foundations of traditional theatre architecture by connecting avant-garde ideas with commercial entertainment. Conversely, shopping-mall developers looked the other way. Business was good and there seemed to be no need to contemplate change. By the time themed malls started to emerge, the consequences were apparent. Instead of moving towards progressive architectural and theatrical concepts, developers held onto the neo-traditional theming strategies put forward in Disneyland. As a result, themed malls became static shells of images that lacked any ability to adapt: they used scenography's capacity to imitate reality but left out its performativity and power to reflect dramatic content through spatial and atmospheric developments. In the process of merging scenography with architecture, performativity was thus left behind, and an important connection that could have kept up with the continuously evolving patterns of retail commerce was never formed.

Even though the success of the daring architectural experiments of the 1960s is difficult to gauge because they were never built, they still have the potential to serve as inspiration and a challenge to search for new solutions appropriate to our times, which would be able not only to follow the rhythm of economic fluctuations but also to stay ahead of them. They present a view of architecture as an agent that 'would enable things to happen ... it would rid itself of its conventional expectations and concentrate on the possibilities of its use' (Pimlott 2007: 288). At the moment, the dominant urban-design strategies for revitalising and transforming shopping malls to cater to contemporary needs usually involve demolition and rebuilding (Williamson in Lepik et al. 2016: 219–27). Demographic shifts, changes in consumer behaviour and general market saturation are often given as the reasons for some shopping malls' inability to stand the test of time on the free capitalist market (Williamson in Lepik et al. 2016: 222). However, the experience of the last sixty years suggests that flexibility in terms of both theming and use of space could give these urban environments long-term appeal for contemporary consumers as well as for subsequent generations whose shopping habits will, undoubtedly, be different. 'Flexibility of retailing', Sallie A. Marston and Ali Modarres argue, 'enables both producers and consumers to enter into the exchange relationship in a whole range of sites that satisfy both economic as well as cultural needs and desires' (Marston et al. 2002: 90). Expanding the scope of revitalisation strategies could deliver a more sustainable approach. It is also necessary to take into account the significant financial investments required by current strategies such as re-inhabiting, re-developing and re-greening in order to revive city districts or suburban areas (Williamson in Lepik et al. 2016: 221–7). A scenographic approach to themed shopping malls could facilitate the modification of infrastructure and, consequently, of concept design, creating spaces structurally able to shift and grow. If we wish to keep up with the pace of modern technology, exploring this option seems a matter not so much of choice as of necessity.

At the same time, taking such a step would signify a final break from the misuse of scenography in an architectural context, as well as from its negative connotations of superficiality and artificiality. It could remove the last obstacle to grasping the full potential of combining architecture and scenography in spatial design. Establishing a connection between the theatrical and architectonic, fluid and stable, flexible and solid would lead towards more ephemeral structures in which theming would become the catalyst for experiencing specific sensory qualities. Therefore, a deeper understanding of the complexity inherent in the wide range of scenography could be beneficial for everyone involved in the future development, conception and design of themed shopping malls.

Even if this strangely echoes Walt Disney's original intention constantly to expand existing themed infrastructure and so to secure returning visitors, in other words to reinvent themed consumption through scenographic hyper-bodies (Oosterhuis 2003: 17f), a construction that can change its physical shape has nothing in common with Disney's ambition to make illusion believable. Looking at our case studies, the practice of theming established by Disney after the Second World War seems resistant to modification. The scenographic approach described above is a chance not only to move social structures into the future but also to step away from grand narratives and tap into more fragmented, fluid spatial constructs. Taking into consideration the lack of history in newly built places, scenography is a valuable asset when it comes to designing shopping malls. It paves the way for creative spatial interventions that, unlike the current practice of theming, could potentially provide innovative constructs free from direct associations with other places and previous experiences. In turn, this would prevent the mingling of memory and perception, and consequently prevent our responses from becoming automated.[13] As scenography directs our attention towards sensing the immediate impulses of urban environments, we can better reflect upon and react to our surroundings without losing sight of the fundamental aim of public spaces – even if they are privately funded – to enhance feelings of participation and inclusion in city life.

Drawing on Henri Bergson's *Matter and Memory* (1911), Crary reminds us of Bergson's approach to the question of attention as the intersection between memory and perception, and our capacity to have variable responses to stimuli from our surroundings (2001: 319; Bergson 1911: 163). The gap 'between awareness of stimulation and reaction to it ... is equivalent to lived experience, and it is where attention performs a pivotal role' (Crary 2001: 317). According to Bergson, the way sensation is processed 'decides not only the nature of one's perception but the degree of freedom of one's own existence' (Bergson 1911: 244–5; Crary 2001: 317). Locating theming between simulation and reaction could bring back 'lived experience', a component that went missing as a result not of the gradual displacement of the marketplace into enclosed spaces over several centuries, long before themed shopping malls came around, but of the attempts to recreate an archaic image of the city that does not even exist as a real place. If it exists at all, then it is as a collective memory. Crary highlights Bergson's observation that 'the degree of vital autonomy possessed by an individual is proportional to the very indetermination and imprecision with which memory intersects with perception. The more "determined", that is, the more habitual and repetitive one's perceptual response to one's environment, the less autonomy and freedom characterize that individual existence' (2001: 317). In the context of theming, regaining the lived experience and its associated autonomy would mean stepping away from a literal interpretation of exotic and/or historical references. Rather, investing in the creation of innovative scenographic landscapes that allow referentiality,[14] thus opening perceptual responses to new sensory experiences, could prove effective in terms of boosting our imagination and provoking feelings of freedom.

Resistance requires space, and it is here that the conditions for conquering that space might be able to emerge. Gottdiener remarks that the restriction of themed environments 'to domains dominated by consumption' opens the possibility 'for personal self-expression and self-realization through the mode of resistance' (1997: 157–8). But, while consumers can, in theory, practise such resistance by refusing to go to shopping malls at all and, instead, move in the direction of alternative means of consumption, the scenography of themed malls today stands stiff and passive, stripped of its ability to reflect and comment on the silently fanciful versions of the faraway places it references. As such, it cannot support any kind of resistance, whether in terms of physical behaviour or mental exercise (Gottdiener 1997: 158).

Somewhat ironically in this age of information, overexposure to digital images and rapid technological developments, themed shopping malls still cling on to old-fashioned scenographic methods. They do not even attempt to deliver Fredric Jameson's notion of pastiche (Sarup 1993: 146),[15] a melange of references to a 'dead style' that creates an original idea of a place that has never actually existed. Instead, the malls use iconographic allusions to guide us through a three-dimensional image of a dreamland, a warped kind of Neverland where the 'lost' consumers do not stop ageing but disintegrate into abstraction. Drawing a parallel with *Alice's Adventures in Wonderland*, Lefebvre asks, 'So what escape can there be from a space thus shattered into images, into signs, into connected-yet-disconnected data directed to a "subject" itself doomed to abstraction? For space offers itself like a mirror to the thinking "subject", but, after the manner of Lewis Carroll, the "subject" passes through the looking-glass and becomes a lived abstraction' (1991: 313–14). This seems to suggest that, for a day, we might escape all the troubles of reality by giving free rein to our abstract selves. As all forms of escapism, however, it is of course extremely short-lived. The only thing we are left to hold on to is the fantasy, which remains for as long as we buy things. When it is all over, our pockets will be empty but our purchases will still be there, letting us continue to imagine that it was not just a dream and that, in fact, we lived by consuming the make-believe.

7.3 Double-crossed by urban dreams

Changes in cultural conditioning brought about by the aesthetics of commerce visible in today's themed shopping malls are the outcome of a long development process (Bittner 2016: 75). Regina Bittner uses Raymond Williams's notion of culture as a social practice and way of life in order to explain the shift in perception that occurred in the first decades following the

Second World War. This shift has led to identifying consumption in shopping malls with a cultural practice (2016: 75–6). Considering the shopping malls' sociocultural dimension as a way of learning about the world, Alain Thierstein stresses the importance of spatial and relational proximity for the creation and accumulation of knowledge (2016: 140). This occurs 'through the interaction of individuals who are close to and familiar with one another, both spatially as well as through networks, and who are both prepared and capable for such interaction' (2016: 140). Some studies, such as that conducted by Ana Aceska and Barbara Heer on malls in the divided cities of Johannesburg and Mostar,[16] draw attention to the mall's potential 'to rework boundaries of race, class, religion and ethnicity' (Aceska et al. 2019: 47). As places where social encounters and exchange are combined with physical nearness, Thierstein expects shopping malls to stay relevant despite the presumed expansion of e-commerce (Aceska et al. 2019: 47). According to Aldo Legnaro and Almut Birenheide, the origins of the term 'consumption' correspond to ideas of accomplishment and completion. This line of reasoning suggests that the world of commodities offers consumers a glimpse of what they might become. In doing so, it shows the path to achieving the highest degree of this experience, namely freedom (Legnaro et al. 2007: 273).

Rem Koolhaas raises the same topic, noting the promise of liberty reflected in strolling through the shopping mall (2001a: 412). As a capitalist marketplace, however, the mall offers only the semblance of freedom (Haslett 2000: 75). In her discussion on culture and ideology in *Marxist Literary and Cultural Theories*, Moyra Haslett remembers Karl Marx's perspective and the fundamental inequality inherent not only in the production but also in the exchange of commodities (2000: 76). The Marxist position holds that the loss of freedom starts at the very beginning of the production process – in the exchange of labour for liberty (2000: 76). The end result is social alienation, as the only relationships are 'between things, and relations between persons become material' (2000: 76). If the capitalist market's relationship to materiality necessarily implies alienated social relations based on the loss of liberty, how can consumers in the scenographed environment of the shopping mall, whether their presence there is 'aimless or purposeful', then have anything at all to do with an experience of freedom? At best, Haslett argues, this experience might bear traces of what Marx called 'commodity fetishism', a phenomenon based not on social relations but on monetary value (2000: 76). As social relations are thus sidelined, there is no possibility for personal freedom, which, according to Marx, is only possible within a community (Haslett 2000: 35).

Looking at our cognitive capacities, Crary highlights Bergson's argument: 'The fact that our nervous systems not only can delay response to a stimulus but have the possibility of "variable" responses is a precondition of a free and autonomous subject' (Crary 2001: 319). This indicates that environmental scenography is able to satisfy the human need for social encounters by enhancing culture as a social practice, and to expand the limits of freedom in shopping malls by going beyond flatness, artificiality and aestheticisation. In the early 1960s, Jane Jacobs warned that the over-aestheticisation of city streets could easily become pretentious and that reducing the approach to architectural accentuation could achieve more interesting results (1993: 197). Her work evaluates the role played by accents in the city, which can distinguish themselves from their surroundings either by their physical characteristics or by their function (1993: 197). Jacobs stresses the importance of non-commercial accents in the city, even if these are just empty spaces, for bringing visual balance to public life, especially in districts dominated by trade (1993: 198). The consequence here is that, ultimately, the only way to 'break free' in the shopping mall environment is to break (out of) its structure, to use scenography as a tool to catapult consumers out of the world of commodities and back into life itself.

As markets, shopping malls stand between a limitless number of offers and an equal amount of mistrust.[17] The shiny world they project dazzles consumers into denial regarding the conditions in which the products are made (Böhme A. 2012: 134). In themed shopping malls, this effect is even more significant. As they submerge consumers in their theatrical settings, the distance needed for ideological criticism is diminished (Tabački 2015: 75–6). Ritzer remarks on the risk of drifting into the 'dreamworld of consumption' because it is difficult for consumers to see 'the realities of the economic system in which they are immersed' (2005: 65). The result is a significant reduction in scenography's capacity to reflect critically upon architecture and its representational role in the media-driven phase of late capitalism, challenging the way in which it 'might work as cultural critique' (Rufford 2015: 18). Drawing on architectural historians Louise Pelletier, Dalibor Veselý and Hilde Heynen, Juliet Rufford highlights mimesis as an important scenographic approach to advance 'architecture's social, cultural or political dimensions' (2015: 21). Nevertheless, the potential of scenography to address social, cultural and political issues by imitating architecture comes up short in the 'expression and interrogation of human thought, action and experience' due to market demands, especially in places where capital is realised (2015: 25–6). In themed malls, the use of scenographic architecture to convey 'abstract ideas and conceptual structures' and to reflect on everyday life is not exactly what investors are looking for. On the contrary, it is a denial of the outside world and the attendant security of oblivion that draw consumers and ensure financial survival, especially in times of crisis.

Themed shopping malls not only mirror the relationship between theatre and architecture, but they also highlight the contradiction between the critical possibilities of scenographic architecture and the conditions dictated by the realities of late capitalism and private ownership (Heynen 1999: 198, cited in Rufford 2015: 28–9). Chuihua Judy Chung observes that the 'use of commercial private space as public property has become so commonplace that themed commercial districts and shopping malls are preferred over outdoor plazas and streets for public activity' (2001a: 280). In contrast with the transitory and connecting nature of arcades and department stores, which form an integral part of the open city environment, the 'cultural experience' established by staged interiors and promotional events is internal, occurring within the inward-looking spiral of the shopping mall (Böhme A. 2012: 70). Here, scenographed escapism and a parallel reality replace the connection to urban infrastructure, even in shopping malls located within the city (Terminal 21, for example). Some theoreticians point out the decline of enclosed shopping malls, looking at the current trend of bringing the heightened consumption aesthetics of retail complexes to open urban spaces (2012: 65–6). Even though themed shopping malls are predominantly bounded, controlled environments, they still clearly aspire to participate in the trend through their themed narratives. This aspiration, unfortunately, is doomed to failure. Michel de Certeau explains that the city concept functions as 'a site of transformations and appropriations, the object of interventions, but also a subject continually being enriched with new attributes: simultaneously the plant and the hero of modernity' (1985: 127). As the city, he elaborates, 'acts as a totalizing and almost mythic gauge of socio-economic and political strategies, urban life allows what has been excluded from it by the urbanistic plan to increase even further'. In other words, the city setup directly contradicts the socioeconomic politics of shopping malls (1985: 127). When the city 'is no longer a theatre for programmed, controlled operations' (de Certeau 1985: 128), themed commercial environments can make no claim to either a real urban feeling or the aesthetics of urban space.

Apart from the split between the themed environment and the city, the alienation experienced in shopping malls also comes from another direction. The expanded reach of scenography in themed malls as 'sensorialised'[18] space and its interactive effect on consumers showcase the advantage of commercial environments over the theatre. In traditional stage settings, the performance is usually separated from the audience. Theming, on the other hand, transforms scenography into a commodity, which can then be consumed by our senses as an experience. As such, these constructed spaces can facilitate a feeling of belonging in a way totally different from regular consumption: the theatricality of themed shopping malls makes it a two-way process. The 'experience economy' of late capitalism is not only about a set of financial transactions whereby products change hands and belong to consumers. Rather, it offers a larger dimension of consumption. Exposed to the scenographic environment of the themed mall, consumers risk being 'consumed' themselves, perhaps not by zombies, as in George

A. Romero's horror classic *Dawn of the Dead*,[19] but by the equally theatrical politics of space. 'They don't know what they want,' says Ken Foree's character Peter about the zombies attacking the shopping mall, 'but they remember that they felt good here'. In Romero's film, the mall is simultaneously safe (the protagonists have everything they need to survive) and a place of imminent danger (from their 'former selves'). Above all, however, it is a battlefield of human alienation in the middle of a consumer paradise. In real-life malls, the scenographic strategies implemented to immerse consumers in the themed environment leave hardly any possibilities of escape. Baudrillard's metaphor of the shop windows as 'sites of consumption', mirrors in which we cannot see our own reflections, emphasises alienation through consumption (1998: 192). According to Baudrillard, 'the individual ... is absorbed in the contemplation of multiple signs/objects, is absorbed into the order of signifiers of social status, etc. He is not reflected in that order, but absorbed and abolished' (1998: 192). As Baudrillard repeats the word, so the scenography of themed shopping malls uses all its available sensory arsenal again and again to absorb consumers into the theatricality of the place. In doing so, it completes the process of alienation by fully separating them from themselves. It is a kind of modern-day Mephistophelian enchantment – the extraction of the soul through the exposure of the body. Emphasising its 'ludic' aspects, Baudrillard refers to consumption as 'the tragic dimension of identity' (1998: 192).

7.4 Responsibility in the final act

Defining site-specificity as a theatrical term, Arnold Aronson describes a three-way exchange: between the scenography and the site, between the site and the spectator, and between the spectator and the performance (2018: 194). At first glance, themed shopping malls seem to embody all three relationships. A performance text in the traditional sense, which converses with the site, is exchanged for the narrative provided by the place itself. This equates with the general tendency in environmental theatre to shift the focus 'from the text and its meanings, to the signification of the physical space and to the centrality of the spectator within that space' (Aronson 2018: 211). Hiding the bare, meaningless construction underneath, the scenographed fronts of shopping streets invite mall visitors to stroll and discover. They impose layers of signification, tell stories about past times and civilisations, provoke 'communication' with the surroundings through signs and the mimicry of exotic places. But the themes are artificial and do not bear any connection to the site of the shopping mall; even though they 'talk' to consumers, aiming to amuse, fascinate, even educate, as scenography does in the traditional theatre, they neglect the immediate urban space. The result is a gap between inside and outside, between the structure and location of the site and its scenography.

The relationship between the site and the spectator is just as tricky as the one between scenography and the site (Aronson 2018: 194). The shops and restaurants indisputably involve consumers in a dialogue with sales and service personnel, though to a far lesser extent than with the products. After all, consumption is still the main goal of a visit to a mall. They are tested (gadgets), moved around (objects), tried on (clothes), eaten (food) and utilised (amusement park infrastructure). They are bought, exchanged, refunded and, in some cases, even stolen. They are not only admired, desired, praised, but also disliked and rejected. Throughout all this activity, the question remains, which site do we mean when we talk about themed shopping malls? Is it the interior, because this is where the transformation happens? Is it the imagined place of their themed narrative? Or is it the site of the building itself? Whichever position we take changes the themed place's site-specificity and theatricality. However, as utterly inward-orientated environments, themed shopping malls, like theme parks, allow performativity to happen only within the staged space.

Finally, the third aspect of site-specificity is the conversation 'between the spectator and the performance' itself (2018: 194). In the themed environment, there is a constant, ongoing transformation of the spectator/consumer into a performer/consumer and vice-versa, facilitated through physical presence and activity. In one of the central aspects that constitute the performativity of everyday places, the consumer is an inseparable part of the performance (2018: 204). Therefore, the conversation that takes place at this level is a negotiation within the consumer themselves, a kind of living situated between performing and observing, acting and standing aside.

Site-specific theatricality did not come about solely through the deliberate intentions of developers. The phenomenon, recognised by Debord in the 1960s as 'the society of the spectacle', was also a result of the neo-liberal capitalist agenda, which misused theatricality to disguise its own essence, namely profit. Applied scenography, used for centuries to support the accumulation of capital, became a mask moulded around meaningless spaces, elevating them to the status of tourist attractions that consumers had to visit in order to experience their uniqueness. As Jon Goss notes, 'Sophisticated techniques of illusion and allusion enable [developers] to create an appropriate and convincing context where the relationship of the individual to mass consumption and of the commodity to its context is mystified' (1993: 21). Over time, the early Modernist 'nostalgia for authentic community' and the promotion of shopping centres 'as an alternative focus for modern community life' have given way to extravagantly themed concepts (Goss 1993: 22). Developers and designers have constantly expanded the scope of spaces' added value. As a result, scenographic settings have become increasingly elaborate, seeking emotional and behavioural responses through environmental conditioning (1993: 30). Looking at the phenomenon from a global perspective, different shopping malls that have the same theme come very close to what Nicholas Jewell describes as a 'universal model', which is, by definition, less and less site-specific (2001: 329). Representing an idea rather than a real place, the Venice experienced in shopping malls in Doha, Las Vegas, Macau and Greater Noida is a product of a 'consumerist belief-system' and, as such, not particularly different in all these locations (2001: 329). In spite of all the efforts to establish a unique shopping environment by promising a certain lifestyle or even culture, the spread of a specific theme weakens diversity. As themed malls celebrate a single unified concept around the world, local features are ignored or undermined, accentuating the identity crisis inherent in malls as a 'global product' (2001: 329–30).

It is nevertheless important to acknowledge that theming is also 'a systemscape that encourages variety and differentiation' (Bryman 2004: 168). Although perhaps within limits, it does still allow variation and diversity, a chance to break out of the cultural homogeneity imposed by globalisation (2004: 168). To paraphrase Schechner, regardless of whether the themed mall is a new manifestation of a sacred place, it is undeniably a special kind of immersive stage.[20] Through culture, as 'the human mode of adaptation', we use these malls to re-establish the relationship between ourselves and the environment (Ingold 1992: 39). Montecasino, the Ibn Battuta Mall, the Villaggio and Terminal 21 all reflect globalisation as a process implemented not from the outside but by developers from within the region, who have modified their chosen themes according to their own cultural milieux, even in cases where that theme has been followed rather literally. In any case, feeling or sensing a 'place' is not necessarily related to its physicality.

Where theming fails as a scenographic strategy is not only in its inability to provide a deeper historical context or, in an anthropological sense, locality (Jewell 2001: 337) but also in its insistence on blending out the power structures that accompany that context. This is reflected in theming's abridged representation of history,[21] especially when meant for educational purposes. In general, the simplification of architectural styles neglects the political systems, terms of labour and inherent exploitation that built them. Knowledge of these systems leads to a better understanding of the socioeconomic conditions of a historical period, which cannot be separated from the period's architecture. This does not mean that themed places should be obliged to deliver only totally accurate reconstructions of historical facades. On the contrary, scenography offers a unique opportunity to engage with the past creatively – to exaggerate, caricature, emphasise and extract, but all in order to convey the true essence of the atmosphere and power of the historical period in question. 'Reasoning about history', Debord argues, 'is inseparably reasoning about power' (1970: §134). The danger for theming and scenography lies in remaining between these two approaches, which, unfortunately, is exactly where all the shopping malls we have discussed are situated. They neither offer the full complexity of the past nor are they daring enough to transmit atmosphere through an artistic interpretation of past times. At best, they merely satisfy curiosity: 'The consumer's relation to the real world, to politics, to history, to culture is not a relation of interest, investment or committed responsibility – nor is it one of total indifference: it is a relation of curiosity' (Baudrillard 1998: 34). Furthermore, Baudrillard sees the attendant denial of reality as occurring through overexposure to signs and warns us to 'beware of interpreting this gigantic enterprise of production of the artificial and the cosmetic, of pseudo-objects and pseudo-events, which is invading our daily existence, as a denaturing or falsifying of an "authentic" content' (1998: 34, 126).

In their aim to establish a clear identity, some themed malls fabricate a clash of different cultural references, blending them together into one eclectic whole (Jewell 2001: 341). The resulting amalgam of stage sets satisfies the curiosity Baudrillard talks about but also confuses and disorientates (Pimlott 2007: 298), making the stretch between local and global difficult to grasp. The question is, however, whether it is really appropriate, nowadays, to insist on architectural and anthropological authenticity and locality in shopping malls. Is it not designers' task to address changes both in retail business and in 'individual identity in relation to space and place' (Jewell 2001: 345), to provide alternatives to existing concepts in urban spaces instead of trying to mimic the long-lost image of the agora, forum, bazaar and medieval town square? A deeper understanding and evaluation of scenography as a cultural practice could prove its capacity to confront the tension between local and global beyond a dull imitation of architectural forms. Should our task not then be to target the resolution of the form in order to enable reconciliation with its image?[22] This may be our only chance to reintroduce newness into urban settings since it was lost in the transition of the marketplace into enclosed spaces. Intertwining and exchange between architecture and scenography as spatial design disciplines has been fruitful throughout the history of theatre, triggering new concepts in both fields. As the nature of the marketplace continues to evolve, would it not be astute to take something from it and, following Lyotard's advice about the transfer of knowledge, use everything we have learned so far, rearrange it and so invent a new game (Lyotard 1984: 43–4, 51–2; Sarup 1993: 139)?

Overall, it is clear that the theming of the marketplace cannot be viewed separately from scenographic techniques and their manipulative influence on place and locality. What has changed in the course of time, as critics have noted, is a gradual shift from the consumption of goods and services towards the consumption of place in the form of experience (Ritzer 2005: 156). The themed shopping mall, as a truly Postmodern phenomenon, celebrates this tendency by collapsing the binary relation between 'real' and 'imaginary' and by acknowledging polyculturalism, kitsch and popular culture (Sarup 1993: 166). Regardless of the current decline in traditional sales channels, they firmly stand their ground. A consumer survey conducted by Christopher Donnelly and Renato Scaff at Accenture Retail clearly shows the dominance of buying experiences over purchasing things.[23] According to them, 82 per cent of millennials[24] prefer conventional stores to shopping online (Donnelly et al. 2013: 4). In order to improve performance, Donnelly and Scaff suggest retailers make 'the customer experience just as important as [the] product' (2013: 7). Theming, as a marketing strategy to tackle difficulties in profit realisation, forms an unbreakable bond between a 'desirable personal experience and the corporate activity of money-making' (Gottdiener 1997: 126). Ultimately, as Terry Eagleton observes, the driving force of 'mass' culture, in shopping malls as well as everywhere else, 'is not the inevitable product of "industrial" society, but the offspring of a particular form of industrialism which organizes production for profit rather than for use, which concerns itself with what will sell rather than with what is valuable' (2003: 30).

This change in focus, along with the Postmodernist bias towards 'figural signification' based on visual sensibility (Sarup 1993: 168), has propelled scenographic techniques into places of commerce as a design approach to the simulation of 'otherness'. Looking more closely at Postmodern signification shows that it essentially asks the same question raised by Kathleen Irwin in regard to the showing-doing of scenographic agency: What do cultural practices actually *do*? (Irwin 2017: 111–23; Sarup 1993: 168). In the realms of popular and consumer culture, scenography sets the stage for the simulation of parallel realities, adding to Postmodern confusion and the increasingly troubled differentiation between what is 'simulated' and what is 'real' (Haslett 2000: 79–80). It opens the stage door to consumers, allowing them to become part of a theatrical performance in which they can choose their own roles. This, however, comes at a price in both the literal and metaphorical senses. High commissions have to be paid in the business of exchanging money for experiences, where one needs to consume in order to participate and, thereby, belong. Following Walt Disney's escapist idea of immersion in a fantasy as a way of forgetting the daily grind (Bryman 2004: 109), the scenography of themed shopping malls is stripped of the function that would set it apart from mere decoration, namely, of engaging critically with the world by holding a mirror to it, reacting to its aesthetic, social, economic and political issues. No matter how spectacular themed spaces are, their one-dimensional meanings and fundamental inability to respond to the dynamics of life are also in danger of becoming dated and boring (Beyard et al. 2001: 254; Jewell 2001: 333; Ritzer 2005: 175). Some scholars, such as Pine II et al., suggest that the 'economy must learn how to stage revolving productions, just as theatres did long ago', in order to secure returning visitors who will be willing to pay their admission (1999: 67).

In Disneyland, Walt Disney aspired to create a themed environment that would continue to grow and adapt, offering visitors something new every time they returned. Judging by visitor numbers and annual revenues, the gradual extension of existing attractions with new experiences, in themed shopping malls as in Disney resorts, drives the economy forward. It ensures demand for goods and services, and thus supports the foundation of the experience economy as laid out by Pine II et al. (1999: 67). From the scenographic point of view, however, this approach does not solve the problem. In fact, it multiplies it by expanding 'simulacra'. Rob Shields describes the nature of this transformation, which neglects 'the spatial metaphors expressing social status ... power, time, prestige, order ... reason, etc.', as removing the sense of place and denying locality (1989: 6). None of this is much of a surprise. The application of scenography in commercial themed settings and environmental simulations is a logical next step in the long history of interdependence between the theatre and the marketplace. The more significant issue here seems to be the way scenography is used to 'imitate the topography of the town', to facilitate 'a transformation of everyday space into festival space' using 'spectacular decor, crowd control, and even mass emotional manipulation', and to mimic fairs, carnivals and amusement parks, altogether exploiting the ancient human need for gatherings (Aronson 2018: 30). As a result, themed shopping malls are not only contemporary manifestations of the fairs and festivities held in town squares (2018: 30); they are a special kind of theatre building wrapped in an envelope of consumption.

This situation is not, by any means, a new one. Since the Renaissance, Marvin Carlson points out, commercially oriented theatres 'have sought the business heart of the city, the marketplace, and have developed much closer architectural affinities to such commercial structures as banks and shops than to museums and churches, typically individualistic and isolated from the street facade row' (1989: 98). Before theatre was transferred into permanent facilities, Carlson says, 'companies set up their booths in the fairs and marketplaces alongside those of the purveyors of vegetables, chickens, clothing, and gingerbread' (1989: 98). The incorporation of theatres into mixed-use cultural structures, such as art centres, during the second half of the twentieth century weakened the architectural identity of theatre buildings that was established in the nineteenth century. Together with the environmental and site-specific tendencies that developed from the 1960s onwards, this led to theatrical space being enclosed in broader urban infrastructure, similarly to court theatres being incorporated into Renaissance palaces (1989: 96–7). Nowadays, of course, real-estate interests lead this transformation, 'using the theatre as a cultural emblem for the enhancement of surrounding commercial property' (1989: 97).

In the realm of consumerism, themed shopping malls as theatres provide the stage and scenography for a sudden see-saw of roles between performers and audience at any given moment, depending on the way we choose to participate. They provide a safe zone for consumers to go beyond their association with a particular social group, and to define themselves instead according to a certain lifestyle (Jewell 2001: 372). Their specific commercial context, which attracts so many people every year, means that themed shopping malls have to deal with the issue of theatrical representation in society, of how the performances of such places 'are to be interpreted and integrated into the rest of [the spectator's] social and cultural life' (Carlson 1989: 2). As they grapple with this question, the malls offer a legitimate alternative to the existing options available in cities. Unfortunately, the misuse of theatrical techniques for superficial cosmetics and an unproductive exchange between architecture and scenography clearly indicate the necessity for change. The possibility is there, no doubt about that. We only need to figure out how to redirect future developments towards addressing communities' need for theatricality and finding ways in which scenography could meaningfully carry out its social purpose within this particular commercial dimension.[25]

Consumers have different expectations for different shopping malls, which are reflected in their buying behaviour (Dennis 2005: 54). Bearing this in mind, the sensible appropriation of theatricality in themed commercial environments in order to enrich cultural life, instead of being used exclusively to empty consumers' pockets, could prove beneficial for the shopping malls' longevity. If we assume that people will continue to go out and engage with places of consumption, regardless of the obvious expansion of 'dematerialised' shopping (Ritzer 2005: 209), scenographic strategies will likewise continue to make an impact on consumers. But, while the malls continue to redefine the 'marketplace as icon', shifting the paradigm of how we define place and space (Warnaby et al. 2018: 281), scenographic agency is stumbling around in the dark. In these settings, the question is no longer what scenography *does* but rather what it might *enable* if used to its full potential.

A rising aversion to enclosed spaces, a growing demand for the uniqueness of the open, natural environment of the city (Coleman 2006: 4–5), a 'renewed interest in synaesthesia in art, architecture and design', and an awareness that the 'relationship between ourselves and buildings can no longer be merely visual' (Ursprung 2014: 21) collectively offer an opportunity to rethink the possibilities of scenographic interventions in an urban context. 'With the decline of star architecture', Philip Ursprung argues, 'demand for buildings that act on various senses simultaneously, buildings that one can touch, smell or hear, that evoke mental images and resonate in one's memory' has been spreading (2014: 21). Imaginary scenographic representations of the 'ideal city' once inspired real cities' architecture, as the principles of perspective from Baldassare Lanci's set for *La Vedova* (1569) were applied in the design of Florence (Carlson 1989: 23–5). The ability to effect change in the audience's perception of the urban setting seems to have been lost over the centuries. Yet if we tried to pinpoint the dramaturgy of the shopping mall, a story weaving together a variety of different tales from each shop, service and entertainment venue, it would be a drama of the marketplace and of the city itself. In this regard, the choice of scenographic narrative in themed shopping malls follows a logical path. Nonetheless, the use of scenography to imitate existing urban structures instead of exploiting a unique opportunity to experiment and push boundaries, aping old concepts rather than testing new ones, seems to be a misfire on a rather grand scale.

Of course, as has been acknowledged here, the mall's primary purpose is to make money, not to engage with progressive architectural and theatrical concepts. Still, considering the interdependent relationship between people and their surroundings, a process of 'forming and constructing' the self through the environment and 'forming and constructing' the environment through human interaction clearly demonstrates the power of scenography to alter existing structures through its own agency (Haslett 2000: 36). Despite the necessarily predetermined commercial identity of the shopping mall, scenographic vocabulary offers the tools to 'work upon and transform those contexts' (Haslett 2000: 36). Precisely because it remains within the domain of ideology, scenography, as art itself, communicates with us, in Louis Althusser's words, 'in the form of "seeing", "perceiving" and "feeling", which is not the form of knowing'[26] but a 'sense from the inside' – 'the ideology from which it is born, in which it bathes, from which it detaches itself as art, and to which it alludes' (1984: 174–5, cited in Haslett 2000: 66–7). Therefore, even if it means taking a step back to recall Modernism, which defined itself, at least in part, through a reactive approach to commodification, we must recognize that it is designers' task to take the current situation as a challenge 'not to be a commodity, to devise an aesthetic language incapable of offering commodity satisfaction, and resistant to instrumentalization' (Jameson 1979: 135).

Instead of creating 'dream' worlds, dreaming about exposing the hidden and subconscious makes all the difference. Real life, in shopping malls or elsewhere, as Lewis Mumford reminds us, provides more than enough material for both dream and culture, but we have to keep in mind that 'both are warped by pressure of fear, power, ancient traumas, or newly awakened desires' (1996: 60). The overlap between reality and fantasy in themed malls pushes us into a somnambulant state of mind. Like the lost soul of Special Agent Dale Cooper,[27] we drift between identical rooms veiled with theatrical red curtains, which are drawn aside to show us a different setting every time we step through them. We do so only to discover that while our bodies are awake, we remain in a dream, though not our own. If shaking the body alone does not help us find our way out of this double-layered dream dimension and hypnosis, shall we then not try to concentrate on how we could use scenography to 'key up' attention in an attempt to wake up our minds?

As we think about how to break out of the loop in which we are caught, and how to reach for the stars, this 'in-between' state is actually not as bad a place to be as one might think. On the contrary, dreaming is not, depending on how you look at it, reserved exclusively for escapism: it is also a creative hub where anything might be possible. It is the place where innovation starts, is it not? And if so, is this not also where responsibility begins?

Notes

Introduction

1. Alan Bryman defines 'anticipatory localisation' as a process whereby 'firms adapt the principles of Disneyization (or indeed any globalizing force) to local conditions in anticipation of how they are likely to be received' (2004: 162).
2. König (2008: 13).
3. Gernot Böhme explains how, in the developed phase of capitalism, *needs* (das Bedürfnis) are exchanged for *desires* (das Begehren) (1995: 64). See also König (2008: 15).
4. 'Urban entertainment centre' is a general term designating a mixed-use type of shopping mall that combines retail with a variety of entertainment offers (Hahn 2002: 10).
5. According to Arnold Aronson, 'site-specific theatre should be a performance that is created specifically for a particular site' (2018: 174). In the context of themed shopping malls, site-specific theatricality is triggered by mutual interaction between scenography created for a particular site and performativity set in motion by consumer's actions in it.
6. See Rem Koolhaas and Hans Ulrich Obrist, 'An Interview with Denise Scott Brown and Robert Venturi' (in Chung et al. 2001b: 595).
7. See *Learning from Las Vegas* (Venturi et al. 1979).
8. In today's Las Vegas, Mark Gottdiener notes that a 'nostalgic yearning for the ambience of urban pedestrian culture continues to grow and define new themed environments' (1997: 152).
9. See Haslett's reading of Althusser's concept of total ideology (Haslett 2000: 66).
10. Bryman (2004: 48).

Chapter 1

1. Until 1912, the sultans held the executions of rebels and criminals at the Djamaa-el-Fna market in Marrakesh (Baran 2004: 14).
2. According to Jon Goss, places traditionally associated with liminoid experiences include 'seaports and exotic tropical tourist destinations, and

NOTES

Greek agora, Italian piazza, and other traditional marketplaces' (1993: 28; Turner 1982).

3   A covered walkway or porch in the ancient Greek architecture of an agora, meant for public use.

4   *Qaysariyya* refers to the roofed streets or buildings used as a market in Islamic architecture (Goitein 1999: 194; Hmood 2017: 264). A *khan* is a building with a colonnaded courtyard used for the storage and exchange of goods, as well as for lodgings (Hmood 2017: 264). The typology is similar to the caravanserai, which hosted merchants, animals and goods along trade roads (Hmood 2017: 268). A *wakala* is an urban building that combines the functions of a khan, a warehouse and a market (Petersen 2002: 302). According to Walter M. Weiss, archaeological sites in Syria, Turkey and Morocco enable us to trace the origins of bazaars as roof-covered halls and arcaded courtyards back to the fourth century BCE (1994: 58). See Sze Tsung Leong's diagram 'Evolution of retail types' (2001: 28).

5   See 'Marketing and Scenographic Seduction' (Hann 2019: 108–11).

6   See 'A Tale of Two Stoas' (McK. Camp 2015).

7   'Whether the configuration of mannequins or the ordering of fruit baskets, these are acts of staging that are of scenographic order' (Hann 2019: 126).

8   In the latter cases, ground floors either were transformed into shops with arched colonnades along the facades, as in Ypres Cloth Hall, Belgium, or included separate covered walkways as part of larger structures built for trading, as in the Ring in Wroclaw, Poland (Coleman 2006: 20–2).

9   Engraving entitled 'Covered market' by Bertrand, fifteenth century. Available online: www.alamy.com. Image ID: DC9B92. Accessed: 12 June 2019.

10 The richly ornamented, neo-gothic Antwerp Exchange (1531) initially had an open courtyard, which, in the nineteenth century, was covered with a glass roof supported by an iron construction extravagantly decorated with floral ornaments.

11 Sabil-Kuttab-Wakala of Sultan Qa'it Bay (1477), Cairo, Egypt.

12 In the Ottoman Empire, apart from the souks and halls for selling merchandise, they incorporated wells, baths, lodgings for caravan travellers, stables for camels and storage areas (Weiss 1994: 59–60).

13 See images in Coleman (2006: 24–5).

14 'Architecture … may contribute to [man's] mental health, power, and pleasure' (Ruskin 1898: 13).

15 For a detailed description of the typology of passages and arcades, see Geist (1982: 24–6). See also Böhme A. (2012: 51–3).

16 'In 1857 the first electric streetlights in Paris (near the Louvre)' (Benjamin 1999: 834).

17 See Geist (1982: 29). For panorama and diorama, see Brockett et al. (2010: 168–70, 185–7).

18 'Setup of the panoramas: View from a raised platform, surrounded by a balustrade, of surfaces lying round about and beneath. The painting runs along a cylindrical wall approximately a hundred meters long and twenty meters high' (Benjamin 1999: 528).

19 See a list of the most important shopping arcades built between 1788 and 1925 in Geist (1982: 94–5, 97).

20 See a watercolour painting of Passage des Panoramas from 1810 that illustrates the obstruction of a narrow passage for visitors because of overhung and protruding goods in front of the shops: image 202 in the catalogue section, Geist (1982). See also image 222 in the same section of Passage Choiseul as an example of scenographic signs in the shapes of products and protrusions of display boxes and vitrines in front of the shops.

21 See the catalogue section in Geist (1982): the Galleria Vittorio Emanuele II (images 131–49).

22 For arcade images, see the catalogue section in Geist (1982): the Galleria Umberto I in Naples (images 175–6), the Upper Trading Rows in Moscow (images 160–5) and Cleveland Arcade (images 64–6).

23 See Jules Claretie, La Vie à Paris, 1895 (Paris 1896), pp. 47ff. as quoted in Benjamin (1999: 121).

24 See the catalogue list of shopping arcades and passages in Geist (1982: 122–8).

25 Some shopping arcades also had shops on the upper galleries, for example, The Strand Arcade in Sydney (1891).

26 Images of KaDeWe's White Week interiors: ID 249133, 249134 at the Landesarchiv Berlin. Images of Tietz department store: ID 40004147, 40004148, 40004149 at the Stiftung Preußischer Kulturbesitz. Available online: https://www.bpk-bildagentur.de/shop. Accessed: 19 September 2019.

27 For shop window dressing in KaDeWe during White Week, see image ID: 249135 at the Landesarchiv Berlin. See also Whitaker (2013: 77).

28 Warenhaus Tietz, Leipzigerstraße, Berlin, 1900.

29 Kaufhaus Tietz, Alexanderplatz, Berlin, 1911. Landesarchiv Berlin, image ID: 201 828.

30 As Richard Longstreth asserts, this development initially prompted department stores to establish branches on city peripheries to attract suburban shoppers (2016: 53). This approach was not very successful, however, because they had no influence on the type of stores subsequently erected around these outlying branches, which often created opportunities for competing businesses instead of securing their own profits (Hahn 2002: 35). Instead, developers offered department stores with better rent conditions and allowed them to choose retailers that would complement their assortment of goods, thus reducing competition from emerging chain stores (Hahn 2002: 36). Taking over the strategies used by department stores since their very beginnings, Longstreth also notes, the environments created in shopping malls continued to support the idea of consumption as a leisure activity, and so the legacy of shopping arcades and department stores was carried over into the prosperous decades following the war (2016: 53).

31 In some cases, department stores even initiated the construction of such malls (Hahn 2002: 35; Longstreth 2016: 53).

32 One of the most prominent examples is Market Square in Lake Forest (1916), which has been referred to as 'the first planned outdoor shopping center' (Ritzer 2005: 11). It is essentially a town square with two groups of terraced houses positioned across from each other. Each group contains shops lining the ground floor and residential apartments above them.
33 See Oc et al. (1997: 8).
34 'By 1976, branch sales amounted to nearly 78 per cent of total department-store business nationwide' (Cohen 1996: 1067).
35 Some of the most prominent examples include Cameron Village in Raleigh (1949), Northgate Mall in Seattle (1948–50), Shoppers' World in Framingham (1948–51), the Emporium in San Francisco (1950–2), Northland in Detroit (1954) and Marshall Field's Old Orchard Shopping Center in Skokie, a suburb of Chicago (1956), to name only a few (Hahn 2002: 33).
36 See a chronology of shopping malls in the United States in Chung et al. (2001b: 461).
37 According to Gruen, his first draft of the shopping-mall concept was presented in the article he wrote for a special issue of the *Architectural Forum* journal in 1943. The illustrations were done by Elsie Krummeck. See Gruen et al. (2014: 126, 166–7).
38 Because of his involvement in the Viennese Theatre Group, Gruen had the opportunity to see many successful shows on Broadway in the late 1930s. He collaborated with influential stage designers such as Donald Oenslager with the Viennese Theatre Group, and with Norman Bel Geddes on the world exhibition's 'Futurama' pavilion for General Motors.
39 Gruen describes how the showcases in Lederer de Paris were lit with strong reflectors 'like the ones used in the theatre' (Gruen et al. 2014: 140). Simone Bader mentions how Gruen's theatrical background is demonstrated in the extravagant facade of Grayson's in New York (Lepik et al. 2016: 13).
40 See 'Air Conditioning' for a description of Southdale's air conditioning system (Leong et al. 2001: 117–20).
41 Frank Lloyd Wright has criticised Southdale for environmental damage (Gruen et al. 2014: 303).
42 'On a Sunday soon after its opening, when the stores were closed for the Sabbath, 75,000 people drove to Southdale just to walk around the new complex and window shop' (Teaford 2016: 108).

Chapter 2

1 According to Tanner Oc and Steven Tiesdell, there were over 20,000 suburban malls by the end of the 1970s. See Oc et al. (1997: 1–20) as cited in Warnaby et al. (2018: 277).
2 See 'the effects of mall renovation on shopping values, satisfaction and spending behaviour' (Chebat et al. 2014).

3   Barbara Hahn credits Kirwan (2000); Muhlebach (1998: 73); Shields (1992: 1–2) as the source of the term 'entertainment or lifestyle retailing'. See Hahn (2002: 115).

4   See package holiday offers to visit the Mall of America for a day or explore the West Edmonton Mall for four days. Available online: https://www.mallofamerica.com/visit/packages; http://www.andersonvacations.ca/products/explore-west-edmonton-mall. Accessed: 23 June 2017. See also König (2008: 76).

5   They include Galaxyland Amusement Park, Mayfield Toyota Ice Palace, BRBN St., World Waterpark, Deep Sea Adventure and Adventure Golf Course.

6   There are beds in the shape of a Victorian coach and a truck, while elsewhere the themes take inspiration from waterparks and igloos. The Polynesian rooms, for example, include a rocky wall with vegetation between the stones that surround a bathtub, richly sculpted bed legs drawn out into fish-shaped columns, artificial palms, bamboo furniture and a mural of a seascape.

7   Coleman (2006: 78).

8   Four submarines, introduced in the mid-1980s, were used to take visitors on an underwater tour of the lake. The sea life, including fish, sharks and turtles, was not the only attraction: the bottom of the lake was scenographed with rocks, ornaments and sunken riches, all of which added to the overall experience of the underwater adventure. Because of a decline in public interest and high maintenance costs, the submarine tours were discontinued in 2005, leaving the submarines to function as stationary scenography in the lake till 2012, when they were eventually removed.

9   The third themed street in the mall, organised around T&T Supermarket on the second floor, still retains architectural and decorative elements associated with China, even though the 'Chinatown' sign was removed in 2012. The strong orthogonal geometry of the railing, simplified *paifang* (arch construction) and red lanterns are scenographic details that still give this area a themed aspect despite the fact that it is not currently restricted to businesses conceived around a single theme.

10 The amusement park's initial theme, which included Camp Snoopy, ended when the rights to Charles M. Schultz's Peanuts franchise were lost, and was replaced with the Nickelodeon Universe in 2008.

11 Coleman (2006: 83).

12 Crayola, Lego and American Girl.

13 Barbara Hahn mentions a group of five stores in suburban Riverside, Illinois (1870), as well as small commercial centres in Roland Park, Maryland (1890), Lake Forest, Illinois (1913), Forest Hill Gardens, New York (1909–12) and Tyrone, New Mexico (1914–15). As Hahn emphasises, all these early examples of collected shops provided only comestible goods, which contradicts the conception of the mall as providing a variety of services and goods. See Hahn (2002: 30).

14 See the Missouri Department of Natural Resources report 'Country Club Plaza: History and Significance'. Available online: https://dnr.mo.gov/shpo/survey/JAAS072-R.pdf. Accessed: 25 May 2019.

15 See the Missouri Department of Natural Resources report 'Country Club Plaza: History and Significance', map Country Club Plaza Shopping Center, figure 2: *c.* 1940. Available online: https://dnr.mo.gov/shpo/survey/JAAS072-R.pdf. Accessed: 25 May 2019.

16 'Es simuliert und ersetzt als ideale und angepasste künstliche Version eine andernorts bestehende echte Struktur' ('It [the mall] simulates and replaces an actual structure that exists elsewhere as an ideal and adapted artificial version') (Böhme A. 2012: 60).

17 For a historical overview of Highland Park Village, see this article published in *D Magazine* in 1988: https://www.dmagazine.com/publications/d-magazine/1988/april/highland-park-village/. Accessed: 25 May 2019.

18 *Mudéjar* is a rich architectural style in which Islamic decorative elements are applied to medieval European styles, characteristic for post-Islamic Iberia.

19 See Said (1979: 49–72); Jones (2012: 76) regarding the term 'imaginative geographies'.

20 Edward Said gives the example of Western representations of the Orient (Said 1979: 49–72, 68).

21 For a detailed case study of Desert Passage, see Beyard et al. (2001: 160–7).

22 Available online: https://www.citymetric.com/horizons/doha-building-shopping-centre-outdoor-air-conditioning-878; https://ecgolf.com/News/December_2018/Nine_upcoming_attractions_in_Qatar_2019. Accessed: 7 April 2019.

23 Available online: http://www.air2o.net. Accessed: 7 April 2019.

24 The Center for Gaming Research at the University of Nevada, Las Vegas.

25 See Parmley 2017.

26 As Bryman recognises, the 'expenses associated with supplying the physical embodiment of the theme in terms of visual, auditory and even tactile stimuli and the costs of training staff to behave in ways consonant with the theme' are a significant part of the investment in keeping the illusion alive (2004: 17).

27 See the plate 'Royal Menagerie, Exeter 'Change, Strand' by Thomas Rowlandson, British Library, 192.b.19.

28 Tracy C. Davis gives the example of public rejection and outrage at the suggestion to exhibit a Canadian moose in the West Edmonton Mall, while dolphins and Arctic foxes were generally accepted (Davis 1991: 8).

29 Gernot Böhme draws on German philosopher Wolfgang Fritz Haug and his *Critique of Commodity Aesthetics* (1986), published in German in 1971, who recognised the change in late capitalism towards the domination of design and packaging that put the 'exchange value' ahead of the 'use-value' of commodities as status symbols. It is not their use that matters, but the monetary ability to own it (Böhme 1995: 45–6).

30 'Bühnen- und Altagswirklichkeit sind so in einander verschlungen; Fantasie als "Unwirklichkeit" und Gegensatz zur "Wirklichkeit" ist für die Spielzeit aufgehoben, ein Ort in dem man die Dinge anders wahrnimmt' (Schechner 1990: 214).

31 'Darstellen heißt entweder ein Abbild von dem zu machen, was ist, ode rein Vorbild für das, was sein soll' (Böhme 2012: 41; Flusser 1994: 35).

32 A critique of seeing shopping malls through a theatrical lens is repeatedly addressed in architectural discourse, among others in *Harvard Design School Guide to Shopping* and *Project on the City II: The Harvard Guide to Shopping* (Koolhaas 2001a: 202).

33 One of its themed venues was in the South African mall Gateway Theatre of Shopping in Durban between 2002 and 2016, when it closed due to economic reasons and a leasing dispute (Suter 2016: 2).

Chapter 3

1 See https://www.bentel.net/portfolio-items/monte-casino/. Accessed: 16 March 2019.

2 See https://www.bentel.net/portfolio-items/monte-casino/. Accessed: 16 March 2019.

3 Lucca, Grosseto, Magliano, San Gimignano and Monteriggioni have walls around their historic centres, built in medieval times to protect villages from the Florentines. Available online: https://www.visittuscany.com/en/ideas/5-stunning-walled-towns-in-tuscany/. Accessed: 9 March 2019.

4 Situated between regional route R511 and Witkoppen Road, the latter bordered on both sides with kilometre-long protective walls, Montecasino stands out among the business compounds and showrooms of motor corporations (Toyota, Lexus, Kawasaki) and the Fourways commercial and residential hub that are its neighbours.

5 The Creative Kingdom Inc.'s in-house publication, *The Creative Kingdom Herald* (volume 1, 2002) gives an overview of the company's activities at the time, including the Montecasino complex.

6 'Montecasino's Nu Metro complex has 15 separate theatres with a total of 3,137 seats, with 560 of these from Il Grande alone' (Saunders 2012).

7 In one corner of the casino area, the monotony of the vast deep blue 'sky' is broken by a sunset painted onto the ceiling.

8 This technique was applied also in the Desert Passage, a themed shopping mall on Las Vegas Strip, before it was revamped into Miracle Mile Shops (Beyard et al. 2001: 164).

9 The side of the Teatro with the stage entrance is especially aged and, on its single surface, shows the images of multiple buildings side-by-side, as in the manner of film and stage sets.

10 Data according to the Dewan Architects + Engineers website. Available online: http://www.dewan-architects.com/work-retail-ibn-batutta.html. Accessed: 13 January 2019.

11 The fountain is enclosed by eight columns whose capitals hold an eight-point star architrave decorated with geometrically patterned grilles (*jali*). The architrave continues upwards to an octagonal semi-dome (*muqarnas*) with incorporated grilles and relief patterns.

12 The *jali*, colourful tiles, ornamental reliefs, merlons in different historical shapes, and blue doors and windows reinforce the Tunisian aura.

13 The column shafts and the walls are covered with painted hieroglyphics and narrative compositions resembling the interiors of ancient Egyptian temples and palaces. The painted surfaces also extend to the ceilings: in one of the shopping alleys, they create a suggestion of a starry night sky, characteristic of the interiors of residential buildings in ancient Egypt.

14 They include elements such as pilasters, mouldings, friezes and engrailed arches. A group of seven double columns in the central hall, above which the architrave holds a red-painted dome, dominates the space. A huge chandelier hanging from the dome illuminates the floral arabesque mouldings that grace its inner surface. Overall, only ochre and earthy orange are added to the monochromatic colour scheme. Yellow, blue and light pink are hidden in corners, used to embellish the floor in the court's central area.

15 The design of the columns, arches and light sources recalls elements of the Sawan Pavilion in the Red Fort, the interior of the Palace of Winds and the Taj Mahal, emblems of Indo-Islamic style from the seventeenth and eighteenth centuries.

16 Although red dominates the colour range, the beams and ornaments are highlighted with violet, blue, yellow, turquoise and green, adding to the intense vibrancy on display.

17 The only exception is the Louis Vuitton shop front. Unlike the others, it has only one additional floor, with huge arched windows between ionic pilasters, a balustrade railing with urns above the cornice and the beginning of a rooftop. The upper levels of neighbouring shops are recessed next to it, creating balustraded balconies decorated with urns on both sides and enabling the Louis Vuitton shop to stand out.

18 A repetitive row of cannelured ionic pilasters also fills the first level above the shop fronts. Impressive mouldings on the door and window frames reference sixteenth-century Italian architecture.

19 Black-and-white tiles and their patterns elevate the visual impact of the floor design from the rest of the mall, where unified tiles allude to the paved streets and walkways in Venice.

20 The lower ground floor houses shops, a supermarket and food stalls.

21 They include triumphal arches, a mosaic floor, ionic pilasters, the geometry of the door grilles, fountains, and crowned lion heads in the men's restroom that mask the taps and shoot water from their open mouths. In the ladies' restroom, a round marble basin with multiple taps stands free like a fountain, surrounded on three sides by huge mirrors between ionic pilasters. Above the circular basin, a frieze frames a rectangular light panel, suggesting an atrium around the *impluvium* in a way characteristic of ancient Roman *domus* architecture. Unlike the rest of the themed elements thus inspired by the city of Rome, the fourth wall is covered with a huge print of the Jardin du Luxembourg with a view towards the Pantheon in Paris. Multiplied in its mirrored reflections, this image announces the theme on the next floor.

22 The wall along the walkway towards the restrooms is moulded into a cartoon version of a train at a station, with silhouettes of passengers cut out of the large mirror inserted between the open doors of the carriage. The yellow line indicating the gap between the train and the edge of the platform stretches along the wall and leads towards the restroom entrances. Underground

signs decorate the wall and the floor in front of the doors, which are painted red with tube-shaped glass windows. Inside the restrooms, the walls combine mock bricks and white tiles, while the yellow line along the floor and an enlarged print of the London tube map extending across the cubicle and restroom walls maintain associations with the Underground.

23   The fourth and fifth levels of the mall are food courts.

24   A sign in the form of a giant rolling pin indicates the restroom entrance on the fourth floor. Inside, exposed brick walls serve as the background for differently coloured basins that look like kitchen bowls, above which the exact same bowls serve as lamp shades. A mirror frame in the shape of a chopping board and compositions of crockery in the alcoves continue associations with the food court. In line with the theme of Fisherman's Wharf, a sculpture of a crab holds the restroom sign above the door on the fifth floor. The walls here are covered with dark slatted wood. Additional design elements include round mirrors that look like portholes, ring buoys framing the mirrors and wooden barrels serving as basins.

25   The sixth floor is occupied by the Cineplex, as well as a few extra shops and services.

26   Even though the mall's overarching theme is an airport terminal, the building's interior, which houses various themed segments, is just basic contemporary architecture. It is indeed stylistically characteristic of modern airport terminals, but there is nothing specifically 'terminal-esque' about it; this type of interior design is applied to all sorts of buildings. All the other examples discussed here are immersed in the themed concept with very few references to contemporary architecture, or none at all.

Chapter 4

1   Alan Bryman differentiates between the terms *Disneyization* and *disneyfication*: the latter is used to refer to the 'trivialisation and sanitisation' of the literature (e.g. fairy tale narratives) and history. In a more general sense, it means to take something and simplify it for the market and merchandising. *Disneyization*, on the other hand, relates to the application of the principles of the Disney theme parks/resorts in wider social, economical and recreational sectors, including restaurants, shopping malls, resorts etc. (Bryman 2004: 5–13).

2   Although there are some exceptions, merchandising, as extended form of consumption of goods derived from the brand, rarely relates to the spatial scenographic settings, but to the theme or brand itself. Themed casino-hotel Luxor in Las Vegas has a shop selling variety of products related to the Egyptian theme (Bryman 2004: 94). The gift shop of the German Historical Museum in Berlin sells 'themed' mugs, plates, postcards and other items with prints of Karl Friedrich Schinkel's scenography for *The Magic Flute* as light motif. For more details on merchandising, see Beyard et al. (2001: 127, 130); Bryman (2004: 79ff).

NOTES

3 Bryman distinguishes between two kinds of themed narrative: *external narratives* that depict a source not necessarily related to sold goods and services and *brand narratives* developed around the brand image of the store (Bryman 2004: 38–40).
4 The Disneyland training manual emphasises the importance of an honest smile that comes from within (Bryman 2004: 108).
5 'Economies of scope refer to the advantages that accrue when different products and services are combined' (Thierstein, cited in Lepik and Bader 2016: 133).
6 Bruegmann (2016: 93–4).
7 Of course, the birds are not alive; they are merely realistic-looking props.
8 This practice still continues today. A 250-metre-long aeroplane is installed in front of Terminal 21 in Pattaya.
9 Chung gives this information on different scales applied to the architecture and transportation at Disneyland (2001a: 276).
10 Explaining the role of scenography, Anna Viebrock points out that scenography holds a 'mirror to social reality' by means of heightened stylisation (Brejzek 2017: 64–5).
11 See *Popular Mechanics*, issue May 1913, 669. The department stores Saks and Lord & Taylor were among the first to use hydraulic compartment lifts for their shop windows. See also Bird (2007: 25–6).
12 See *Popular Mechanics*, May 1913: 669.
13 See *Popular Mechanics*, February 1932: 306.
14 See *Popular Mechanics*, July 1941: 147.
15 See *Popular Mechanics*, July 1941: 147.
16 212 feet.
17 See Fritsch (2018); also: https://lumipixels.com/#. Accessed: 17 July 2019.
18 Aaron Tam reports $645,000 spent by Harbour City Mall on Christmas displays in 2013 (2013).
19 See https://www.bellagio.com/en/entertainment/fountains-of-bellagio.html. Accessed: 17 July 2019.
20 See Wee (2017); also 'Spectra, Marina Bay Sands Light Show: New Water and Light Spectacular'. *Little Day Out*, 31 May 2017. http://www.littledayout.com/2017/05/31/spectra-marina-bay-sands-light-show-new-water-light-spectacular/. Accessed: 31 July 2017.
21 See http://www.laservision.com.au/portfolio/marina-bay-sands/. Accessed: 31 July 2017.
22 See http://www.laservision.com.au/portfolio/marina-bay-sands/. Accessed: 31 July 2017.
23 See Aedes https://www.aedas.com/en/what-we-do/architecture/mixed-use/the-venetian-macao-. Accessed: 17 July 2019.
24 See Aronson (2018: 41).

Chapter 5

1. 'Until ca. 1870 the carriage ruled. *Flânerie*, on foot, took place principally in the arcades' (Benjamin 1999: 841).
2. Desert Passage (today Miracle Mile Shops) 'hosted 300 000 visitors its first weekend and had welcomed 1 million visitors by its 12th day of operation' (Beyard et al. 2001: 162). According to its website, the Villaggio Mall reports over 1.5 million visitors each month (Available online: https://www.qatarliving.com/shoppingretail/villaggio-mall. Accessed: 11 February 2020). In 2017, the Ibn Batutta Mall welcomed 21 million visitors. Available online: https://www.menaherald.com/en/business/retail-entertainment/ibn-battuta-mall-welcomes-21-million-visitors-2017. Accessed: 13 September 2019.
3. Marc Augé referred to the shopping centre as a 'non-place' (Bader 2016: 11).
4. 'I take leave of you now to travel to Inaba, but if you tell me that you'll wait for me like the pine trees that grow there, I'll be sure to come back soon.' Translated from Japanese by Yuka Yanagihara.
5. The poster announcing *Tosca* dates from the 1930s, while the one advertising *Così Fan Tutte* from the 1980s.
6. 'Es wird nicht zuerst etwas wahrgenommen, dem dann – in einem Akt der Interpretation – die Bedeutung von etwas anderem zugesprochen wird, sondern Bedeutung entsteht bereits im Akt der Wahrnehmung' (Fischer-Lichte et al. 2005: 20).
7. It is widely accepted that a pleasant ambient odour has an effect on both consumers' duration of stay and the perceived value of the merchandise (Shashikala et al. 2103: 12). See also Air Aroma, a firm specialising in scent marketing, whose clients include SLS Hotel & Casinos, Nissan and The Ritz Carlton, among others. Available online: https://www.air-aroma.com/clients. Accessed: 5 May 2019.
8. Available online: https://allsense.com.my/retailers/. Accessed: 23 October 2019.
9. See Artaud (1958: 96–7); Aronson (2018: 66).
10. 'Shophouse-style storefronts are often reduced to 5/8 scale (as in Disney's theme parks) to give shoppers an exaggerated sense of importance, transporting them into a looking glass world' (Goss 1993: 32).
11. The shopping malls are 'kept perfect and ageless by personnel who may be employed to do nothing else but constantly polish or touch up the spotless shiny surfaces' (Goss 1993: 32).
12. See also 'Rappel à l'ordre, the Case for the Tectonic' (Frampton 1996).
13. The Triple Five Group reports that the Mall of America has 40 million and West Edmonton Mall 30 million annual visitors. Available online: http://triplefive.com/en/pages/moa/tourism-facts. Accessed: 5 May 2019. The MENA Herald reported 21 million visitors to the Ibn Battuta Mall in 2017. Available online: https://www.menaherald.com/en/business/retail-entertainment/ibn-battuta-mall-welcomes-21-million-visitors-2017. Accessed: 5 May 2019.
14. Available online: http://www.annualreports.com/HostedData/AnnualReports/PDF/NYSE_LVS_2017.pdf. Accessed: 5 May 2019.

Chapter 6

1. See Schechner (1990: 119).
2. The term 'cathedral of consumption' was used by Émile Zola in his novel *Au bonheur des dames* (1882–3) to refer to a department store (Rooch 2009: 17, 19).
3. Available from 2018. https://www.businessinsider.de/why-dubai-has-so-many-malls-2018-11?r=US&IR=T. Accessed: 23 October 2019.
4. See Friemert (1984), plates 62, 67, 72, 75, 81, 98, 104, 113, 114, 126, 128, 130, 133–5, 140, 142, 144–55, 157.
5. Mitchell (1989: 232–3).
6. 'Pastiche is, like parody, the imitation of a peculiar or unique, idiosyncratic style, the wearing of a linguistic mask, speech in a dead language' (Jameson 1991: 17). 'The culture of the simulacrum comes to *life* in a society where exchange-value has been generalized to the point at which the very memory of use-value is effaced, a society of which Guy Debord has observed, in an extraordinary phrase, that in it "the image has become the final form of commodity reification" (*The Society of the Spectacle*)' (Jameson 1991: 18).
7. See Augé (2008).
8. Drawing on Robert Olson's notion of 'the mythotype' (1999), Kozinets et al. list ten characteristics of successful 'mythotypes' that help unfold the narratives behind themed concepts in brand stores (2008: 94): the story needs an open end, realistic content, highly developed technologies, to support order in consciousness, to allow circularity and a return to the starting point, to create a sense of mystery through restricted divulgence of information, to express universal emotions, to immerse the consumer in the content, to assure its omnipresence, and, finally, to include spectacular effects (Kozinets et al. 2008: 94).
9. 'A questionnaire composed of 44 items was successfully administered on, and completed by, 1230 respondents, whose composition is: 298 from Kururu Shopping Center; 216 from Pitt Street Mall; 324 from White Oaks Mall and 392 from Roosevelt Field Mall' (Tsai 2010: 327).
10. Branding identity of the mall.
11. According to research, product arrangement does not relate only to attractive product displays, but also to a 'wide selection of stores, adequate assortments of product brands, quality assurance, reasonable pricing, informative product descriptions, and convenient layout of shopping area' (Tsai 2010: 335).
12. Inspired by Gruen's ideas from *The Heart of Our Cities*, Buckminster Fuller's dome construction to control the climate and Le Corbusier's 'Radiant City', Disney developed the model of a City of Tomorrow, known today as the EPCOT Center, in the Walt Disney World Resort (Chung et al. 2001a: 288).
13. Beiró et al. carried out empirical research in sixteen malls in Santiago, Chile (Beiró et al. 2018: 15). See also Ritzer (2005: 194).

14 See Peter Maxwill, 'Wie ein Bürgermeister seine Stadt rettet' in *Spiegel Online:* http://www.spiegel.de/panorama/gesellschaft/mechelen-wie-bart-somers-die-dreckigste-stadt-belgiens-gerettet-hat-a-1191163.html. Accessed: 12 February 2018.
15 Moilin (1869: 26–9), 'Aspect des rues-galeries'. Cited in Benjamin (1999: 55).
16 'Pocketstop, a notification software vender, said its business was up 33% over the past year among shopping centers' (Leonhardt 2016).
17 Bryman cites Frances Clarke Sayers, who criticised Walt Disney for 'leaving "nothing to the imagination of the child"'. See Bryman (2004: 6); Sayers (1965: 604).

Chapter 7

1 Appropriate terminology for this kind of transformation, where architectural typology morphs into a commercial product by means of spatial design, was introduced in 1987 by Peter Rummell, president of Disney Design and Development, at the American Institute of Architects (Chung et al. 2001a: 289; Lepik 2016: 6). He coined the term 'entertainment architecture' to designate the concept behind Disneyland (Chung et al. 2001a: 289; Lepik 2016: 6), a vocabulary that was subsequently taken up by architects like Jon Jerde. The latter adapted the idea of the mall, seeking to activate attention in order to boost spending by emphasising the spectacular in an urban environment.
2 Disneyland: 12 million visitors per year, Walt Disney World Resort: 30 million visitors per year (Chung 2001a: 289).
3 The Walt Disney Company earned $46.8 billion in 2017. See The Walt Disney Company, Fiscal year 2017, Annual financial report. Available online: http://www.annualreports.com/HostedData/AnnualReports/PDF/NYSE_DIS_2017.pdf. Accessed: 16 February 2019.
4 The essay was originally published in 1990.
5 For more information on the Celebration community, see Ritzer (2005: 112).
6 See Goss (1993: 39).
7 See the *Theatre and Performance Design* journal, special issue on video and projections, volume 3, issues 3–4 (2017).
8 For detailed analyses of South China Mall, see Jewell (2015: 115–25).
9 See Johan Nylander, 'Chinese "Ghost Mall" Back from the Dead?' *CNN International Edition*, 24 June 2015. Available online: https://edition.cnn.com/2015/04/28/asia/china-ghost-mall-return-to-life/index.html. Accessed: 18 February 2019.
10 Mall manager Huang Jincheng explains the difficulties in running the first shopping mall of this size in China. See *Utopia, Part 3: The World's Largest Shopping Mall* (6:45) by Sam Green. Available online: https://vimeo.com/122128694. Accessed: 18 February 2019.
11 Nelson Blackly from the National Retail Research Knowledge Exchange Centre at the Nottingham Business School, who specialises in closing the

gap between academic research in retail and the UK retail sector, argues that the shift towards the experience economy is advisable for the shopping centres' revitalisation (Harby 2018).

12. As Marinic explains, architects and interior designers were not involved in the interior transformation of the Euclid Square Mall (Marinic 2016: 61–2).
13. See Crary's reading of *Matter and Memory* (1911) and *Time and Free Will: An Essay on the Immediate Data of Consciousness* (1960) by Henri Bergson (2001: 317–19).
14. Referential: 'Relating to a referent, in particular having the external world rather than a text or language as a referent' (Oxford Dictionaries). Available online: https://www.lexico.com/en/definition/referential. Accessed: 30 July 2019.
15. 'The poststructuralists argue against this; in their view the concept of the unique individual and the theoretical basis of individualism are ideological. Not only is the bourgeois individual subject a thing of the past, it is also a myth, it never really existed in the first place; it was just a mystification. And so, in a world in which stylistic innovation is no longer possible, all that is left, Jameson suggests, is pastiche. The practice of pastiche, the imitation of dead styles, can be seen in the "nostalgia film"' (Sarup 1993: 146).
16. Case study examples include Greenstone Shopping Centre in Johannesburg and Tržni centar Rondo in Mostar.
17. 'Ich kauf mir einen Hackerangriff' (Seibt 2018). Available online: http://www.spiegel.de/netzwelt/web/darknet-so-sieht-es-in-der-internet-parallelwelt-aus-a-1181621.html. Accessed: 1 March 2019.
18. Pine II et al. (1999: 18).
19. Warnaby et al. (2018: 278).
20. 'Ob die Bühne heilig ist oder nicht, etwas Besonderes ist sie allemal' (Schechner 1990: 219).
21. Bryman calls this aspect the 'distortion of history and place' (Bryman 2004: 169).
22. 'The limitation of the shopping mall lies partly in the fact that it is incapable of finding an expression of "place" that reconciles form and image in a meaningful relationship' (Jewell 2001: 351).
23. See Donnelly et al. (2013). See also Lintec of America's 'Decorative Digital Interiors for Today's Retail Spaces' by Digital Window Graphics.
24. People born between 1980 and 2000.
25. In his analysis of the Postmodern spatial turn through the planning discourse of mall architects, Ian Woodward argues that contemporary shopping centres 'need to be planned with an understanding of community and sense of social purpose, or at least a representation of it, to have longevity' (Woodward 1998: 52).
26. According to Althusser, art allows us to 'see, perceive or feel ideology; science to "know" it' (Haslett 2000: 67).
27. A fictional character in the television series 'Twin Peaks' by David Lynch (1990–1, 2017).

References

Abel, Alexandra, and Bernd Rudolf. 2018. *Architektur Wahrnehmen*. Bielefeld: Transcript.
Aceska, Ana, and Barbara Heer. 2019. 'Everyday Encounters in the Shopping Mall: (Un)Making Boundaries in the Divided Cities of Johannesburg and Mostar'. *Anthropological Forum* 29, no. 1: 47–61. https://doi.org/10.1080/00664677.2019.1588100. Accessed: 14 August 2019.
Adamczyk, Alicia. 2014. 'Holiday Window Displays Light Up New York City'. *Forbes*, 25 November 2014. https://www.forbes.com/sites/aliciaadamczyk/2014/11/25/holiday-window-displays-light-up-new-york-city/#374ab8436d07. Accessed: 25 May 2019.
Ajzinberg, Aleksandar, and Biljana Sovilj. 2010. *Stilovi Od Praistorije Do Secesije. Arhitektura, Enterijer, Nameštaj*. Belgrade: Gradjevinska knjiga.
Althusser, Louis. 1984. *Essays on Ideology*. London: Verso.
Altick, Richard. 1978. *The Shows of London*. Cambridge, MA: Harvard University Press.
Arnold, Ellis. 2019. '5 Things to Know: CityCenter, Downtown Redevelopment in Englewood. City Hopeful for Hotel, Apartment, Retail Revamp at City Hall'. *Englewood Herald* (blog), 18 February 2019. https://englewoodherald.net/stories/5-things-to-know-citycenter-downtown-redevelopment,276868? Accessed: 14 August 2019.
Aronson, Arnold. 1977. 'The Total Theatrical Environment: Impression Management in the Parks'. *Theatre Crafts*, no. 11: 35–73.
Aronson, Arnold. 2014. 'The Stage as Simulacrum of Reality'. *The Cultural Magazine of Pro Helvetia* 63, no. 2: 14–16.
Aronson, Arnold. 2018. *The History and Theory of Environmental Scenography*. London: Bloomsbury, Methuen Drama.
Artaud, Antonin. 1958. *The Theater and Its Double*. New York: Grove Press.
Augé, Marc. 2008. *Non-Places: An Introduction to Supermodernity*. London and New York: Verso.
Bader, Vera Simone. 2016. 'The Architecture of the Shopping Mall'. In *World of Malls*, edited by Andreas Lepik and Vera Simone Bader, 11–21. Ostfildern: Hatje Cantz.
Bala, Sruti. 2018. 'What Is the Impact of Theatre and Performance?' In *Thinking through Theatre and Performance*, edited by Maaike Bleeker, Adrian Kear, Joe Kelleher and Heike Roms, 186–99. London: Bloomsbury, Methuen Drama.
Barad, Karen. 2012. '"Matter Feels, Converses, Suffers, Desires, Yearns and Remembers": Interview with Karen Barad'. In *New Materialism: Interviews and Cartographies*, edited by Rick Dolphijn and Iris van der Tuin. Open Humanities Press. Available online: http://openhumanitiespress.org/books/download/Dolphijn-van-der-Tuin_2013_New-Materialism.pdf. Accessed: 18 January 2020.

REFERENCES

Baran, Claudie. 2004. *Souks: Märkte und Basare von Aleppo bis Sanaa*. Munich: Christian Verlag.
Baudrillard, Jean. 1998. *The Consumer Society: Myth and Structures*. London: Sage.
Bauman, Zygmunt. 1997. *Flaneure, Spieler und Touristen: Essays zu postmodernen Lebensformen*. Hamburg: Hamburger.
Becker, Jeffrey. n.d. 'Forum and Markets of Trajan'. Khan Academy. *Art and Humanities* (blog). https://www.khanacademy.org/humanities/ap-art-history/ancient-mediterranean-ap/ap-ancient-rome/a/forum-and-market-of-trajan. Accessed: 23 November 2018.
Beiró, Mariano G., Loreto Bravo, Diego Caro, Ciro Cattuto, Leo Ferres and Eduardo Graells-Garrido. 2018. 'Shopping Mall Attraction and Social Mixing at a City Scale'. *EPJ Data Science* 7, no. 28: 1–21. https://doi.org/10.1140/epjds/s13688-018-0157-5. Accessed: 25 May 2019.
Benjamin, Walter. 1968. 'The Work of Art in the Age of Mechanical Reproduction'. In *Illuminations: Essays and Reflections*, edited by Hannah Arendt, 217–53. New York: Schocken Books.
Benjamin, Walter. 1999. *The Arcades Project*. Cambridge, MA: The Belknap Press of Harvard University Press.
Bergson, Henri. 1911. *Matter and Memory*, translated by Nancy Margaret Paul and W. Scott Palmer. London: George Allen and Unwin.
Berry, Helen. 2002. 'Polite Consumption: Shopping in Eighteenth-Century England'. *Transactions of the Royal Historical Society* 12: 375–94.
Beyard, Michael D., Raymond E. Braun, Herbert McLaughlin, Patric L. Phillips and Michael S. Rubin. 2001. *Developing Retail Entertainment Destinations*. Washington: Urban Land Institute.
Bird, Jon. 2018. 'The Future of the Shopping Mall Is Not about Shopping'. *Forbes*, 17 June 2018. https://www.forbes.com/sites/jonbird1/2018/06/17/the-future-of-the-shopping-mall-is-not-about-shopping/#7a88978b5cf2. Accessed: 25 May 2019.
Bird, William L., Jr. 2007. *Holidays on Display*. New York: Princeton Architectural Press.
Bittner, Regina. 2016. 'Futures Past: The Shopping Mall as Megastructure'. In *World of Malls: Architectures of Consumption*, edited by Andreas Lepik and Vera Simone Bader, 68–78. Ostfildern: Hatje Cantz.
Böhme, Antje. 2012. *Träumen Sie schön: Ästhetischer Schein und gesellschaftliches Sein am Beispiel des Shoppingcenters*. Bielefeld: Aisthesis Verlag.
Böhme, Gernot. 1995. *Atmosphäre: Essays zur neuen Ästhetik*. Frankfurt am Main: Suhrkamp.
Brejzek, Thea. 2015. 'The Scenographic (Re-)Turn: Figures of Surface, Space and Spectator in Theatre and Architecture Theory 1680–1980'. *Theatre and Performance Design* 1, no. 1–2: 17–30.
Brejzek, Thea. 2017. 'Between Symbolic Representation and New Critical Realism: Architecture as Scenography and Scenography as Architecture'. In *Scenography Expanded: An Introduction to Contemporary Performance Design*, edited by Joslin McKinney and Scott Palmer, 63–78. London and New York: Bloomsbury.
Brockett, Oscar, Margaret Mitchell and Linda Hardberger. 2010. *Making the Scene: A History of Stage Design and Technology in Europe and the United States*. San Antonio, TX: Tobin Theatre Arts Fund.

Bruegmann, Robert. 2016. 'Shopping Reshapes the Metropolis'. In *World of Malls: Architectures of Consumption*, edited by Andreas Lepic and Vera Simone Bader, 90–8. Ostfildern: Hatje Cantz.
Brune, Walter, and Holger Pump-Uhlmann. 2011. *Vom Kaufhaus zur Stadtgalerie: Bauten für den Handel von Walter Brune*. Berlin: Jovis.
Bryman, Alan. 2004. *The Disneyization of Society*. London: Sage.
Buether, Axel. 2018. 'Die Sprache des Raums'. In *Architektur Wahrnehmen*, edited by Alexandra Abel and Bernd Rudolf, 1–80. Bielefeld: Transcript.
Campbell, Colin. 2005. *The Romantic Ethic and the Spirit of Modern Consumerism*. York: Blackwell Publishers.
Carlson, Marvin. 1989. *Places of Performance: The Semiotics of Theatre Architecture*. Ithaca, NY and London: Cornell University Press.
Chebat, J. C., R. Michon, N. Haj-Salem and S. Oliveira. 2014. 'The Effects of Mall Renovation on Shopping Values, Satisfaction and Spending Behaviour'. *Journal of Retailing and Consumer Services* 21, no. 4: 610–18.
Choay, Françoise. 1986. 'Urbanism and Semiology'. In *The City and the Sign: An Introduction to Urban Semiotics*, edited by M. Gottdiener and Alexandros Ph Lagopoulos, 160–75. New York: Columbia University Press.
Chung, Chuihua Judy. 2001a. 'Disney Space'. In *Harvard Design School Guide to Shopping*, edited by Chuihua Judy Chung et al. Cologne: Taschen.
Chung, Chuihua Judy, Jeffrey Inaba, Rem Koolhaas, Sze Tsung Leong and Tae-wook Cha, Harvard University, Graduate School of Design, and Harvard Project on the City. 2001b. *Harvard Design School Guide to Shopping*. Cologne and New York: Taschen.
Cloke, Paul, Philip Crang and Mark Goodwin. 2014. *Introducing Human Geographies*. New York: Routledge.
Cohen, Lisabeth. 1996. 'From Town Center to Shopping Center: The Reconfiguration of Community Marketplaces in Postwar America'. *American Historical Review* 101, no. 4: 1050–81. http://nrs.harvard.edu/urn-3: HUL.InstRepos:4699748. Accessed: 25 May 2019.
Coleman, Peter. 2006. *Shopping Environments: Evolution, Planning and Design*. Oxford: Architectural Press.
Copeland, Roger. 1990. 'The Presence of Mediation'. *TDR (1988–)* 34, no. 4: 28–44. Cambridge, MA: MIT Press.
Covoto, Gabriele, and Giorgio Limonta. 2015. 'Shopping Centres in Italy: New Polarities and Deadmalls'. In *The Shopping Centre 1943–2013. The Rise and Demise of a Ubiquitous Collective Architecture*, edited by Janina Gosseye and Tom Avermaete, 173–85. Delft: Delft University of Technology.
Crary, Jonathan. 2001. *Suspensions of Perception: Attention, Spectacle and Modern Culture*. Cambridge, MA: MIT Press.
Cucheval-Clarigny, Athanase. 1894. *Souvenir offert par les magasins du Bon Marché fondés par Aristide Boucicaut*. Paris: Imp. Gauthier-Villars. http://catalog.hathitrust.org/api/volumes/oclc/47976405.html. Accessed: 13 June 2019.
Davidson, Joyce, and Christine Milligan. 2004. 'Embodying Emotion Sensing Space: Introducing Emotional Geographies'. *Social & Cultural Geography* 5, no. 4: 523–32.
Davis, Heidi. 2012. 'A Brief History of Christmas Lights'. *Popular Mechanics* 21, 12 December. https://www.popularmechanics.com/technology/gadgets/g1018/a-brief-history-of-christmas-lights/. Accessed: 25 May 2019.
Davis, Mike. 2006. 'Fear and Money in Dubai'. *New Left Review*, no. 41: 47–68.

Davis, Tracy C. 1991. 'Theatrical Antecedents of the Mall That Ate Downtown'. *Popular Culture* 24, no. 4: 1–15. https://onlinelibrary.wiley.com/doi/abs/10.1111/j.0022-3840.1991.2404_1.x. Accessed: 25 May 2019.

De Cauter, Lieven. 2014. 'The Experience Economy'. *Passages: The Cultural Magazine of Pro Helvetia* 63, no. 2: 30.

De Certeau, Michel. 1985. 'Practices of Space'. In *On Signs*, edited by Marshall Blonsky, 122–45. Baltimore, MD: Johns Hopkins University Press.

Debord, Guy. 1970. *Society of the Spectacle*. Detroit: Black & Red.

Den Oudsten, Frank. 2017. *space.time.narrative: The Exhibition as Post-Spectacular Stage*. London: Routledge.

Dennis, Charles. 2005. *Objects of Desire: Consumer Behaviour in Shopping Centre Choices*. London: Palgrave Macmillan.

Di Benedetto, Stephen. 2017. 'Cognitive Approaches to Performance Design, or How the Dead Materialize and Other Spectacular Design Solutions'. In *Scenography Expanded: An Introduction to Contemporary Performance Design*, edited by Joslin McKinney and Scott Palmer, 155–66. London and New York: Bloomsbury, Methuen Drama.

Digital Window Graphics. 2018. 'Decorative Digital Interiors for Today's Retail Spaces'. https://cdn2.hubspot.net/hubfs/3783266/Market%20Veep%20Content/Decorative%20Digital%20Interiors%20for%20Todays%20Retail%20Spaces/Decorative%20Digital%20Interiors%20for%20Todays%20Retail%20Spaces.pdf. Accessed: 25 May 2019.

Diltz, Colin. 2018. 'From the Archives: Look at Northgate Mall in the 1950s, When It Was an Outdoor Shopping Center'. *The Seattle Times*, 31 May 2018. https://www.seattletimes.com/seattle-news/from-the-archives-look-at-northgate-mall-in-the-1950s-when-it-was-an-outdoor-shopping-center/. Accessed: 25 May 2019.

Donnelly, Christopher, and Renato Scaff. 2013. 'Who Are the Millennial Shoppers? And What Do They *Really* Want?' *Outlook: Accenture's Journal of High-Performance Business*, no. 2. Available online: https://www.accenture.com/us-en/insight-outlook-who-are-millennial-shoppers-what-do-they-really-want-retail. Accessed: 8 February 2020.

Driver, Felix. 2014. 'Imaginative Geographies'. In *Introducing Human Geographies*, edited by Paul Cloke, Philip Crang and Mark Goodwin, 234–48. London and New York: Routledge.

Dunham-Jones, Ellen, and June Williamson. 2017. 'Dead and Dying Shopping Malls, Re-Inhabited'. *Architectural Design* 87, no. 5: 84–91.

Durgin, Frank H. 2009. 'When Walking Makes Perception Better'. *Current Directions in Psychological Science* 18, no. 1: 43–7.

Eagleton, Terry. 2003. *Literary Theory: An Introduction*. Minneapolis: The University of Minnesota Press.

Eco, Umberto. 1986. *Travels in Hyperreality*. London: Pan, in association with Secker & Warburg.

Erben, Dietrich. 2016. 'Conspicuous Architecture: The Shopping Arcade, the Department Store, and Consumer Culture'. In *World of Malls: Architectures of Consumption*, edited by Andres Lepik and Vera Simone Bader, 24–35. Ostfildern: Hatje Cantz.

Ervolino, Bill. 2017. 'Remember the Giant Santa at GSP? A Look at Holiday Mall Decor, Then and Now'. northjersey.com, 8 December 2017. https://eu.northjersey.com/story/entertainment/2017/11/27/deck-malls-holiday-decor-then-and-now/843374001/. Accessed: 25 May 2019.

Eynat-Confino, Irène. 1987. *Beyond the Mask: Gordon Craig, Movement, and the Actor*. Carbondale and Edwardsville: Southern Illinois University Press.
Filingeri, D., D. Fournet, S. Hodder and G. Havenith. 2014. 'Why Wet Feels Wet? A Neurophysiological Model of Human Cutaneous Wetness Sensitivity'. *Journal of Neurophysiology* 112, no. 6: 1457–69.
Fischer-Lichte, Erika, and Benjamin Wihstutz. 2013. *Performance and the Politics of Space: Theatre and Topology*. New York: Routledge.
Fischer-Lichte, Erika, and D. Kolesch. 2005. *Metzler Lexikon Theatertheorie*. Stuttgart and Weimar: J. B. Metzler.
Flusser, Vilém. 1994. 'Abbild – Vorbild'. In *Was heißt Darstellen?*, edited by Christiaan L. Hart Nibbrig, 34–48. Frankfurt am Main: Suhrkamp.
Frampton, Keneth. 1996. 'Rappel à l'ordre: The Case for the Tectonic (1990)'. In *Theorizing a New Agenda for Architecture: An Anthology of Architectural Theory 1965–1995*, edited by Kate Nesbitt, 516–29. New York: Princeton Architectural Press.
Friemert, Chup. 1984. *Die Gläserne Arche: Kristallpalast London 1851 und 1854*. Dresden: VEB Verlag der Kunst.
Fritsch, Eileen. 2018. 'A Peek into Retail Store Window Design Trends'. *Wide-Format Impressions* (blog), 26 September 2018. https://www.wideformatimpressions.com/article/a-peek-into-retail-store-window-design-trends/. Accessed: 25 May 2019.
Geist, Johann Friedrich. 1982. *Passagen. Ein Bautyp Des 19. Jahrhunderts*. Munich: Prestel.
Gibson, James J. 1950. *The Perception of the Visual World*. Cambridge, MA: The Riverside Press.
Giesekam, Greg. 2007. *Staging the Screen: The Use of Film and Video in Theatre*. New York: Palgrave Macmillan.
Glogowski, Dominika. 2009. 'Daniel Libeskind – Westside Shoppingcenter in Bern, Schweiz'. *Architektur Aktuell*, Shopping, no. 01/02/2009: 56. Wien: Architektur aktuell GmbH.
Goitein, Shelomo Dov. 1999. *A Mediterranean Society: The Jewish Communities of the Arab World as Portrayed in the Documents of the Cairo Geniza*. Berkeley: University of California Press.
Goldberger, Paul. 1986. 'In Downtown San Diego, a Freewheeling Fantasy'. *The New York Times*, 19 March 1986.
Goldstein, Bruce E. 1981. 'The Ecology of J. J. Gibson´s Perception'. *Leonardo* 14, no. 3: 191–5.
Goldthwaite, Richard. 2002. 'The Empire of Things: Consumer Demand in Renaissance Italy'. In *Patronage, Art, and Society in Renaissance Italy*, edited by F. W. Kent, Patricia Somons and John Christopher Eade, 153–75. Oxford and New York: Oxford University Press.
Gomes, Renata Maria, and Fabio Paula. 2016. 'Shopping Mall Image: Systematic Review of 40 Years of Research'. *The International Review of Retail, Distribution and Consumer Research* 27, no. 1: 1–27.
Goss, Jon. 1993. 'The "Magic of the Mall": An Analysis of Form, Function, and Meaning in the Contemporary Retail Built Environment'. *Annals of the Association of American Geographers* 83, no. 1: 18–47.
Gottdiener, Mark. 1997. *The Theming of America*. Boulder, CO, and Oxford: Westview Press.

Gottdiener, Mark. 1998. 'Themed Environments of Everyday Life'. In *The Postmodern Presence Readings on Postmodernism in American Culture and Society*, edited by Arthur Asa Berger, 85. Walnut Creek, CA: AltaMira Press.
Gottdiener, Mark, and Alexandros Lagopoulos. 1986. *The City and the Sign: An Introduction to Urban Semiotics*. New York: Columbia University Press.
Graham, Wade. 2017. *Dream Cities: Seven Urban Ideas That Shape the World*. New York: Harper Perennial.
Green, Sam. 2009. *Utopia Part 3: The World's Largest Shopping Mall*. https://vimeo.com/122128694. Accessed: 25 May 2019.
Gruen, Victor, and Anette Baldauf. 2014. *Shopping Town: Memoiren Eines Stadtplaners (1903–1980)*. Vienna and Cologne: Böhlau Verlag.
Günel, Gökçe. 2011. 'A Flying Man, a Scuttled Ship, and a Timekeeping Device: Reflections on Ibn Battuta Mall'. *Public Culture* 23, no. 3: 541–9.
Hahn, Barbara. 2002. *50 Jahre Shopping Center in den USA*. Passau: L.I.S. Verlag.
Hann, Rachel. 2019. *Beyond Scenography*. London: Routledge.
Hampel, Annika. 2010. *Der Museumsshop als Schnittstelle von Konsum und Kultur: Kommerzialisierung der Kultur oder Kulturalisierung des Konsums?* Hamburg: Diplomica Verlag.
Harby, Jennifer. 2018. 'More Than 200 UK Shopping Centres "in Crisis"'. *BBC News* (blog), 1 November 2018. https://www.bbc.com/news/uk-england-45707529. Accessed: 25 May 2019.
Hardwick, Jeffrey M. 2010. *Mall Maker: Victor Gruen, Architect of an American Dream*. Philadelphia: University of Pennsylvania Press.
Harvie, Jen, and Dan Rebellato. 2015. *Theatre & Architecture*. London: Palgrave Macmillan.
Haslett, Moyra. 2000. *Marxist Literary and Cultural Theories*. New York: St. Martin's Press.
Hassell, Greg. 1996. 'Malls Slipping as Shopping Meccas'. *Houston Chronicle*, 9 October 1996, 1.
Haug, Wolfgang Fritz. 1986. *Critique of Commodity Aesthetics: Appearance, Sexuality and Advertising in Capitalist Society*. Cambridge: Polity Press.
Haug, Wolfgang Fritz. 2009. 'Warenästhetik im High-Tech-Kapitalismus'. *Kritik der Warenästhetik*, 211–350. Frankfurt am Main: Suhrkamp.
Hellmann, Kai-Uwe, and Guido Zurstiegeeds. 2008. *Räume des Konsums. Über den Funktionswandel von Räumlichkeit Im Zeitalter des Kunsumismus*. Wiesbaden: VS Verlag.
Herman, Daniel. 2001. 'Jerde Transfer: Spatial Assault'. In *Harvard Design School Guide to Shopping*, edited by Chuihua Judy Chung et al., 402–7. Cologne: Taschen.
Heynen, Hilde. 1999. *Architecture and Modernity: A Critique*. Cambridge, MA: MIT Press.
Hmood, K. F. 2017. 'Traditional Markets in Islamic Architecture: Successful Past Experiences'. *WIT Trans. Built Environ. WIT Transactions on the Built Environment* 171: 263–73.
Hosoya, Hiromi, and Markus Schaefer. 2001. 'Brand Zone'. In *Harvard Design School Guide to Shopping*, edited by Chuihua Judy Chung et al., 164–73. Köln: Taschen.
Howard, Pamela. 2008. *What Is Scenography?* London: Routledge.

Husserl, Edmund. 1983. *Ideas Pertaining to a Pure Phenomenology and to a Phenomenological Philosophy*. The Hague, Boston, Lancaster: Martinus Nijhoff Publishers.

Husserl, Edmund. 1989. *Ideas Pertaining to a Pure Phenomenology and to a Phenomenological Philosophy Second Book, Second Book*. Dordrecht, Boston and London: Kluwer Academic Publishers.

Ingold, Tim. 1992. 'Culture and the Perception of the Environment'. In *Bush Base: Forest Farm. Culture, Environment and Development*, edited by Elisabeth Croll and David Parkin, 39–56. London and New York: Routledge.

Ingold, Tim. 2000. *The Perception of the Environment*. London and New York: Routledge.

Irwin, Kathleen. 2017. 'Scenographic Agency: A Showing-Doing and a Responsibility for Showing-Doing'. In *Scenography Expanded: An Introduction to Contemporary Performance Design*, edited by Joslin McKinney and Scott Palmer, 111–23. London and New York: Bloomsbury, Methuen Drama.

Jacobs, Jane. 1993. *Tod Und Leben Großer Amerikanischer Städte (The Death and Life of Great American Cities)*. Braunschweig/Wiesbaden: Fried. Vieweg & Sohn Verlagsgesellschaft mbH.

Jameson, Fredric. 1979. 'Reification and Utopia in Mass Culture'. *Social Text*, no. 1: 130–48.

Jameson, Fredric. 1991. *Postmodernism, or, the Cultural Logic of Late Capitalism*. Durham: Duke University Press.

Jewell, Nicholas. 2001. 'The Fall and Rise of the British Mall'. *The Journal of Architecture* 6, no. 4: 317–78. https://doi.org/10.1080/13602360110071450. Accessed: 12 June 2019.

Jewell, Nicholas. 2015. *Shopping Malls and Public Space in Modern China*. Farnham: Ashgate Publishing Limited.

Jones, Andrew. 2012. *Human Geography: The Basics*. New York: Routledge.

Julien, Selina. 2018. 'Dubai Unveils Plans for $2 Billion Tech-Driven Mega Mall'. CNN. *CNN Travel* (blog). https://edition.cnn.com/travel/article/dubai-square-mall-dubai-creek/index.html. Accessed: 16 January 2020.

Kent, Gordon. 2018. 'Lollipop Headdress Statue Removed at West Edmonton Mall after Complaints of Racism'. *Edmonton Journal* (blog). https://edmontonjournal.com/news/local-news/lollipop-headdress-statue-removed-at-west-edmonton-mall-after-complaints-of-racism. Accessed: 18 January 2020.

Kim, Ji Wan, Freddy Lee and Yong Gu Suh. 2015. 'Satisfaction and Loyalty from Shopping Mall Experience and Brand Personality'. *Services Marketing Quarterly*, no. 36: 62–76.

König, Wolfgang. 2008. *Kleine Geschichte der Konsumgesellschaft: Konsum als Lebensform der Moderne*. Stuttgart: Franz Steiner Verlag.

Koolhaas, Rem. 2001a. 'Junkspace'. In *Project on the City II: The Harvard Guide to Shopping*. Cologne: Taschen.

Koolhaas, Rem. 2001b. 'Koolhaas on Shopping'. *Architectural Research Quarterly* 5, no. 3: 201–3.

Kopytoff, Verne G. 1999. 'Computers Are the Balanchine behind Those Dancing Fountains'. *The New York Times*, 21 October 1999. https://www.nytimes.com/1999/10/21/technology/computers-are-the-balanchine-behind-those-dancing-fountains.html. Accessed: 12 June 2019.

Kozinets, Robert V., John F. Sherry, Jr., Benét DeBerry-Spence, Adam Duhachek, Krittinee Nuttavuthisit and Diana Storm. 2008. 'Themed Flagship Brand Stores in the New Millennium'. In *Räume des Konsums. Über Den Funktionswandel von Räumlichkeit Im Zeitalter des Konsumismus*, edited by Kai-Uwe Hellmann and Guido Zurstiege, 87–118. Wiesbaden: VS Verlag für Sozialwissenschaften.

Kutnicki, Saul. 'Wayfinding Media and Neutralizing Control at the Shopping Mall'. *Critical Studies in Media Communication* 35, no. 5: 401–19. https://doi.org/10.1080/15295036.2018.1490024. Accessed: 12 June 2019.

Lefebvre, Henri. 1991. *The Production of Space*. Oxford: Blackwell.

Legnaro, Aldo, and Almut Birenheide. 2005. *Stätten der späten Moderne: Reiseführer durch Bahnhöfe, shopping malls, Disneyland Paris*. Wiesbaden: VS Verlag für Sozialwissenschaften.

Legnaro, Aldo, and Almut Birenheide. 2007. 'Die Mall als ein Ort kommoder Freiheit'. In *Shopping Malls: Interdisziplinäre Betrachtungen eines neuen Raumtyps*, edited by Jan Wehrheim, 261–75. Wiesbaden: VS Verlag für Sozialwissenschaften.

Leong, Sze Tsung. 2001. '... And Then There Was Shopping: The Last Remaining Form of Public Life'. In *Harvard Design School Guide to Shopping*, edited by Chuihua Judy Chung et al., 130–1. Cologne: Taschen.

Leong, Sze Tsung, and Srdjan Jovanovic Weiss. 2001. 'Air Conditioning'. In *Harvard Design School Guide to Shopping*, edited by Chuihua Judy Chung et al., 117–20. Cologne: Taschen.

Leonhardt, Megan. 2016. 'Shopping Malls Are Using Facial Recognition, License Plate Scanning to Improve Safety'. *Money* (blog), 3 October 2016. http://time.com/money/4515264/shopping-malls-security/. Accessed: 12 June 2019.

Lepik, Andres, and Vera Simone Bader. 2016. *World of Malls: Architectures of Consumption*. Ostfildern: Hatje Cantz.

London, Bianca. 2013. 'All Aboard the Harrods Express!' *Mail Online*, 6 November 2013. https://www.dailymail.co.uk/femail/article-2488250/All-aboard-Harrods-express-First-look-luxury-stores-iconic-Christmas-2013-window-display.html. Accessed: 12 June 2019.

Longstreth, Richard. 2016. 'The Concept of the Regional Shopping Mall at Its Inception, 1945–60'. In *World of Malls: Architectures of Consumption*, edited by Andres Lepik and Vera Simone Bader, 48–55. Ostfildern: Hatje Cantz.

Lyotard, Jean François. 1984. *The Postmodern Condition: A Report on Knowledge*. Manchester: Manchester University Press.

Macpherson, Kerrie L. 2016. *Asian Department Stores*. London: Taylor & Francis.

Marinic, Gregory. 2016. 'Internal Appropriations: Multiculturalism and the American Shopping Mall'. *Journal of Interior Design* 41, no. 3: 47–67.

Marston, Sallie A., and Ali Modarres. 2002. 'Flexible Retailing: Gap Inc. and the Multiple Spaces of Shopping in the United States'. *Tijdschrift Voor Economische En Sociale Geografie* 93, no. 1: 83–99.

Marx, Karl, and Friedrich Engels. 2000. *A Critique of the German Ideology*. Moscow: Progress Publishers. https://www.marxists.org/archive/marx/works/download/Marx_The_German_Ideology.pdf. Accessed: 12 June 2019.

Mbembe, Achille. 2004. 'Aesthetics of Superfluity'. *Public Culture* 16, no. 3: 373–405.

McK Camp II, John. 2015. 'A Tale of Two Stoas'. *Greece Is – Democracy* (blog), 9 October 2015. http://www.greece-is.com/a-tale-of-two-stoas-2/. Accessed: 4 October 2019.

McKinney, Joslin. 2012. 'Kinesthetic Empathy in Creative and Cultural Practices.' In *Kinesthetic Empathy in Creative and Cultural Practices*, edited by Dee Reynolds and Matthew Reason, 221–35. Bristol: Intellect.

McKinney, Joslin, and Philip Butterworth. 2009. *The Cambridge Introduction to Scenography*. Cambridge, UK, and New York: Cambridge University Press.

McKinney, Joslin, and Scott Palmer, eds. 2017. *Scenography Expanded: An Introduction to Contemporary Performance Design*. London and New York: Bloomsbury, Methuen Drama.

McMorrough, John. 2001. 'City of Shopping'. In *City of Shopping. In Project on the City II: The Harvard Guide to Shopping*, edited by Chuihua Judy Chung et al., 374–9. Cologne: Taschen.

Merleau-Ponty, Maurice. 1962. *Phenomenology of Perception*. London and New York: Routledge.

Merleau-Ponty, Maurice. 1964. 'Eye and Mind', translated by. C. Dallery. In *The Primacy of Perception, and Other Essays on Phenomenological Psychology, the Philosophy of Art, History and Politics*, edited by J. M. Edie, 159–90. Evanstone: Northwestern University Press.

Miller, Jacob C. 2014. 'Affect, Consumption, and Identity at the Buenos Aires Shopping Mall'. *Environment and Planning* A 2014, no. 46: 46–61.

Mitchell, Timothy. 1989, 'The World as Exhibition'. *Comparative Studies in Society and History* 31: 232–3.

Mitrovic, Branko. 2013. *Visuality for Architects. Architectural Creativity and Modern Theories of Perception and Imagination*. Charlottesville and London: University of Virginia Press.

Moilin, Tony. 1869. *Paris en l'an 2000*, Paris. 26–9.

Mooney, Paul, and Simon Webb. 2014. 'Huge Thai Security Force Deployment Stifles Coup Protests'. *Reuters*, 1 June 2014. https://www.reuters.com/article/us-thailand-politics/huge-thai-security-force-deployment-stifles-coup-protests-idUSKBN0EC11Q20140601. Accessed: 12 June 2019.

Mraz, Stephen. 2003. 'Application Profile: The Motors, Pumps, and Valves That Make Water Dance'. *Machine Design* (blog), 9 January 2003. http://www.machinedesign.com/recreation/application-profile-motors-pumps-and-valves-make-water-dance. Accessed: 12 June 2019.

Mumford, Lewis. 1996. *The Culture of Cities*. San Diego: Harcourt Brace Jovanovich.

Nylander, Johan. 2015. 'Chinese "Ghost Mall" Back from the Dead?' *CNN Regions/International Edition* (blog), 24 June 2015. https://edition.cnn.com/2015/04/28/asia/china-ghost-mall-return-to-life/index.html. Accessed: 11 February 2020.

Oc, Tanner, and Steven Tiesdell. 1997. *Safer City Centres: Reviving the Public Realm*. London: Paul Chapman Publishing.

Olson, Scott Robert. 1999. *Hollywood Planet: Global Media and the Competitive Advantage of Narrative Transparency*. Mahwah, NJ, and London: Lawrence Erlbaum Associates Publishers.

Oosterhuis, Kas. 2003. *Hyperbodies: Toward an E-motive Architecture*. Basel: Birkhäuser.

Oteíza, Marcela. 2017. 'City as Site: Street Performance and Site Permeability during the Festival Internacional Teatro a Mil, Chile, 2012–2015'. In *Scenography Expanded: An Introduction to Contemporary Performance*

Design, edited by Joslin McKinney and Scott Palmer, 79–92. London and New York: Bloomsbury, Methuen Drama.
Pacione, Michael. 2005. 'City Profile: Dubai'. *Cities* 22, no. 2: 255–65.
Pallasmaa, Juhani. 2005. *The Eyes of the Skin*. Chichester: John Wiley and Sons.
Parmley, Suzette. 2017. 'Las Vegas Casinos Bet on Shopping Malls to Capture Tourist Dollars'. *The Seattle Times*, 12 June. https://www.seattletimes.com/business/retail/las-vegas-casinos-bet-on-shopping-malls-to-capture-tourist-dollars/. Accessed: 12 June 2019.
Petersen, Andrew. 2002. *Dictionary of Islamic Architecture*. London and New York: Routledge.
Pilgrim, Barry. 2017. 'Use of Location-Based Technology Improves Customer Experience'. *Gofindo* (blog), 9 October 2017. https://www.gofindo.com/blog/post/how-beacon-technology-is-transforming-shopping-mall-experience. Accessed: 12 June 2019.
Pimlott, Mark. 2007. *Without and Within: Essays on Territory and the Interior*. Rotterdam: Episode.
Pine II, B. Joseph, and James H. Gilmore. 1999. *The Experience Economy*. Boston, MA: Harvard Business School Press.
Power, Cormac. 2008. *Presence in Play: A Critique of Theories of Presence in the Theatre*. Amsterdam and New York: Rodopi.
Pump-Uhlmann, Holger. 2011. *Vom Kaufhaus zur Stadtgalerie: Bauten für den Handel von Walter Brune*. Berlin: Jovis.
Richter, Peter G. 2018. 'Warum hat es moderne Architektur so schwer?' In *Architektur Wahrnehmen*, edited by Alexandra Abel and Bernd Rudolf, 153–75. Bielefeld: Transcript.
Ritzer, George. 2005. *Enchanting a Disenchanted World: Revolutionizing the Means of Consumption*. Thousand Oaks, CA: Pine Forge Press.
Rooch, Alarich. 2009. 'Warenhäuser: Inszenierungsräume Der Konsumkultur. Von Der Jahrhundertwende Bis 1930'. In *Bürgertum Und Bürgerlichkeit Zwischen Kaiserreich Und Nationalsozialismus*, edited by Wrner Plumpe and Jörg Lesczenski, 17–30. Mainz: Philipp von Zabern Verlag.
Rufford, Juliet. 2015. *Theatre & Architecture*. London: Palgrave Macmillan.
Rufford, Juliet. 2018. 'Scenography and the Political Economy of Design'. In *Anthology of Essays on Contemporary Performance*, edited by K. Kipphoff and S. Graffer. Oslo: Vigarorlaget. Available online: https://www.academia.edu/39123470/Scenography_and_the_Political_Economy_of_Design. Accessed: 12 February 2020.
Ruskin, John. 1898. *The Seven Lamps of Architecture*. New York: D. Appleton.
Said, Edward. 1979. *Orientalism*. New York: First Vintage Books.
Sarup, Madan. 1993. *An Introductory Guide to Post-Structuralism and Postmodernism*. Athens, GA: University of Georgia Press.
Saunders, Evan. 2012. 'One of the Top Cinemas in South Africa?' Fortress. https://www.fortressofsolitude.co.za/nu-metro-il-grande/. Accessed: 14 January 2020.
Sayers, Frances Clarke. 1965. *Summoned by Books: Essays and Speeches by Frances Clarke Sayers*. Compiled by Marjeanne Jensen Blinn. New York: Viking Press.

Schechner, Richard. 1968. '6 Axioms for Environmental Theatre'. *The Drama Review* 12, no. 3: 41–64.
Schechner, Richard. 1990. *Theater-Anthropologie: Spiel und Ritual im Kulturvergleich*. Hamburg: Rowohlt Taschenbuch Verlag.
Schechner, Richard. 1994. *Environmental Theater*. New York: Aplaus Theatre & Cinema Books.
Schwartz, David G. 2019. 'Nevada Casinos: Departmental Revenues, 1984–2018'. Las Vegas: Center for Gaming Research, University Libraries, University of Nevada Las Vegas. https://gaming.unlv.edu/reports/NV_departments_historic.pdf. Accessed: 12 June 2019.
Seibt, Philipp. 2018. 'Marktplätze im Darknet: Ich kauf mir einen Hackerangriff'. *Spiegel Online*, 7 January. http://www.spiegel.de/netzwelt/web/darknet-so-sieht-es-in-der-internet-parallelwelt-aus-a-1181621.html. Accessed: 12 June 2019.
Shashikala, R., and A. M. Suresh. 2013. 'Building Consumer Loyalty through Servicescape in Shopping Malls'. *IOSR Journal of Business and Management (IOSR-JBM)* 10, no. 6: 11–17.
Shields, Robert. 1989. 'Social Spatialization and the Built Environment: The West Edmonton Mall'. *Environment and Planning D: Society and Space* 7, no. 2: 147–64.
Suter, Billy. 2016. 'Barnyard to Close Doors after 15 Years'. *The Mercury*, 25 November. https://www.pressreader.com/south-africa/the-mercury/20161125/282535837971018. Accessed: 12 June 2019.
Tabački, Nebojša. 2014. *Kinetische Bühnen. Sean Kenny und Josef Svoboda – Die Szenografen als Wiedererfinder des Theaters*. Bielefeld: Transcript.
Tabački, Nebojša. 2015. 'Diving into the Abyss: Scenography for Contemporary Aquatic Theatres'. *Theatre and Performance Design* 1, no. 1–2: 64–78.
Tabački, Nebojša. 2017a. 'Make Me Feel: Sensing Technology in Contemporary Scenography'. *Theatre and Performance Design* 3, no. 3–4: 119–39.
Tabački, Nebojša. 2017b. 'The Matter of Water: Bodily Experience of Scenography in Contemporary Spectacle'. In *Scenography Expanded: An Introduction to Contemporary Performance Design*, edited by Joslin McKinney and Scott Palmer, 169–81. London and New York: Bloomsbury, Methuen Drama.
Tam, Aaron. 2013. 'Battle of the Christmas Decorations for Hong Kong Malls'. *Rappler* (blog), 24 December 2013. https://www.rappler.com/life-and-style/46567-battle-of-christmas-decorations-for-hong-kong-malls. Accessed: 12 June 2019.
Teaford, Jon C. 2016. *The Twentieth-Century American City: Problem, Promise, and Reality*. Baltimore, MD: Johns Hopkins University Press.
Thierstein, Alain. 2016. 'The Shopping Mall: How Do I Organize the Human Need for Encounter in a Spatially Efficient Way?' In *World of Malls*, edited by Andres Lepik and Vera Simone Bader, 132–42. Ostfildern: Hatje Cantz.
Tsai, Shu-pei. 2010. 'Shopping Mall Management and Entertainment Experience: A Cross-Regional Investigation'. *Service Industries Journal* 30, no. 3: 321–37.
Turner, V. 1982. *From Ritual to Theater*. New York: Performing Arts Publications.
Twitchell, James B. 1999. *Lead Us into Temptation: The Triumph of American Materialism*. New York: Columbia University Press.
Underhill, Paco. 2004. *Call of the Mall*. New York: Simon & Schuster.
Unwin, Tim. 2000. 'A Waste of Space? Towards a Critique of the Social Production of Space'. *Transactions of the Institute of British Geographers. New Series* 25, no. 1: 11–30.

Ursprung, Philip. 2014. 'Presence: The Light Touch of Architecture'. In *Sensing Spaces: Architecture Reimagined*, edited by Kate Goodwin and Philip Ursprung, 13–27. London: Royal Academy of Arts.

Varman, Rohit, and Russell W. Belk. 2012. 'Consuming Postcolonial Shopping Malls'. *Journal of Marketing Management* 28, no. 1–2: 62–84.

Venturi, Robert, Denise Scott Brown and Steven Izenour. 1979. *Lernen von Las Vegas zur Ikonographie und Architektursymbolik der Geschäftsstadt*. Basel, Boston and Berlin: Birkenhäuser.

Wall, Alex. 2005. *Victor Gruen: From Urban Shop to New City*. Barcelona: Actar.

Walsh, Claire. 1995. 'The Design of London Goldsmiths' Shops in the Early Eighteenth Century'. In *Goldsmiths, Silversmiths and Bankers*, edited by David Mitchell, 96–111. Oxford: Oxford University Press.

'The Walt Disney Company, Annual Financial Report, Fiscal Year 2017'. 2017. Financial Report. Washington, DC: United States Securities and Exchange Commisssion. http://www.annualreports.com/HostedData/AnnualReports/PDF/NYSE_DIS_2017.pdf. Accessed: 12 June 2019.

Warnaby, Gary, and Dominic Medway. 2018. 'Marketplace Icons: Shopping Malls'. *Consumption Markets & Culture* 21, no. 3: 275–82.

Wee, Lea. 2017. 'New Light-and-Sound Shows to Catch at Marina Bay Sands, Sentosa and Gardens by the Bay'. *Straits Times*, 1 August 2017. https://www.straitstimes.com/lifestyle/new-light-and-sound-shows-to-catch-at-marina-bay-sands-sentosa-and-gardens-by-the-bay. Accessed: 12 June 2019.

Wehrheim, Jan, ed. 2007. *Shopping Malls: Interdisziplinäre Betrachtungen eines neuen Raumtyps*. Wiesbaden: VS Verlag.

Weiss, Walter M. 1994. *Der Basar: Mittelpunkt des Lebens in der islamischen Welt: Geschichte und Gegenwart eines menschengerechten Stadtmodells*. Vienna: Dt. Taschenbuch-Verl.

Whitaker, Jan. 2013. *Wunderwelt Warenhaus: Eine internationale Geschichte*. Hildesheim: Gerstenberg Verlag.

Wiles, David. 2003. *A Short History of Western Performance Space*. Cambridge and New York: Cambridge University Press.

Williamson, Janice. 1992. 'Notes from Storyville North: Circling the Mall'. In *Lifestyle Shopping: The Subject of Consumption*, edited by Rob Shields, 216–32. London: Routledge.

Williamson, June. 2016. 'The Once and Future Shopping Mall: Retrofitting Suburbia for Twenty-First-Century Challenges'. In *World of Malls*, edited by Andres Lepik and Vera Simone Bader, 218–28. Ostfildern: Hatje Cantz.

Woodward, Ian. 1998. 'The Shopping Mall, Postmodern Space and Architectural Practice: Theorising the Postmodern Spatial Turn through the Planning Discourse of Mall Architects'. *Architectural Theory Review* 3, no. 2: 45–56. https://doi.org/10.1080/13264829809478344. Accessed: 12 June 2019.

Film/TV programme

Disneyland's 10th Anniversary Show HD (1965), [TV programme], Dir. Hamilton Luske.

Index

added-value strategy 35
adjacent attraction 34
aesthetic drama 46
agency
    aesthetics of 126–7
    images and signs of 114
    ritual and entertainment 46
    scenographic 4, 7, 35, 141, 147–8, 159, 161–2
    theatrical and performative 4
aircraft exhibitions 22
animated films 3, 75, 81, 87, 143
anticipatory localization 1
Aronson, Arnold 31, 33–4, 43–4, 81, 96, 99, 101–2, 114–15, 128, 155–6, 160
atmosphere 2–3, 5, 10–12, 14–15, 34, 36, 39, 42, 44–5, 47, 49, 54, 57, 59, 77, 79, 80, 83, 93, 121, 128–9, 131, 146, 157–8
audience 2, 4, 31, 36, 42–3, 45, 47–8, 78–81, 97, 101, 108, 114–15, 121, 127, 143, 154, 161–2

Bader, Vera Simone 25, 117–18
Baudrillard, Jean 15, 108–9, 116, 118, 123, 125–6, 132–3, 139, 155, 158
Benedetto, Stephen di 36
Benjamin, Walter 15–16, 18, 21, 41, 99, 101, 103–4, 121, 134
Bergson, Henri 150, 152
Bird, William L. 21–2, 37, 41, 51–2, 85–6
Bliss, James Albert 20–1
Böhme, Antje 47, 113, 128, 153–4
Böhme, Gernot 36, 42, 83, 118, 126
Bon Marché department store 20–1, 23

Boucicaut, Aristide 21
branding 1, 4, 26, 82
Brejzek, Thea. 2, 83–4, 140, 147–8
Brune, Walter 19, 23–4, 25–6, 42, 80
Bryman, Alan 1–2, 31, 34–5, 38, 40, 43, 45, 48, 75–8, 81, 84, 118, 133–5, 142, 157, 159

Campbell, Colin 14, 47, 103, 135
capitalism 2, 4, 16–18, 32, 42, 109, 123, 132, 134, 147
Carlson, Marvin 16, 19, 44, 48, 92, 120, 160–2
Cheek, James 33
Christmas lighting 86, 89–90
Chung, Chuihua Judy 80–2, 110, 112, 131, 139–40, 142, 154
Cohen, Lisabeth 24–6, 44, 95, 125, 130, 134, 136–7
Coleman, Peter 1, 11–12, 14, 18–19, 27–8, 32, 36, 82, 133, 161
commercial retail industry, sustainable approach 146–7
consumer(s)
    and architectural symbols 108–14
    buying behaviour 2, 36, 77, 147, 149, 161
    scenographic strategies, impact on 114–17
    seduction 3, 9–10, 14, 16, 23
    themed shopping malls 101–4, 108–10, 113, 115–18
    transformation 45
consumerism 14, 22, 108, 110, 120, 125–6, 161
consumption
    in affluent society 2
    freedom and 132–4, 152–3
    hybrid 75–7

INDEX

mode of resistance 151
of place 34, 39, 117, 159
Country Club Plaza 40
Craig, Edward Gordon 47
Crary, Jonathan 16–17, 84–5, 90, 99, 104, 122, 124–6, 150, 152–3
culture/cultural, as social practice 1, 46, 75, 83, 109, 121, 141, 151–3, 158–9

Davis, Mike 40–1, 67, 81, 86, 132, 137
Davis, Tracy C. 40–1
De Cauter, Lieven 2
Debord, Guy 16, 48, 113, 126, 130, 135, 156, 158
Delk, Edward Buehler 32
demonstration/political protest 136–8
department stores
    exhibitions 22
    holiday displays, Christmas 85–6
    nineteenth-century theming 37, 42, 79, 84, 122
    personalized spaces 100–1
    technology-based displays 85–8
    theatrical techniques 21, 26
digital technology 97, 142–3
diorama 15, 41
Disney, Walt 3, 75, 79, 81, 131, 138, 142, 149, 159–60. *See also* Disneyization; Disneyland
Disneyization
    hybrid consumption 76–7
    merchandising 172 n.2
    performative labour 75–6
    theming 75–82
Disneyland 3, 34–35, 46, 67, 78–81, 103, 138, 140, 142, 148, 160
display 5, 10–17, 19–22, 24, 41, 54, 56–7, 59, 62, 69, 73, 84–9, 91–5, 111, 122, 136–7, 166, 173, 175, 178–9, 185
Dougall Design Associates 37
Dunham-Jones, Ellen 145

early themed settings 22
embodied experience 36, 107, 113, 117
enclosed market spaces. *See also* roofed markets

arcades and department stores 14–23
classical civilisations 9–14
medieval Europe 10–13
shopping malls 23–6
souks and bazaars 13–14
themed resorts 39–40
entertainment or lifestyle retailing 28
entertainment-oriented shopping destinations 28
Erben, Dietrich 45
Exchange's Royal Menagerie 40
exhibitions 10, 19–20, 22, 41, 76, 95, 124–5
experience economy 4, 35–6, 40, 83, 130, 132, 144–5, 147, 154, 160

festival 43–4, 120, 123–4, 160
Fischer-Lichte, Erika 42–4, 113, 139
flagship stores 46
flânerie 99, 103–4, 108, 144, 174 n.1
flâneurs 5, 19, 30, 99, 103–4
FlatIron Crossing 36
flexible theatre structures 148–9
FlyOver America 31
Fooshee, Marion 33
The Forum Shops 37–9, 77, 89
fountains 5, 20, 26, 37, 52, 54, 57, 61, 67, 70, 89, 92–4, 97, 132

The Galaxyland Amusement Park 29, 168 n.5
Gateway Ekamai Shopping Mall 96
Geddes, Norman Bel 20
Geist, Johann Friedrich 15–18, 165–6
Gest, Morris 20
Gilmore, James H. 35
globalization 1, 5, 35, 157
Goss, Jon 9, 32, 87, 93, 103, 111, 116, 123, 135–7, 142–3, 156
Gottdiener, Mark 2, 19, 21–2, 30–1, 33, 45, 78, 84, 99, 103, 109–10, 112–14, 123, 128, 135, 142, 149
Graham, Wade 45
Grand Canal Shoppes 38–9, 62, 67, 78, 96
Grand Venice Mall 96, 128
Gruen, Victor 25–6, 36, 93, 131, 145

Hahn, Barbara 25, 27–8, 44, 82, 86, 147
Hann, Rachel 3, 7, 147
Hales, Landy R. 20
haptic sense 37, 116. *See also* touch, touching
Harbour City Mall 88
Highland Park Village 33
Hosoya, Hiromi 35–6, 82
Husserl, Edmund 107–8
hyperrealistic scenography 35

Ibn Battuta Mall
　aesthetic ideas 57–62, 83
　architectural and decorative references 57–62
　Christmas decoration 89–90
　design concept 57–8
　thematic concept 79–80
identity
　architectural 160
　consumer's 16
　corporate 4
　local 67, 82, 141
　mall's 3, 32, 47, 158, 162
　place/spatial 34, 37, 40, 103, 141
　themed 39
　visual 1, 28, 31, 33, 90
imaginative geographies 34–5, 39–40, 124
immersion 2, 38, 41, 47, 57, 103, 108, 115, 128, 132, 135, 159
Ingold, Tim 45, 99, 105, 107–8, 110, 113, 135, 157

Jameson, Fredric 6, 92, 124, 126, 129, 138, 162
Jerde, Jon 30
Jewell, Nicholas 47, 103, 108, 114, 133–4, 146, 157–8, 161
Jones, Andrew 34–5, 123–4, 145

KaDeWe 22–3
Kapali Carsi 13
Katara Plaza 39
Kessler, George E. 32
Kiesler, Frederick 2, 20, 101–2
kinaesthetic sense 31, 37, 41, 44, 96–7

König, Wolfgang 25, 67, 102, 125–6, 132
Koolhaas, Rem 112, 132–3, 138, 152

Lefebvre, Henri 102, 117, 119, 127, 151
Lepik, Andres 9, 25, 144, 149
liminality 9
Longstreth, Richard 24–5, 166 n.30

Macy's 20, 85, 87
Madrid's Xanadu Shopping Mall 96
The Mall of America 28–31, 37, 41, 110, 144, 168 n.4
Marx, Karl 123, 152
materiality 2, 5–6, 13, 32, 36–7, 56, 64, 77–8, 115–16, 121, 132, 136, 152
Mayfield Mall 145
Mbembe, Achille 137, 140–1
McArthurGlen development and management company 33
memory 117, 150, 162
Merleau-Ponty, Maurice 107–8
Miracle Mile Shops 39
Montecasino
　aesthetic ideas 51–6, 83
　bird garden 41, 51–2
　consumerism symbols 110, 113–14
　design concept 51–2
　holiday displays, Christmas 89–90
　scenographic techniques 56, 79, 125, 128
　theatre in 48–9
Moss, John 22
Mumford, Lewis 12, 120, 162

neo-liberalism 133, 157
Neville Wakefield 34
New South China Mall 144
Nichols, Jesse Clyde 32

oriental bazaars 13, 17, 25
ornamentation 5, 83, 86, 90, 109–10, 120, 141

panorama 16, 38, 41, 84, 165 n.17
Park Meadows Mall 36
Parker, Louis Napoleon 44

INDEX

participatory spectatorship, participation 5, 33–4, 43–5, 47, 104, 130, 150
Passage des Panoramas 15–16
perception 3–7, 16–17, 22–3, 31–2, 37, 45, 47, 49, 80–4, 97, 99, 101, 104–9, 113, 115, 117–18, 121, 128, 134, 139, 141, 144, 147, 150–1, 162, 181–2, 184, 186
phenomenology 107. *See also* Husserl, Edmund; Merleau-Ponty, Maurice
Pine II, B. Joseph 35, 82, 130, 160
Prévost, Pierre 16, 41

recreation of identity 45
retail entertainment destinations 28
Ritzer, George 1, 19, 37, 48, 77, 102, 121, 127–8, 131–5, 140, 153, 159–61
robotic technology 31, 94
roofed markets 3, 10–11, 13, 15, 17, 89, 165. *See also* enclosed market spaces
Rufford, Juliet 3, 7, 42, 46, 138, 153–4

Sarup, Madan 76, 108, 116, 118, 147, 151, 158–9
scenography
    aesthetic appeal 126–30
    aquatic 93–7
    and architecture 3, 6–7, 79, 97, 99, 101, 140, 146, 148–9, 153, 158, 161
    and consumer seduction 3, 9–10, 14, 16, 23
    consumption of 1–2
    as cultural practice 1, 155–8
    in department stores 18–23
    in early enclosed market places 9–14
    environmental 9, 12, 102, 105, 119, 141, 153
    expanded 7, 14, 31, 77–8, 154
    historical themed precedents 32–4
    monetary value 18
    political connotations 133–8
    postmodernist bias 2, 6, 30, 37, 52, 62, 70, 75–6, 92, 109, 111–12, 116, 123–6, 129, 138, 140, 142, 147, 159
    in shopping arcades 14–18
    in shopping malls 23–6 (*see also specific malls*)
    social activity of consumption 130–3
    temporality and adaptability 3, 139–47
Schaefer, Markus 35
Schechner, Richard 2, 5, 44–6, 99–102, 116, 118–21, 157
sea life exhibitions 29, 31, 41
'sensorialised' space 154
Shields, Robert 29–30, 103, 130, 144, 160
Shopper's World 44, 92
shopping arcades, architecture 14–23
site-specific theatre 2, 31, 84, 97, 101–2, 106, 108
Sloan, James Blanding 115
social drama 46
souks and bazaars 10, 13, 59
Southdale shopping mall 25–6, 36, 41, 93, 131
spatial interventions
    emotional impact 128
    role of signs and symbols 112–13, 130
    scenographic approach 125, 132, 139, 142–3, 146–52, 158, 160
    sensory relationships 117–18
spatial negotiation 102, 111, 140
spectacle 4, 6, 16–17, 22, 36, 41, 48, 87, 102, 108, 110–11, 113, 117, 122, 124, 130, 135, 148, 156
staged value 42
staging products 21–2
The Stoa of Attalos 10
Sunderland, Maurice 29
surface semiotics, symbols 109–13

technology as scenography 84–92
Terminal 21
    aesthetic ideas 69–73, 83
    Christmas decoration 89–90
    design concept 73
    employees' performance 76
    sign systems 112
    walkway patterns 100
theatre buildings 43, 148

theme parks 31, 35, 75–76, 81, 84, 99, 131, 133, 135, 138, 140, 142, 144, 156
themed narratives 125, 127, 141, 147, 154
themed retail centres 1
themed shopping malls 1–3, 32–3, 51–73. *See also specific malls*
 design aspects 2
 financial challenges, shopping malls 145
 marketing strategy 158–9
 scenographic architecture 3, 6–7, 9–15, 17–18, 23–4, 30–2, 36, 47, 54, 57, 59, 62, 70, 73, 78–9, 84, 97, 104, 110, 112, 116, 121, 126, 129, 139–42, 146–9, 153, 157–8, 161–2
theming
 as scenographic principle 1
 in shopping environments 32–40, 51–73
 strategies 27–8, 30, 36–7, 39, 142, 148, 156–7
touch, touching 20, 31, 69, 96–7, 107, 116–18, 132, 162. *See also* haptic sense
Trajan's Market 10

untreated strangeness 35
urban entertainment centres 28
Urry, John 34

Venturi, Robert 81, 83, 109–10, 112–13, 140–1
Villaggio Mall, The
 aesthetic ideas 62–8, 127
 Christmas decoration 90
 design concept 64–5, 67
 layout 100, 143, 174 n.2
visual brand identity 28, 31

water as scenography 92–7
Weiss, Walter M. 13, 119
West Edmonton Mall 29–31, 40–1, 67, 95, 130, 134, 138
Whitaker, Jan 18–20, 22–5, 30, 85, 95
White Week 21, 23, 166 n.26
Williamson, June 138, 145, 149
window displays 14, 20–1, 24, 84–5, 87, 91, 136
world fairs, world exhibitions 19